M000198342

Shakespeare
and
Queer Theory

ARDEN SHAKESPEARE AND THEORY

Series Editor: Evelyn Gajowski

AVAILABLE TITLES

Shakespeare and Cultural Materialist Theory
Christopher Marlow
Shakespeare and Economic Theory David Hawkes
Shakespeare and Ecocritical Theory Gabriel Egan
Shakespeare and Ecofeminist Theory Rebecca Laroche
and Jennifer Munroe
Shakespeare and Feminist Theory Marianne Novy
Shakespeare and New Historicist Theory Neema Parvini
Shakespeare and Postcolonial Theory Jyotsna G. Singh
Shakespeare and Posthumanist Theory Karen Raber
Shakespeare and Psychoanalytic Theory Carolyn Brown

FORTHCOMING TITLES

Shakespeare and Adaptation Theory Sujata Iyengar
Shakespeare and Performance Theory David McCandless
Shakespeare and Presentist Theory Evelyn Gajowski
Shakespeare and Race Theory Arthur L. Little, Jr.
Shakespeare and Reception Theory Nigel Wood
Shakespeare and Textual Theory Suzanne Gossett

Shakespeare and Queer Theory

Melissa E. Sanchez

THE ARDEN SHAKESPEARE
LONDON • NEW YORK • OXFORD • NEW DELHI • SYDNEY

THE ARDEN SHAKESPEARE
Bloomsbury Publishing Plc
50 Bedford Square, London, WC1B 3DP, UK
1385 Broadway, New York, NY 10018, USA

BLOOMSBURY, THE ARDEN SHAKESPEARE and the
Arden Shakespeare logo are trademarks of Bloomsbury Publishing Plc

First published in Great Britain 2019
This paperback edition published 2020

Series design by Sutchinda Rangsi Thompson
Cover image © Nick Veasey / Getty Images

A catalogue record for this book is available from the British Library.

A catalog record for this book is available from the Library of Congress.

ISBN:	HB:	978-1-4742-5667-4
	PB:	978-1-4742-5668-1
	ePDF:	978-1-4742-5670-4
	eBook:	978-1-4742-5669-8

Series: Shakespeare and Theory

Typeset by Integra Software Services Pvt. Ltd.
Printed and bound in Great Britain

To find out more about our authors and books visit www.bloomsbury.com
and sign up for our newsletters.

parce que c'était lui; parce que c'était moi

Dedicated to Chris
and in memory of Newman and Algernon

CONTENTS

SERIES EDITOR'S PREFACE

'Asking questions about literary texts – that's literary criticism. Asking "Which questions shall we ask about literary texts?" – that's literary theory'. So goes my explanation of the current state of English studies, and Shakespeare studies, in my never-ending attempt to demystify, and simplify, theory for students in my classrooms. Another way to put it is that theory is a systematic account of the nature of literature, the act of writing and the act of reading.

One of the primary responsibilities of any academic discipline – whether in the natural sciences, the social sciences or the humanities – is to examine its methodologies and tools of analysis. Particularly at a time of great theoretical ferment, such as that which has characterized English studies, and Shakespeare studies, in recent years, it is incumbent upon scholars in a given discipline to provide such reflection and analysis. We all construct meanings in Shakespeare's texts and culture. Shouldering responsibility for our active role in constructing meanings in literary texts, moreover, constitutes a theoretical stance. To the extent that we examine our own critical premises and operations, that theoretical stance requires reflection on our part. It requires honesty, as well. It is thereby a fundamentally radical act. All critical analysis puts into practice a particular set of theoretical premises. Theory occurs from a particular standpoint. There is no critical practice that is somehow devoid of theory. There is no critical practice that is not implicated in theory. A common-sense, transparent encounter with any text is thereby impossible. Indeed, to the extent that theory requires us to question anew that with which we thought we were familiar, that which we thought we understood, theory constitutes a critique of common sense.

Since the advent of postmodernism, the discipline of English studies has undergone a seismic shift. The discipline of Shakespeare studies has been at the epicentre of this shift. Indeed, it has been Shakespeare scholars who have played a major role in several of the theoretical and critical developments (e.g. new historicism, cultural materialism, presentism) that have shaped the discipline of English studies in recent years. Yet a comprehensive scholarly analysis of these crucial developments has yet to be done, and is long overdue. As the first series to foreground analysis of contemporary theoretical developments in the discipline of Shakespeare studies, *Arden Shakespeare and Theory* aims to fill a yawning gap.

To the delight of some and the chagrin of others, since 1980 or so, theory has dominated Shakespeare studies. *Arden Shakespeare and Theory* focuses on the state of the art at the outset of the twenty-first century. For the first time, it provides a comprehensive analysis of the theoretical developments that are emerging at the present moment, as well as those that are dominant or residual in Shakespeare studies.

Each volume in the series aims to offer the reader the following components: to provide a clear definition of a particular theory; to explain its key concepts; to trace its major developments, theorists and critics; to perform a reading of a Shakespeare text; to elucidate a specific theory's intersection with or relationship to other theories; to situate it in the context of contemporary political, social and economic developments; to analyse its significance in Shakespeare studies; and to suggest resources for further investigation. Authors of individual volumes thereby attempt to strike a balance, bringing their unique expertise, experience and perspectives to bear upon particular theories while simultaneously fulfilling the common purpose of the series. Individual volumes in the series are devoted to elucidating particular theoretical perspectives, such as adaptation, cultural materialism, ecocriticism, ecofeminism, economic theory, feminism, film theory, new historicism, postcolonialism, posthumanism, presentism, psychoanalysis, queer theory, and race theory.

Arden Shakespeare and Theory aims to enable scholars, teachers and students alike to define their own theoretical strategies and refine their own critical practices. And students have as much at stake in these theoretical and critical enterprises – in the reading and the writing practices that characterize our discipline – as do scholars and teachers. Janus-like, the series looks forward as well as backward, serving as an inspiration and a guide for new work in Shakespeare studies at the outset of the twenty-first century, on the one hand, and providing a retrospective analysis of the intellectual labour that has been accomplished in recent years, on the other.

To return to the beginning: What is at stake in our reading of literary texts? Once we come to understand the various ways in which theory resonates with not only Shakespeare's texts, and literary texts, but the so-called 'real' world – the world outside the world of the mind, the world outside the world of academia – then we come to understand that theory is capable of powerfully enriching not only our reading of Shakespeare's texts, and literary texts, but our lives.

***

I am indebted to David Avital, publisher at Bloomsbury Academic, who was instrumental in developing the idea of the *Arden Shakespeare and Theory* series. I am also grateful to Margaret Bartley and Mark Dudgeon, publishers for the Arden Shakespeare, for their guidance and support throughout the development of this series.

Evelyn Gajowski
Series Editor
University of Nevada, Las Vegas

ACKNOWLEDGEMENTS

Since I usually feel like an imposter in both of the fields this book discusses – Shakespeare studies and queer theory – I am still a bit surprised that I came to write it, and I am grateful to all who helped make it happen.

Evelyn Gajowski has been in equal parts a rigorous and deeply serious reader, on the one hand, and a nearly saintlike model of patience and generosity, on the other. Her guidance throughout the process has made this a much better book than it otherwise would have been. Stephen Guy-Bray, who I was delighted to learn was a referee for this book, offered vital advice early on. Dorothy Vanderford's eagle eye saved the manuscript from numerous errors and infelicities. Lara Bateman shepherded the manuscript through its final stages with care and grace.

I have learned much from my colleagues and students at the University of Pennsylvania. Conversations with Ania Loomba and David Eng, in particular, informed many of the arguments in this book. And I am especially indebted to the students in my 2016 and 2017 graduate seminars: our discussions helped me work through nearly all of the summaries and readings in the pages to follow. Beyond Penn, those who have influenced and supported me are too numerous to list individually (though many are cited in the pages to follow). But I do feel compelled to single out a few whose generosity has gone beyond any possible call of duty: Kim Coles, Ann Coiro, Carla Freccero, Lowell Gallagher, Aschah Guibbory, Stephen Guy-Bray, Jeff Knapp, Arthur Little, Madhavi Menon, Kathryn Schwarz, Will Stockton, Gordon Teskey, Ayanna Thompson, Valerie Traub and Chris Warley.

One of the unexpected pleasures of writing this book was my correspondence with James Richardson, who generously helped me secure permission to reprint his brilliant poem. That poem is 'In Shakespeare' from *By the Numbers* © 2010 by James Richardson. Reprinted with the permission of The Permissions Company, Inc. on behalf of Copper Canyon Press, www.coppercanyonpress.org.

At home, Chris Diffee, Quincy Sanchez-Diffee, and Phineas and Sabine loved and forgave me (and made me laugh, despite myself) as I struggled through the doubts and frustrations of writing. *Shakespeare and Queer Theory* is dedicated to Chris, whose objections, questions and insights profoundly shaped this book's contents – and with whom I share the memory of the foursome we once formed with Newman and Algernon, along with so much else in the incommunicable past.

Introduction

Shakespeare and Queer Theory

For the past three decades, queer theory has continually offered some of the most creative and generative frameworks for reading literature in the Anglo-American academy. Queer theory's staying power arises from its explicit commitment to self-critique, capaciousness and flexibility. What began as a study of gay and lesbian lives has expanded into an investigation of the opacity and multiplicity of not only sexuality, but also gender, race, subjectivity, temporality, history, epistemology, language, pedagogy and politics more largely. Beyond academia, discussions of same-sex marriage, trans* rights and discrimination against sexual minorities regularly appear in the popular press even as these topics are a common theme in modern film, theatre, television and literature.[1] These representations and debates promise to remain urgent and prominent in the years to come, within and beyond academia. Because Shakespeare endures as, in Marjorie Garber's apt analysis, a cultural 'fetish', queer approaches to his work can dislodge the conservative ideals of desire and subjectivity that great literature is often supposed to bestow to its readers (1990: 250). When we read Shakespeare through a queer lens, we refine our understanding of identification and desire in the present as well as the past.

Shakespeare and Queer Theory offers students and scholars a detailed overview of the history, background, key terms and concepts, and current critical debates at the intersection of queer theory and Shakespeare studies up through the time of this volume's publication. Such an endeavour cannot help but be partial and biased, reflecting my own influences, history and location in the United States as a teacher and scholar. If queer theory, like feminism before it, teaches us anything, it is that description is itself a form of interpretation: all seemingly objective narratives are produced from situations of desire and interest.[2] Queer theory's value inheres in its capaciousness and self-critique, rather than in a single programme. Accordingly, I offer this book not as the 'truth' about the fields it discusses, but as one contribution to an ongoing, productively unwieldy conversation. The only argument of which I hope to persuade you is that queer theory and Shakespeare studies are not only valuable in themselves, but mutually useful and illuminating.

Queer plots, queer feelings

James Richardson's contemporary lyric 'In Shakespeare' provides a fitting opening to a book on the relationship between Shakespeare's writing, Shakespearean criticism and queer theory:

> In Shakespeare a lover turns into an ass
> as you would expect. People confuse
> their consciences with ghosts and witches.
> Old men throw everything away
> when they panic and can't feel their lives.
> They pinch themselves, pierce themselves with twigs,
> cliffs, lightning, to die – yes, finally – in glad pain.

You marry a woman you've never talked to,
a woman you thought was a boy.
Sixteen years go by as a curtain billows
once, twice. Your children are lost,
they come back, you don't remember how.
A love turns to a statue in a dress, the statue
comes back to life. Oh God, it's all so realistic
I can't stand it. *Whereat I weep and sing.*

Such a relief, to burst from the theatre
into our cool, imaginary streets
where we know who's who and what's what,
and command with MetroCards our destinations.
Where no one with a story struggling in him
convulses as it eats its way out,
and no one in an antiseptic corridor,
or in deserts or in downtown darkling plains,
staggers through an Act that just will not end,
eyes burning with the burning of the dead.

([2007] 2010)

Richardson's poem details the multiple ways that Shakespeare's plays are queer. First, there is the level of plot. Lovers become asses (both literally transformed to donkeys, as in *A Midsummer Night's Dream*, or, more commonly, behaving like fools); people confuse human thoughts with supernatural entities; grown men behave irrationally, masochistically; gender is a matter of performance and phenomenology, not biology; human beings turn to lifeless statues, which are themselves revivified. The action and structure of the plays reveal the dimension of human desire and behaviour that cannot be explained according to modern, secular, liberal ideals of self-interest or scientific objectivity. And while queerness is often associated with play and pleasure, Richardson's 'In Shakespeare' accentuates an unbearable and searing confrontation with the elements of eroticism that dismay, disturb, disgust and frighten us. This realization that, in Lauren Berlant's words, 'pleasure is not always fun' is a particularly significant focus of queer theory (Berlant 2001: 436). It is 'a relief, to burst from the theatre/into our cool, imaginary streets' because the plays present us with the abject, shameful, shattering dimensions of attraction and attachment that find no welcome in normative cultural ideals of dignity and domesticity.

Next, there is the level of identification and subjectivity. Richardson's shifting pronouns blur the distinctions between characters and spectators, imagination and reality. 'They', 'you', 'I' and 'we' merge and separate as unpredictably as lovers and asses, statues and humans. 'You', at once the poem's reader and the play's audience, find your own thoughts so strange that 'you' mistake them for 'ghosts and witches'; 'you' are the one who marries a woman disguised as a boy; 'you' have queer desires whose paths cannot be commanded as easily as the choice of a subway line. Even more disturbingly, the very phenomenon of reading collapses the 'you' addressed by the poem into the 'I' of the lyric speaker who responds to Shakespeare's plays by crying, 'Oh God, it's all so realistic / I can't stand it'. And both this intolerable absorption into Shakespeare's worlds and the desire for worlds that are more predictable and manageable is also a communal experience that 'we' all seek as 'we' exit the theatre en masse.

Third, 'In Shakespeare' enacts an experience of subjectivity comprised of a mélange in which immediate and vicarious experience, past and present, original and copy, merge and collide. This identification of past and present is announced in the italicized quotation from Henry Howard, Earl of Surrey, one of the first poets to write sonnets in English. In a poem likely composed in the late 1530s, Surrey laments that although 'all things now do hold their peace', he is left out of this midnight reprieve: 'So am not I, whom love, alas, doth wring, / Bringing before my face the great increase / Of my desires, whereat I weep and sing' (2003: 1, 6–8). Surrey voices a thwarted desire for peace and self-mastery shared by theatrical 'old men' who 'can't feel their lives' and a present-day 'we' who 'know who's who and what's what'. But this seemingly spontaneous expression of erotic agony is itself a loose translation of a sonnet by Francesco Petrarch, whose writing predates Surrey by nearly two centuries. In Richardson's poem, Surrey's words furnish the outburst of an uncertain 'I' nearly crushed by the self-recognition elicited by Shakespeare. To believe that there is 'no one' inhabited by a story that 'convulses as it eats its way out' and no one who 'staggers through an Act that just will not end' is itself to deny the 'imaginary' nature of our own reassuring structures, to boil life down to the reassuring lines of a subway map. Things are queer 'in Shakespeare' because the plays so insistently puncture ideas of stable selfhood, desire, gender and knowledge.

Frequently asked questions

Richardson's 'In Shakespeare' gives us a concrete contemporary explanation of some of the queer dimensions of Shakespearean drama. But even to make that statement is to assume a certain vocabulary and framework that this volume will explore. By way of introducing those, I will answer some of the questions that I am often asked by students and by non-specialists. The brief answers below will be expanded, supplemented and complicated at length in the chapters to follow.

Why is this theory called 'queer'? How does it relate to gay and lesbian history, literature and politics?

The relationship between queer theory and gay and lesbian studies and politics is complex and contingent. Queer theory and gay and lesbian studies both strive to make visible the experiences of sexual minorities and to resist discrimination and violence based on sexual desire or practice. But there are some differences of approach and investment. Gay and lesbian studies and politics tend to focus on the experience, history and politics of homoerotic desires and relationships; queer theory analyses the multitude of incoherencies and contradictions that destabilize the distinction between the normal and the perverse (two interrelated terms that I explore in detail in Chapter 1). As David Halperin puts it,

> Queer is ... *whatever* is at odds with the normal, the legitimate, the dominant. *There is nothing in particular to which it necessarily refers* ... 'Queer,' then, demarcates not a positivity but a positionality vis-à-vis the normative – a positionality that is not restricted to lesbians and gay men but is in fact available to anyone who is or who feels marginalized because of her or his sexual practices ... it describes a horizon of possibility whose precise extent and heterogeneous scope cannot in principle be known in advance. (1995: 62, original emphasis)

In order to understand Halperin's comments, we must understand the convergence of two meanings of the 'normal': (1) the statistical norm (the usual, average, or typical) and (2) the evaluative norm (standard, conventional, expected, allowed). In modern psychiatric medicine, Michel Foucault argues, these 'two usages and two realities of the norm are joined together, mutually adapted, and partially superimposed in a way that is still difficult to theorize', so that 'in the simplest, most everyday conduct, in its most familiar object, psychiatry will deal with something that is *an irregularity in relation to a norm* and that must be at the same time *a pathological dysfunction in relation to the normal*'. Foucault then traces 'how this technology of abnormality encountered other processes of normalization that were not concerned with crime, criminality, or monstrosity, but with something quite different: everyday sexuality' (2003: 162, 163; my emphasis). In the nineteenth century, that is, a conception of abnormality that originated in studies of crime and medicine came to be applied to sexual desire and practice.

One of the most visible ideological formations in which the statistical norm becomes a prescriptive norm, irregularity a sign of pathology, is *heteronormativity*. In the chapters that follow, I assume a distinction between (1) *heterosexual desire*, the desire for erotic contact or intimate relation with someone of a different anatomical or chromosomal sex assignment; (2) *heterosexuality* as a historically specific identity designating a person whose desires are directed at persons of the opposite sex assignment; and (3) *heteronormativity*. Heteronormativity is one of queer theory's most persistent targets of opposition and analysis. *Heteronormativity* is related but not identical to heterosexual desire or heterosexuality. Karma Lochrie economically defines heteronormativity as 'heterosexuality that has become presumptive, that is, heterosexuality that is both descriptive and prescriptive, that defines everything from who we think we are as a nation to what it means to be human ... it is also a heterosexuality that excludes others from these same meanings and communities' (2005: xii). Lauren Berlant and Michael Warner explain that heteronormativity designates 'the institutions, structures of understanding, and practical orientations that make heterosexuality seem not only coherent – that is, organized as a sexuality – but also privileged' (1998: 548, n. 2). Because 'queer' is a relational and contingent term, it can illuminate the ideological work not only of sexual norms but also of the racial, ethnic, national, economic and legal categories often assumed to have nothing to do with sex or gender. Queer theory reveals the queer within the normal and the ordinary. It also reveals, as queer scholars have long argued, the normal and the ordinary within the queer.[3]

I discuss the terminology, history and ongoing debates of queer theory at length in Chapter 1, but for now the topic of same-sex marriage affords a good example of the divergence of queer theory from gay and lesbian politics. In recent decades, a good deal of gay and lesbian activism has sought marriage equality as a common-sense path to greater legal, social, economic and political enfranchisement of the LGBTQ community. Queer theorists, by contrast, have argued that expanding the right to marriage to same-sex couples leaves in place the stigma and material disadvantage of those who choose not to marry. From a queer perspective, a more just goal would be to expand state-sponsored rewards beyond those who chose a life of monogamous coupledom and to offer health, inheritance, housing and immigration benefits to everyone, regardless of marital status. In other words, whereas gay and lesbian studies and politics often focus on challenging discrimination against those who desire persons of the same sex assignment, queer theory and politics more explicitly takes as its object of analysis the discriminatory logic and effects of ideals and institutions (in this instance, respectability, monogamy, marriage and domesticity) that benefit some LGBTQ persons but perpetuate discrimination against those whose sexual lives diverge from these norms (the celibate, the promiscuous, the unmarried and those in relations with more than one person).

Were there gay and lesbian (or queer or homosexual) people in the Renaissance?

No and yes. Because Renaissance societies did not categorize people based on sexual preferences, there were no gay, lesbian or queer persons or communities in the same sense that there are today. In fact, the term 'homosexual' was not part of any European vernacular until the nineteenth century. But the absence of a formal category should not be mistaken for the absence of persons whom we would now describe as gay, lesbian or queer. The term 'heterosexual' did not exist until the nineteenth century either. If there were no 'gay' people before that, neither were there were any 'straight' people.

As I discuss in Chapters 1 and 2, one of the key tenets of queer, gay and lesbian studies is that recovering a history of persons who participated in same-sex practices and relationships, on the one hand, and of the wide range of practices and relationships no longer culturally recognized, on the other, is essential to contesting the discriminatory effects of a belief that monogamous, reproductive, heterosexual relations have been the transhistorical ideal. Same-sex desires and relationships – including unions very close in many respects to marriage – have long been recognized and sometimes privileged over their cross-sex counterparts. But along with recovering this history of same-sex intimacy, it is also important to recognize that the very category of the sexual has shifted across time and space. Rather than understand the past in terms of either strict identity with or difference from the present, queer scholars have explored the relations and identifications between different time periods while also noting that neither can be said to have monolithic or coherent erotic landscapes.

Was Shakespeare gay? Were his characters?

As with the question of whether there were gay people in the Renaissance, the answer might well be 'yes, no, *and* we don't know'. In his edition of Shakespeare's Sonnets, Stephen Booth seeks to bracket the question altogether by pointing to the absence of empirical evidence for Shakespeare's sexual practices: 'Shakespeare was almost certainly homosexual, bisexual, or heterosexual. The Sonnets provide no evidence on the matter … they reveal nothing and suggest nothing about Shakespeare's love life' (1977: 548–9). In one respect, Booth is right: we have no hard evidence of Shakespeare's own proclivities, and literary works cannot be taken as proof of material practices. Booth's glib dismissal, however, assumes several truisms that queer theory has questioned: (1) that modern identity categories were operative in Shakespeare's day; (2) that Shakespeare himself identified exclusively with one of the three categories Booth lists; and (3) that since we cannot know which of these categories Shakespeare can be 'certainly' identified with, taking the erotic hints of his poems too literally distracts us from the aesthetic and rhetorical virtuosity that is the real point of literary study.

The Sonnets (and we can assume that this goes for the plays as well), Booth suggests, ought to be read in terms of formal and generic, not sexual, history. In sum, Booth adopts several of the strategies outlined by Eve Kosofsky Sedgwick by which attention to eroticism that does not cohere with modern norms is rendered 'completely meaningless'. This includes the view, Sedgwick writes, that 'it would be provincial to let so insignificant a fact [as homosexual desire] make any difference at all to our understanding of any serious project of life, writing, or thought'. By declaring sexuality insignificant, 'the most openly repressive projects of censorship ... [are] made perfectly congruent with the smooth, dismissive knowingness of the urbane and the pseudo-urbane' (1990: 52–3). Booth's elegant disdain, Sedgwick allows us to see, closes down discussion of sexuality as decisively as overt prohibition and censorship.

I would revise Booth's answer to say that to ask whether Shakespeare or his characters are homosexual is the wrong question, but not because of the absence of biographical data. Rather, when we confine the meanings of sex and eroticism to modern identity categories, we miss the larger promise of queer theory to challenge the common sense of precisely those categories. In addition to identifying proto-gay-and-lesbian characters in Shakespeare – itself a vital means of challenging a presumption of transhistorical heteronormativity – queer theory allows us to appreciate the wide range of gendered identifications and erotic fantasies that his poems and plays bring to light. The well-known transgender performances and queer desires cited by Richardson's poem ('You marry a woman you've never talked to, / a woman you thought was a boy') are just one example. More expansively, as numerous studies have shown, Shakespeare's poems and plays portray an array of same-sex desires and relationships, along with bestiality; bigamy; incest; promiscuity; impersonal intimacy; cross-generational eroticism; asexuality and celibacy; and fantasies of bondage, domination and sadomasochism (BDSM). Shakespeare's oeuvre, that is, depicts a distinctly queer assortment of desires and acts that do not correspond to modern taxonomies.

Why is the distant past important to queer theory? Shouldn't we focus instead on contemporary lives and politics?

As Chapters 1, 2 and 3 demonstrate in more detail, queer theory's engagement with the past is central to a wider mission of challenging two presumptions shared by both academic and mainstream culture. The first is the view that heterosexual object choice and procreative sexual practice have enjoyed a transhistorical status as the natural, default and ideal forms of intimacy and eroticism.[4] The second is the view that the present is itself coherent and knowable. Accordingly, looking at the past has two benefits. It allows us to piece together a more nuanced picture of sexual desire before the modern homo/hetero divide. And it encourages what Jack Halberstam calls 'perverse presentism', a perspective that affords 'not only a denaturalization of the present but also an application of what we do not know in the present to what we cannot know about the past' (1998: 53). The universalizing aim of theory, the effort to forge abstract principles applicable in all times and places, exists in acknowledged tension with particular, embodied, time-bound instances. The conceptual frameworks offered by theory alter how we perceive particular cultural artefacts (from any historical moment), even as those artefacts might reveal conceptual limitations or blind spots that compel us to refine theoretical abstractions. Recognizing this tension between the particular and the general, most early collections of essays in both gay and lesbian studies and queer theory included scholars whose primary materials were drawn from a range of historical periods, suggesting that pre-modern culture was valuable to queer theory and vice versa.[5]

As queer theory has become increasingly institutionalized, however, it has sometimes fallen victim to the periodizing logics of academic hiring and curricula that it initially offered to disrupt. The result has been, in Valerie Traub's apt critique, that the 'cultural productions of the last century and the current moment' have 'become the occasion for theory, while everything prior to the twentieth century increasingly is positioned as simply history' (2015: 169). Instead, as Stephen Guy-Bray maintains, we must continue to learn from a past 'that is not only queer in itself but also a site that produced queer theory' (2009: xiv).[6] For if, as Lochrie pithily notes, 'heteronormativity is as irrelevant as Coca-Cola is to pre-nineteenth century cultures', the pre-modern archive offers a fundamental site for 'finding the queer in more diffuse and diverse sexual places and imagining a future without heteronormativity, or just perhaps with normativities claimed by other sexualities and identities as well as heterosexuality' (2005: xvi). This requires returning to an earlier queer ethos that recognizes the persistence of the past in the present. A view of theory itself as recursive rather than teleological also disrupts a progressive model of history, whereby secular modernity is understood as the latest stage in a liberation from the past. In an explicit and provocative challenge to this historical narrative of increasing sexual freedom and theoretical sophistication, Madhavi Menon has urged us to take Shakespeare himself seriously as a queer theorist *avant la lettre* (2011a: 11–13).

Granted that the past is important to queer theory, why should we study imaginative literature? Wouldn't we learn more by studying the history of real people and events?

Queer theory would be very different without the important work that has been done from early on recovering and reading legal, medical, social, religious and personal documentation of sexual practice: laws, proclamations and court rolls; medical and anatomical tracts; advice and conduct books; sermons, parochial records and ecclesiastical rules; and diaries, letters and family papers. All of these materials provide vital information about the official cultural views of gendered and sexual behaviour, as well as the actual presence of persons whose sexual practices were not married and reproductive. Scholars continue to scour the archives for such empirical data, and as a result of this work our understanding of sexual practice in the early modern period has grown fuller and more nuanced.

Literary works are also central to the history of sexuality. As Fredric Jameson puts it, the reality of history 'is inaccessible to us except in textual form' (1981: 82). Demographic, legal and medical documents give us only a partial picture of the past: they are written from centres of power that exclude non-elite and female voices, and, as Valerie Traub points out, they tend to employ 'formulaic stock phrases' that obscure the variety and complexity of the past (2015: 138). We can take court records as an example. In his seminal study, Alan Bray observes that although they would seem to be the most direct and reliable evidence of 'real' sexual activity, judicial documents are generally more concerned with recording the procedures of the court than with detailing actual events. Even if we assume that court records accurately describe the sexual acts that brought individuals to trial, itself a dubious view, they give us no insight as to the motive or meaning of those encounters (Bray 1982: 38–42). Similarly, documents such as wills and letters must be understood not as personal confessions of authentic feeling, but as social texts written with the expectation of at least semi-public circulation (Bray 2003; Masten 2016: 69–82).

In light of the interested and incomplete nature of 'factual' records, Frances Dolan has argued, we must 'abandon the notion of an evidentiary point of origin or substratum, thinking instead about charting ripple effects, splatters, aftershocks, feedback loops, and contact networks rather than tracing a line to the beginning or digging down to bottom' (2017: 164). If we want to know more than the behaviours that entered the public record, to learn more about both what early modern persons did and what they *thought* about what they did, factual sources must be supplemented by literary works as evidence of

cultural attitudes and individual fantasies. Bruce Smith rightly
maintains that 'Sexual acts are acts of the imagination as well
as acts of the body' (1991: 15).[7] Precisely because imaginative
literature is not confined to what has really happened, or even
to what could possibly happen, it allows us to glimpse the
otherwise invisible and often contradictory passions, affects,
fantasies and attachments that escape official records and
statistics, then as now. As Carla Freccero elegantly summarizes
queer engagement with the past, 'to the extent that history is
lived as and through fantasy in the form of ideology ... reading
historically may mean reading against what is conventionally
referred to as history' (2006: 4). Because sexuality is both
bodily and imaginative, both visible and invisible, its historical
manifestations appear in discourses that are both grounded
in verifiable fact and in those that describe alternatives to
empirical and quotidian reality.

Why focus on queer readings of a hyper-canonical writer like Shakespeare? Wouldn't we learn more by looking at works that haven't already been discussed by centuries of scholars? Or from popular writing rather than literary culture?

To answer this question, I again turn to Sedgwick, who usefully
explains the value of both the traditional canon and alternative
canons of literature as what she called 'antihomophobic
inquiry' (1990: 14). Accentuating the importance of the latter,
Sedgwick argues that 'a potentially infinite plurality of mini-
canons' can challenge the Western 'master canon' on several
levels. For one, literature written by persons other than elite,
white, straight men can challenge 'the conceptual anonymity
of the master-canon' by making visible that canon's own
gendered, racial and class specificity (1990: 50). The master

canon thereby loses its universal status and is shown to be just as specific and local as literature by women, racial and ethnic minorities, colonized and diasporic subjects and working-class writers.

But if queer theorists were to focus only on alternative canons, we would cede interpretation of the traditional canon to old-school authorities. While a challenge to the master canon is valuable, Sedgwick explains, it nonetheless sustains the view of 'lesbian and gay literature as a minority canon' and thereby obscures the 'nonuniversal functions of literacy and the literary' (1990: 51). In reality, however, 'not only have there been a gay Socrates, Shakespeare, and Proust, but ... their names are Socrates, Shakespeare, Proust; and, beyond that, legion – dozens or hundreds of the most centrally canonic figures in what the monoculturalists are pleased to consider "our" culture, as indeed, always in different forms and sense, in every other' (1990: 52). In collaboration with the formation of new, alternative canons, a re-evaluation of the master cannon challenges the universality of heterosexuality, revealing, as Freccero puts it, 'the queerness at the heart of heteronormative culture' (2006: 21).

Because Shakespeare's drama and poetry continue to provide the scripts for so many mainstream erotic ideals and expressions, his oeuvre offers a significant archive for examining the relationship between past and present representations of desire and identification. Shakespeare's visibility, that is, makes his work a particularly sensitive barometer of cultural and political change more generally. A queer approach to Shakespeare allows us to appreciate the contingency of cultural norms and ideals in the present as well as the past.

Chapter outline

In the chapters to follow, I provide an introduction to both queer theory and Shakespeare. Chapter 1, 'Queer Theory

(Without Shakespeare)', gives an overview of the historical and intellectual forces that led to the emergence of queer theory as a distinct field. I begin by discussing the key investments and innovations signalled by the distinction between queer theory and gay and lesbian studies and politics. I then trace queer theory's conceptual heritage and prehistory in deconstruction and poststructuralism, psychoanalysis, the history of sexuality, gay and lesbian studies and politics, the feminist sex wars, women of colour feminism and HIV/AIDS activism. Finally, I outline some of the key terms and concepts of the foundational queer work of the 1990s and early 2000s, as well as the questions, problems and debates that queer theory has encompassed in roughly the past decade.

In Chapter 2, 'Homoeroticism in Shakespeare Studies', I turn to studies of same-sex eroticism in Shakespeare's world and writing. This chapter discusses themes and concepts that were foundational to queer studies of Shakespeare, including the distinction between sodomy and homosexuality, the publicly significant intimacies available in the early modern period, and the different representations of male and female homoerotic relations and practices in early modern queer criticism. From the earliest to the most recent studies, queer scholars have demonstrated that a presumption that Shakespeare's plots or characters conform to modern heterosexual norms not only supports reactionary politics but also perpetuates bad history. In fact, homosocial relations and homoerotic desires were culturally central, shaping customs of religious devotion, pedagogical training and poetic invention.

In Chapter 3, 'Queerness Beyond Homoeroticism', I discuss forms of queerness that go beyond the gender of object choice. To what extent do historically specific structures of race, gender, class and national identification shape early modern sexual fantasies and practices? How is language itself, including both its material circulation in print and its rhetorical manipulation, a repository of queer desire? More broadly, what does it mean to designate a text, person or practice 'queer'? What are the conceptual advantages and limitations of the term's various grammatical forms and usages (as noun, adjective and verb, to take the most commonly discussed possibilities)? What is the relationship between history and theory? Along with examining the prevalence and value of same-sex intimacies, queer work has traced the effects of normativity on topics that on the surface have little to do with same-sex desires. As this work shows, the challenges to modern heteronormative assumptions that studies of same-sex desire have waged are also vital to rethinking present definitions of sexual normativity as well as race, empire and colonialism; writing, rhetoric and language; and history and temporality.

In Chapter 4, 'How Queer Is the Shakespearean Canon?' I offer brief queer readings of several of Shakespeare's plays and poems across the genres in which he wrote. I first discuss the mobility of desire in *A Midsummer Night's Dream* and *Venus and Adonis*. In both of these works, heterosexuality is infused with ambivalence, aggression, abjection, and cross-species and same-sex desire, revealing love itself to be a fundamentally 'queer feeling' (Berlant 2001). I then consider the relation between race, gender and erotic desire in *The Merchant of Venice* and *Othello*. Both plays understand sexuality as profoundly shaped by race – a concept that in the past as well as the present encompassed not just phenotype or skin colour, but also culture, speech, religion and geographical origin. Finally, I discuss how queer work on political history and the early modern archive can reshape our understanding of temporality and reproduction in *Henry V* and *Hamlet*, particularly as these texts intersect with the question of queer pedagogy.

The final chapter, 'The Politics of Form: Queer Shakespearean Film', examines queer film adaptations of Shakespeare's poems and plays. I begin with a discussion of what I see as the first queer Shakespearean film, Derek Jarman's *The Tempest* (1979), which employs punk and camp to critique the conjoined sexual norms and colonial hierarchies often read into Shakespeare's play. I then discuss two formative instances of the New Queer Cinema that also happen to be adaptations of Renaissance plays: Jarman's *Edward II* finds in the Marlowe play of that name a site of protest against the homophobic policies of Thatcherite England, while Gus Van Sant's *My Own Private Idaho* deploys Shakespeare's Henriad to expose the devastating effects of 'family values' in Reagan–Bush America. Finally, I look at two later 1990s Shakespearean films designed for a popular audience, Baz Luhrmann's *William Shakespeare's Romeo + Juliet* and Julie Taymor's *Titus*. Despite their postmodern aesthetic, I argue, both of these films take a retrograde view of sexuality that treats black, brown, queer and trans* persons as threats to the purity and innocence epitomized by the figure of the white child. Read together, the group of films I discuss in Chapter 5 remind us that sexual politics do not evolve according to an Enlightenment narrative of increased openness and plurality. Rather, to the extent that nostalgia for the good old days helps define progress as recuperation of an idealized past, 'Shakespeare' remains a site of theoretical and political contestation.

Caveat lector

Having outlined the structure of this book, I feel compelled to conclude my introduction with two confessions which are also caveats.

First, you should be aware that the chapter divisions perpetuate a false divide between queer theory, on the one hand, and Shakespeare and early modern studies, on the other. Since the early days of what we now call 'queer theory', Shakespeare and the early modern period have been central to the study of sexual history, practice and normativity. In the 1980s and 1990s, field-changing books by Alan Bray (1982), Bruce Smith (1991), Jonathan Dollimore (1991), Alan Sinfield (1992), Valerie Traub (1992) and Jonathan Goldberg ([1992] 2010) traced the prevalence of same-sex attraction in the period that had been previously taken as the dawn of sexual normativity in the form of companionate marriage. They were part of the emergence of gay and lesbian studies and queer theory as academic fields, and they were intrinsic to an initial queer move to contest academic as well as popular assumptions of transhistorical heteronormativity.

Second, in the very process of narrating the history of Shakespeare and queer theory, I have created a deceptively linear, progressive narrative of field development where it would be more accurate to see the field(s) as recursive and multifaceted. The many influences on queer theory that I trace in Chapter 1, for instance, are accentuated, subordinated and suppressed in different theoretical and polemical contexts. By the same token, I had originally conceived Chapters 2 and 3 as a sequence covering early and recent queer studies of Shakespeare, respectively. But I ultimately realized that this division created a false sense of development, when in fact, *all* of these topics have been vital dimensions of the field from foundational texts through the present moment, a concurrence that I seek to make visible by organizing these chapters by theoretical problem rather than chronology.

In short, you should understand *Shakespeare and Queer Theory* not as telling an exhaustive story but, rather, as offering flashpoints that I have found particularly compelling and useful – a rough roadmap from which I hope that you will stray and which I hope you will revise in your own travels in queer theory. In the spirit of a queer theory that takes for granted its own contingency and obsolescence, my hope is that this volume will be but one moment in an unpredictable and promiscuous exchange between modern queer theory and the equally queer thought that Shakespeare's writing exemplifies.

1

Queer Theory
(Without Shakespeare)

When the field of 'queer theory' first arrived on the academic scene in the 1990s, it appeared to many to have emerged already fully formed, like Athena bursting forth from Zeus's skull. We can appreciate just how unexpected queer theory's rise to prominence and prestige was by contrasting its seemingly instant celebrity with the embattlement and marginalization experienced by scholars of gay and lesbian studies in the years prior. Writing in 1990, Martin Duberman, Martha Vicinus and George Chauncey, Jr, describe the anxiety and resistance with which academics had met the grass-roots assemblage of gay and lesbian histories:

> Some [professional historians] have been reluctant to publish in the field due to fear of the possible consequences for their careers; sympathetic faculty still caution graduate students to avoid linking themselves to so 'controversial' a topic. Many scholars still consider the history of homosexuality a marginal field, if not an embarrassing or distasteful subject of study. (1990: 2)

Within a few years, a sea-change had occurred. Lauren Berlant and Michael Warner note in a 1995 essay on the field that 'Queer theory has already incited a vast labor of metacommentary, a virtual industry ... Yet the term itself is less than five years old,' and they wonder, 'Why do people feel the need to introduce, anatomize, and theorize something that can barely be said yet to exist?' (1995: 343). The same year, Leo Bersani could sardonically comment that

> There have been moments at some universities ... when, to read a bulletin board of upcoming lectures and colloquia, a visitor might think that all the humanities departments had been merged into a single gay and lesbian studies programs. Liberal straights respectfully attend lectures at which their own sexual preferences are confidently assigned to the erotic junkheap of compulsory heterosexuality – a practice into which millions of human beings have apparently been forced and from which they are now invited to liberate themselves. (1995: 14–15)

Writing in retrospect, David Halperin recalls that 'the moment that the scandalous formula "queer theory" was uttered ... it became the name of an already established school of theory, as if it constituted a set of specific doctrines, a singular, substantive perspective on the world, a particular theorization of human experience' (2003: 340).

The apparent speed with which queer theory gained visibility and prestige in US universities, however, obscures the decades of activism and scholarship that laid its political and intellectual foundations. In the first section of this chapter, I examine the history of the term 'queer theory'. Subsequent sections explain the theoretical and political movements that preceded and made possible queer theory: deconstruction and poststructuralism; psychoanalysis; the history of sexuality; gay and lesbian activism and scholarship; the feminist sex wars; women of colour feminism; and HIV/AIDS activism. In the final two sections, I discuss key tenets of the classical queer theory of the 1990s and the more recent concerns and debates of the past decade.

Why 'queer'?

The term 'queer theory' as the name of this field of study is usually credited to Teresa de Lauretis. As de Lauretis explains in the 'Introduction' to a 1991 volume of *differences* on the topic, she chose 'queer' in order to 'problematize some of the discursive constructions and constructed silences in the emergent field of "gay and lesbian studies"' (1991: iii–iv). In conversation with but distinct from gay and lesbian studies, queer studies can analyse and challenge 'the respective and/ or common grounding of current discourses and practices of homo-sexualities in relation to gender and race, with their attendant differences of class or ethnic culture, generational, geographical, and socio-political location' (1991: iii–iv). In choosing the non-identitarian and non-academic term 'queer', de Lauretis repurposes what had previously been a homophobic slur into a term whose capaciousness would enable analysis of the imbrication of sexual normativity with other sources of hierarchy and privilege.

In his introduction to another formative collection of essays, *Fear of a Queer Planet* (1993), Michael Warner explains the utility of the term 'queer' at even greater length. Queer theory, he argues,

> rejects the minoritizing logic of toleration or simple political interest-representation in favor of more thorough resistance to regimes of the normal. Rather than treat gays and lesbians as a distinct minority group defined by same-sex object choice and the demand for tolerance and legal protection, 'queer' gets a critical edge by defining itself against the normal rather than the heterosexual. (1993: xxvi)

Queer theory, in other words, maintains that securing a just and safe world for sexual minorities requires critique of the very concepts of the normal, the private and the political. This means beginning from the premise that the subject of queer politics is neither knowable nor namable in advance.

Whereas gay and lesbian studies generally focus on the history and significance of the homosexual–heterosexual distinction, queer theory examines the relation between queerness and normativity. Because gender of object choice was (and is) the most visible dimension of normativity, gay and lesbian and queer analysis often converge. But as I noted in the introduction, a (perhaps *the*) signal intervention of queer theory is to differentiate heterosexuality (which I'll define as desire for genital contact exclusively with members of the opposite sex assignment) from heteronormativity (the idea that heterosexual desire is uniquely natural and healthy). As Berlant and Warner explain, queer theory allows us to see that heterosexuality's 'coherence is always provisional, and its privilege can take several (sometimes contradictory) forms ... Contexts that have little visible relation to sex practice, such as life narrative and generational identity, can be heteronormative in this sense, while in other contexts forms of sex between men and women might *not* be heteronormative' (1998: 548, n. 2, original emphasis). Berlant and Warner vividly illustrate the distinction between heterosexuality and heteronormativity by describing a leather-bar performance of erotic vomiting. 'A boy, twentyish, very skateboard, comes on the low stage at one end of the bar, wearing lyrca shorts and a dog collar' and 'sits loosely in a restraining chair'; his (male) partner slowly force-feeds him, keeping him just 'at the threshold of gagging'. The performance climaxes when the top inserts his fingers into the boy's throat to induce vomiting, 'insistently offering his own stomach for the repeated climaxes'. Significantly, this 'scene of intimacy and display, control and abandon, ferocity and abjection' excludes the specifically genital contact and gendered desire usually associated with sexuality. Reporting that 'Word has gone around that the boy is straight,' Berlant and Warner ask, 'What does that mean in this context?' (1998: 565). To be 'straight' or 'heterosexual' is not necessarily to be 'normal'.

The project of queer theory is to consider the numerous ways that erotic fantasy, desire and practice exceed and fracture what Berlant and Warner elsewhere call a 'fantasized

mainstream' accorded legal, social and economic benefits
(1995: 345). To focus only on gender of object choice, as Eve
Kosofsky Sedgwick writes in a frequently cited explanation of
the value of queer theory, is to overlook 'the open mesh of
possibilities, gaps, overlaps, dissonances and resonances, lapses
and excesses of meaning when the constituent elements of
anyone's gender, of anyone's sexuality aren't made (or can't be
made) to signify monolithically' (1993: 8). Any firm distinction
between the 'queer' and the 'straight' or the 'normative', in
this analysis, already seeks to manage and limit gendered
and erotic possibilities. Judith Butler, likewise, argues that
'if identity is a necessary error, then the assertion of "queer"
will be necessary as a term of affiliation, but it will not fully
describe those it purports to represent'. The value of the term
lies in its 'contingency' and 'specific historicity', which permit
future generations of scholars and activists to 'expose, affirm,
and rework it' (1993: 230).

The ethical, political and hermeneutic value of 'queer',
for a number of critics, lies in its resistance to assimilation
and categorization. David L. Eng, Jack Halberstam and José
Esteban Muñoz, for instance, argue that queer theory offers
a '"subjectless" critique' that 'disallows any positing of a
proper subject *of* or object *for*' the field, 'no fixed political
referent' or 'positivist assumptions' (2005: 3; original
emphasis). How this resistance to a fixed agenda or subject
would shape queer politics has been the subject of vigorous
debate. Lee Edelman insists that 'queerness can never define
an identity; it can only ever disturb one'; accordingly, politics
understood as a collective project of building a better future
is antithetical to queerness (2004: 17). By contrast, Muñoz
argues that 'The future is queerness's domain ... Queerness
is essentially about the rejection of a here and now and an
insistence on potentiality or concrete possibility for another
world' even as he critiques 'the ontological certitude' that he
understands as 'partnered with the politics of presentist and
pragmatic contemporary gay identity' (2009: 1, 11). In other
words, while they disagree about the political value of a focus

on the future, Eng, Halberstam, Muñoz and Edelman share a rejection of identitarian queerness anchored on substantial or ontological definitions of 'the queer'. The instability of the term itself requires a certain humility about its positions and procedures. As Eng, Halberstam and Muñoz put it, 'one of the field's key theoretical and political promises' is its openness 'to a continuing critique of its exclusionary operations' and recognition that 'we must sometimes relinquish not only our epistemological but also our political certitude' (2005: 3, 15).

The expansiveness and non-referentiality of 'queer' has not been without detractors from within queer and gay and lesbian studies. For some scholars, the shift from gay and lesbian studies to queer theory came at the cost of intellectual rigour and political urgency. Just three years after coining the term 'queer theory', de Lauretis would explicitly distance herself from the field with the charge that it had 'quickly become a conceptually vacuous creature of the publishing industry' (1994: 296). If 'queer' theory amounts to nothing more than 'ludic postmodernism', Donald Morton charges, the material and historical dimensions of sexual desire and identity, along with any serious political agenda, might disappear altogether (1996: 2–3). In its attention to the instability, indeterminacy and constructedness of sexuality, Bersani notes, queer theory can de-specify and disembody homosexuality altogether: 'gays have been de-gaying themselves in the very process of making themselves visible', with the logical end that 'there is no longer any homosexual subject to oppose the homophobic subject' (1995: 32, 56). This de-specification, Brad Epps points out, carries its own ironically identitarian agenda. When queer theory 'makes fluidity a fetish', the result is that 'queer' itself 'becomes a term, if not an identity, to be protected, defended, and preserved, to be fixed, that is, as designating a lack of fixity, a generally free fluidity' in order to disavow its own materiality and limitations, or 'the ideological baggage and national limits of the term *queer* itself' (2001: 413, 415; original emphasis). As a prestigious and politically correct 'game the whole family can play', in Halperin's acerbic evaluation, queer theory is too easily taken up by ambitious scholars with no investment in gay and lesbian politics or the transformation of academic protocol or practice (2003: 342, 343). Or, in Sharon Marcus's more measured précis of this critique, 'if everyone is queer, then no one is – and while this is exactly the point queer theorists want to make, reducing the term's pejorative sting by universalizing the meaning of queer also depletes its explanatory power' (2005: 196).

As I will discuss in the final section of this chapter, debates over the conceptual and political value of 'queer' theory persist. These differences are not a bad thing; they are a sign that the field continues to change and evolve, with obsolescence and invention mutually constitutive elements of the queer endeavour. First, however, I want to move systematically through the manifold perspectives that have shaped this unwieldy, self-contradictory field.

Deconstruction and poststructuralism

The insights of deconstruction and poststructuralism have significantly enabled queer theory's challenge to definitions of subjectivity and sexuality as coherent, rational or monolithic. Deconstruction and poststructuralism at once build on and critique the structural linguistics of Ferdinand de Saussure. In Saussure's structuralist view, 'language is a system of pure values which are determined by nothing except the momentary arrangement of its terms' ([1916] 1994: 80). No individual element can be understood apart from the larger structure that determines its identity and significance. Words do not convey any metaphysical substance, and nothing has meaning in isolation of the rest of the system: 'In language there are only differences' ([1916] 1994: 121). So 'black' signifies, or conveys meaning, only in contrastive relation to 'white', 'woman' only in relation to 'man', and so forth. We do not have access to reality except through the medium of language, which itself structures thought and experience. And language is itself at once arbitrary (there is no intrinsic connection between words and the things or concepts they name) and systematic (the individual inherits rather than invents or determines it). For many scholars writing in the wake of Saussure, structuralism reshaped understandings of self and society beyond language. The structural anthropology of Claude Lévi-Strauss, for instance, adapted Saussure's systematic view of language to the relation between human beings and their cultures, on the one hand, and among different cultures, on the other. In its attention to system rather than individual, structuralism radically questions humanist and Enlightenment views of human autonomy, agency and authenticity. Nonetheless, structuralist thought remains optimistic that systems are themselves orderly and rational. Consequently, observation, data-collection and logical deduction give us access to reliable knowledge about language, culture and the world they mediate.

Deconstructive and poststructuralist theorists agree that such confidence is unwarranted. Jacques Derrida, a founding theorist of deconstruction, argues that the binary oppositions that create significance themselves require a fixed, metaphysical centre of meaning that holds the structure in place. Logically, then, structuralism depends on the presence of something beyond the structure – a belief in extra-linguistic essence or truth that Derrida calls a 'metaphysics of presence' – to which one term in any binary set is attributed greater proximity and therefore greater value (for instance, reason is valued over matter, culture over nature, man over woman). Yet, Derrida further argues, such transcendental meaning is itself a product of language and so always deferred. This is because any given term in a binary set is itself at once overdetermined (it has multiple significations that cannot be fully reconciled) and indeterminate (because we cannot decide which of the irreconcilable meanings to exclude). Rather than presence at the centre of human language, Derrida finds an aporia – a lack conceptualized not as non-existence but as a space from which something inarticulable is missing.[1]

Roland Barthes and Michel Foucault's poststructuralist writings on authorship have profoundly impacted queer conceptions of subjectivity and agency. In 'The Death of the Author', Barthes proposes that the agency, intention and singularity that we associate with authorship and, more generally, individuality is itself a product of competing and contradictory linguistic and cultural forces ([1967] 1977). Writing is not 'expressive' in the sense of Romantic individualism that intentionally conveys singular truth or meaning; writing is a system of signs whose significance is indeterminate, dependent on readers who help create its meaning beyond anything its writer might have thought or intended (Barthes [1973] 1974: 10–16). Foucault considers writing in terms of 'discourse' that challenges the 'author-function', or the construction of a single and controlling origin of a text's meaning. Rather than seek to establish the 'real' author of a text or ask what that text really means, Foucault maintains, we must ask about the discursive conditions that produce particular appearances of individual subjectivity ([1969] 1977: 138).

Barthes and Foucault's challenge to a humanist idea of intentional, original authorship is not limited to studies of literature; it is also a broader challenge to the belief in a subject that precedes the discursive systems that, deconstructive and poststructuralist philosophers argue, create the possibilities of meaning and identification. This emphasis on the contradiction and inconsistency inherent to any system helped enable a queer critique of identity by questioning the ideals of agency, subjectivity and authenticity on which normative views of selfhood, desire and sexuality rest.

Psychoanalysis

Originated by Sigmund Freud at the turn of the twentieth century, psychoanalysis remains a rich and nuanced system for discussing sexuality. To be sure, Freud's work was appropriated by a medical and psychiatric establishment that for decades would contribute to the oppression of sexual minorities. In the United States, for instance, the American Psychiatric Associations *Diagnostic and Statistical Manual of Mental Disorders* (*DSM*) classified homosexuality as a mental illness until 1973, and both medical practice and popular culture treated same-sex desire as a pathology to be cured in the interest of individual and societal health. Yet the work of Freud and his interpreters (some of the most notable were Melanie Klein, Jacques Lacan and Jean Laplanche) has also provided a consistent resource for a queer questioning of the view that heterosexuality is natural and normal.

One of Freud's key insights for queer theory is that perversion is innate and universal; 'normality' is imposed for particular social ends but never with complete success. In a 1905 essay on 'Infantile Sexuality', Freud observes that children are 'polymorphously perverse', and that the ease with which they 'can be led into all possible kinds of sexual irregularities' reveals that 'an aptitude for them is innately present in their disposition' ([1905] 1975: 57). Moreover, 'this same disposition to perversions of every kind is a general and fundamental human characteristic', one that is inhibited to varying degrees by 'shame, disgust, pity and the structures of morality and authority erected by society' ([1905] 1975: 97).[2] As Jonathan Dollimore neatly summarizes Freud's position, 'one does not becomes a pervert but remains one' (1991: 176).

The view that we all remain perverts – or queers – is central to Freud's development of theories of ambivalence, narcissism and masochism, which he sees as complex and counterintuitive responses to both organic and cultural hindrances to satisfaction and mastery.[3] In his later works, especially *Beyond the Pleasure Principle* and *Civilization and Its Discontents*, Freud argues that in its perversity and aggression, the sexual instinct is irreconcilable with the demands of civilization. Positing that 'the price we pay for our advance in civilization is a loss of happiness through the heightening of the sense of guilt', Freud asks, 'may we not be justified in reaching the diagnosis that, under the influence of cultural urges, some civilizations, or some epochs of civilization – possibly the whole of mankind – have become "neurotic?"' ([1929] 1963: 97, 110). Civilization produces the very neurosis that threatens its survival by deeming perverse urges that are natural and universal and requiring their redirection or inhibition.

The writings of Jacque Lacan, who interpreted Freud's work through the frameworks of structuralist and poststructuralist linguistics, anthropology and philosophy, have had an especially strong influence on queer theory. In his seminal 'The Agency of the Letter in the Unconscious or Reason Since Freud', Lacan argues that 'what psychoanalytic experience discovers in the unconscious is the whole structure of language' with the result that 'the notion that the unconscious is merely the seat of the instincts will have to be rethought' ([1966] 1977: 147). What Lacan means by this is that the unconscious is not a primordial or singular core of a person's mind or character, nor are there universal archetypes that shape unconscious experience (as had been argued by Carl Jung). Understood through the framework of structural linguistics, the unconscious is structured like a language in that it is a complex and contradictory system of drives and impressions that have no positive significance in themselves. They rather acquire significance only relationally, much as words acquire meaning through grammar, syntax and distinction from other words both at the definitional level and, more fundamentally, at the level of the material letters that comprise them. As a result, in Lacanian psychoanalysis there is no essential self or identity to be recovered from neurosis or trauma. Psychic life is instead comprised of three realms, or orders. The Imaginary encompasses the realm of images that appear clear and coherent, beginning with the infant's identification with its reflection in the mirror as a single, bounded being. The Symbolic describes the order of language and signification; this is the realm of the Other from which the individual learns its place within a larger order ('you are a boy'; 'you are a son'). The Real, not to be confused with 'reality', describes that which escapes full perception or signification.

It is the traumatic and unfathomable wholeness and loss of distinction that is differentiated into navigable order by the realms of images and language.

A key Lacanian axiom is that 'desire is the desire of the Other' (Lacan [1973] 1981: 235). Desire, in this view, does not emerge from some authentic core unconscious. Like self-identification as such, desire is oddly 'impersonal' ([1966] 1977: 298). Desires are given to us by the Other, that authoritative Symbolic realm of linguistic and social meaning that itself structures the unconscious. Consequently, we are always alienated from our desires, as the several overlapping meanings of Lacan's axiom suggest. First, we desire to be desired by the Other; our desires are shaped by the wish to be desirable, to be recognized, to attract love. Second, we desire what the Other desires; that is, we desire an object not because it is intrinsically attractive but because it has already been judged desirable by the Symbolic order. Third, because the subject's initial, infantile encounter with the Other is also the encounter with the mother (understood more broadly as the primary caretaker), desire is fractured between love for that which sustains life and resentment or aggression against the power that the mother/object/Other is felt to have over the self ([1966] 1977: 1–7, 8–29).

These insights point to a larger insight of Lacanian psychoanalysis: because our desire is never for a concrete person or object, love is itself a fantasy whose particular objects are interchangeable. Any single object of desire is a placeholder for an impossible yearning for unconditional, exclusive and eternal love and satisfaction: desire, in effect, strives to abolish itself by achieving a state of wholeness that leaves nothing else to be desired. Because all objects will fall short of delivering the eternal completion at which desire aims, desire is restless, frustrated and tinged with aggression toward its inevitably treacherous and disappointing objects. This aggression is itself a source of *jouissance*, the French term for enjoyment as well as for orgasm. For Lacan, *jouissance* represents not a positive, sustainable pleasure but the ecstatic moment at which intolerable stimulation or excitement is extinguished. *Jouissance* can more widely be seen as coterminous with the Freudian death drive as an impulse to mastery and violation that renders incoherent any systematic distinction between self and other, sadism and masochism, pleasure and pain – or, ultimately, the normal and the perverse (Lacan [1986] 1992: 167–240).[4]

Foucault and *The History of Sexuality*

One of the most direct influences on queer theory was Foucault's *The History of Sexuality*, particularly Volume I, which was first published in France in 1976 and translated into English two years later. Here, Foucault challenges what he called the 'repressive hypothesis', the view that modern society represses sexuality. To the contrary, Foucault argues, sexuality itself has a history; that is, it takes on particular forms and meanings in relation to the discursive orders of particular historical moments. Rather than repress sex, Foucault writes of modernity, 'the techniques of power exercised over sex have not obeyed a principle of rigorous selection, but rather one of dissemination and implantation of polymorphous sexualities', and 'the will to knowledge has not come to a halt in the face of a taboo that must not be lifted, but has persisted in constituting – despite many mistakes, of course – a science of sexuality' ([1978] 1990: 12–13). An important corollary of the insistence that sexuality is not repressed but continually constituted by discourse is that there is no authentic or uninhibited eroticism that is prior to social order or that can be liberated from social constraints: 'We must not think that by saying yes to sex, one says no to power; on the contrary, one tracks along the course laid out by the general deployment of sexuality' ([1978] 1990: 157). Social, medical and legal systems for managing populations demand that their subjects articulate the truth of their desires. Power does not coach us to just say no to sex. It pleads, 'Yes, tell me more. Yes, say that. Say that and say much more than that' (Foucault [1972] 1998: 119).

Consequently, Foucault argues, in modern Western society the religious, moral and medical 'incitement to discourse' is equally a 'perverse implantation' whereby sex is transformed from singular acts into a taxonomic system of discrete identities deemed normal or pathological. While originally focused on children, criminals, homosexuals and the mentally ill, this taxonomy, as I noted in the introduction, also came to encompass 'everyday sexuality' (Foucault 2003: 163). For queer studies, one of Foucault's signal interventions was the observation that 'this new persecution of the peripheral sexualities entailed an *incorporation of perversions* and a new *specification of individuals*' ([1978] 1990: 42–3; original emphasis). Whereas the perversions had once been viewed as singular acts that anyone could do, they now became understood as revelations of a hidden, core identity.

The difference between sodomy, which could include any non-reproductive sexual activity, and homosexuality, understood as the desire for intimacy with persons of one's own sex, provides a concise example of this shift. Foucault explains, 'As defined by the ancient civil or canonical codes, sodomy was a category of forbidden acts; their perpetrator was nothing more than the juridical subject of them'. Foucault contrasts the *juridical* (legal, administrative) category of the sodomite – a category akin to the thief or the adulterer – to the *psychological, psychiatric, medical* category of the homosexual: 'The nineteenth-century homosexual became a personage, a past, a case history, and a childhood, in addition to being a type of life, a life form, and a morphology, with an indiscreet anatomy and possibly a mysterious physiology. Nothing that went into his total composition was unaffected by his sexuality' ([1978] 1990: 43). In the history Foucault reconstructs, modern psychiatric medicine and psychotherapy are secular versions of the medieval confessional practices by which sexuality came to be understood as expressing the 'truth' of the self. It was only with the emergence of medicalized psychology in the nineteenth century that sexual desire and practice were understood as distinguishing among distinct kinds of persons.

Foucault's work further proposes that when individuals name and classify sexual desires and practices, they do not so much submit to repression as participate in their own administration. In Western modernity, 'Pleasure and power do not cancel or turn back against one another; they seek out, overlap, and reinforce one another' ([1978] 1990: 48). A simple binary of oppression and resistance, or domination and agency, is insufficient to account for 'The omnipresence of power: not because it has the privilege of consolidating everything under its invincible unity, but because it is produced from one moment to the next, at every point, or rather in every relation from one point to another. Power is everywhere; not because it embraces everything, but because it comes from everywhere' ([1978] 1990: 93). In contrast to pre-modern feudal regimes, in which sovereign power inhered in the right to put to death, modern regimes centre on biopower (or biopolitics), the right to determine which lives to foster. The administrative state's study of populations, developmental norms and institutional organization disallows certain sexual choices not through juridical prosecution and punishment but instead through withholding of the institutional and material means to survive. To demand inclusion or recognition within a given political order is, therefore, to participate in the administrative apparatus whose exclusions one opposes.

Gay and lesbian scholarship and activism

Modern research on sexuality began in the late nineteenth century, with the historical, sociological and medical studies of John Addington Symonds, Havelock Ellis and, of course, Freud. Academic research on sexual history and practice began to gain a significant presence in the US academy in the mid-twentieth century with the establishment of the Kinsey Institute for Sex Research in 1947 and the ONE Institute for Homophile Studies in 1956. At roughly the same time, gay and lesbian political organizations became more prominent. The Mattachine Society, formed in 1951, was the first long-term gay rights organization and the first to admit women (Meeker 2001). The urgency of gay and lesbian activism in the United States increased with President Dwight D. Eisenhower's 1953 Executive Order declaring gay men and lesbians a threat to US security and prohibiting them from employment by the US government. The consequent 'Lavender Scare' caused thousands of persons to be publicly exposed as homosexuals and dismissed from their positions (Johnson 2004). In response, the Mattachine Society, along with organizations such as Vanguard, the Daughters of Bilitis and the international Gay Liberation Front, began to organize public protests against harassment and discrimination. These increased after the 1969 Stonewall Riots brought the struggle for gay and lesbian rights into the American public eye (Duberman 1994). In the 1970s, a series of homophobic events and movements in the United States drew further attention to the need for gay and lesbian coalitions: the 1977 assassination of Harvey Milk, the first openly gay man elected to public office; Anita Bryant's national 'Save Our Children' campaign to repeal standing gay rights ordinances and prevent new ones; and the 1978 'Briggs Initiative', a California ballot initiative proposing to fire all gay and lesbian public schoolteachers. The first National March on Washington for Lesbian and Gay Rights took place in 1979.

It was amidst this atmosphere of grassroots and national political organization that gay and lesbian studies began to appear in universities. Early work tended to focus not only on reclaiming a history of homosexual desire and practice but also on documenting past persecution and resistance.[5] These pioneering studies tended to offer a broad historical sweep that stressed the persistence and prominence of same-sex desire across decades, and even centuries, of Western culture.

The 1970s also saw the emergence of theoretical accounts of same-sex desire and politics. Foucault's writings remain the most prominent, but there were other instances of queer theory *avant la lettre* written in Europe and quickly translated into English. Guy Hocquenghem's *Homosexual Desire* ([1972] 1993), one of the first theoretical accounts of homosexuality, brought together psychoanalytic and Marxist theory to examine the social, economic and psychic constitution of the modern 'homosexual'. Another early theoretical work was Mario Mieli's *Homosexuality and Liberation: Elements of a Gay Critique* ([1976] 1980), which drew on Freud and Marx to call for a liberatory sexual revolution. French lesbian feminist writing analysed the conjunction of gendered and sexual norms. Monique Wittig's famous declaration that 'a lesbian is not a woman' and Luce Irigaray's analysis of the complex construction of anatomical, psychic, erotic and economic differentiation made sexuality central to female identity and provided the groundwork for Butler's *Gender Trouble* (1990), one of the foundational works of 1990s queer theory.

The feminist sex wars

A good deal of theory and politics that paved the way for the distinct field of queer theory grew out of conflicts within feminism over women's sexual desires and relationships. In the late 1960s and early 1970s, this disagreement took the form of tension between heterosexual and lesbian feminists, the latter of which Betty Friedan described as a 'lavender menace' that threatened to discredit the women's movement in the eyes of mainstream culture. In response, a number of lesbian feminists broke from both the Gay Liberation Front, which they felt prioritized gay male rights, and the National Organization for Women, which took homophobic positions, in order to form a group focused on lesbian rights. Originally called the Lavender Menace in a send-up of Friedan's remark and later renamed

Radicalesbians, the group's most significant legacy was the pamphlet 'The Woman Identified Woman', which argued that heterosexuality supported male rule. Also in the 1970s and early 1980s, lesbian feminists such as Adrienne Rich, Carol Gilligan and Carol Smith-Rosenberg produced important essays that challenged the binary of heterosexuality and homosexuality. Though they had different topics and focuses, these writers brought to view a reality in which women's relationships to one another had long existed on, in Rich's influential phrase, a 'lesbian continuum' ([1980] 1986: 69). Whether or not a woman had or wanted to have sex with other women, Rich argued, the emotional support and intensity of women's relations challenged the view that heterosexual relations were foremost, or even necessary, in women's lives. At the same time, the dominance of heterosexuality as an institution – its centrality to social, economic and legal conditions of existence – made it virtually compulsory, thereby preventing women from seeking out alternatives.

By the early 1980s, tensions over sexuality within the women's movement would erupt in a series of battles within feminism over BDSM, butch–femme relations and pornography. On the one side, both lesbian separatist and anti-pornography feminists understood these practices as a product of patriarchal false consciousness that taught women to take pleasure in their own subjugation. On the other, sex-radical feminists charged that in the name of protecting women, feminists were aligning themselves with the social conservatism of the religious right, which was notoriously hostile to both the women's and gay liberation movements. These debates came to a head at the Barnard Conference on Women and Sexuality in 1982, which was boycotted by many mainstream feminists and vocally protested by the group Women Against Pornography (WAP).[6] Many foundational propositions of what would come to be called queer theory were initially presented at this conference, including Gayle Rubin's 'Thinking Sex: Notes for a Radical Theory of the Politics of Sexuality'. Here, Rubin critiques sexual hierarchies that elevated some practices (heterosexual, married, monogamous, procreative, non-commercial, in pairs, in a relationship, same generation, in private, no pornography, bodies only, vanilla) above others (homosexual, in sin, promiscuous, non-procreative, commercial, alone or in groups, casual, cross-generational, in public, pornography, with manufactured objects, sadomasochistic). Diagnosing the coercive work of normativity, Rubin observes that

> Individuals whose behavior stands high in this hierarchy are rewarded with certified mental health, respectability, legality, social and physical mobility, institutional support, and material benefits. As sexual behaviors fall lower on the scale, the individuals who practice them are subjected to a presumption of mental illness, disreputability, criminality, restricted social and physical mobility, loss of institutional support, and economic sanctions. ([1984] 1992: 279)

Instead, she argues, we need a 'radical theory of sex' that can 'identify, describe, explain, and denounce erotic injustice and sexual oppression' ([1984] 1992: 275). Rubin's call for a 'theory of benign sexual variation' represented a break from both feminist traditions that focused on patriarchal oppression, on the one hand, and those that saw lesbian culture as a refuge from the dominance and violence associated with masculinity, on the other ([1984] 1992: 278). In focusing on fantasy and practice, rather than simply gender of object choice, sex-radical feminists developed a vocabulary for challenging ideals of romance, monogamy and sexual innocence along with heterosexism. If, as Heather Love writes, 'Giving up the myth of lesbian purity, lesbian difference, and the transformative power of love between women is quite a letdown', it also turns lesbianism toward a more comprehensive analysis of 'some intractable problems: gender isn't easy; power is unevenly distributed in relationships; love is always strange, and often ugly' (2000: 110). The sex-radical investment in destigmatizing BDSM, pornography, promiscuity, prostitution, butch–femme roles and other 'perversions' is important to the development of queer theory because it moves the discussion of sexuality away from a homo/hetero binary and toward attention to the imbrication of the queer and the normative.

Women of colour feminism[7]

Frequently understood apart from the feminist sex wars and queer theory alike, the writing now often described as 'women of colour feminism' is best known for its challenges to the racial and sexual exclusions of mainstream second-wave feminism. As José Esteban Muñoz (1999: 1–34) and Roderick A. Ferguson (2004: 1–29) have shown, this body of writing also helped provide some of the intellectual foundations for queer theory. Black, Chicana, Third World and postcolonial feminists in the 1970s and 1980s exposed the role played by Western ideals of the nuclear family in naturalizing the hierarchies of race, class and nation that slavery, colonialism and capitalism required and with which white feminist writers and activists were often complicit. Modern sexual types, this work allowed us to see, are artefacts of a long history of racialized domination and vulnerability – from the systematic ravishment of enslaved women to the myth of the black rapist to the pathologization of the kinship structures of Asian, African and indigenous peoples.

The idea that racial and sexual identities were mutually constituted was a central insight of women of colour feminism well before the term 'intersectionality' entered the critical lexicon in the early 1990s. The Combahee River Collective Statement, one of the earliest and most influential manifestos of black feminist solidarity, declares that 'we are actively committed to struggling against racial, sexual, heterosexual, and class oppression, and see as our particular task the development of integrated analysis and practice based upon the fact that the major systems of oppression are interlocking' ([1977] 1982: 1). Audre Lorde offers a structural critique of these interlocking oppressions: 'The need for sharing deep feeling is a human need. But within the european-american tradition, this need is satisfied by certain proscribed comings-together' ([1978] 1984: 58–9; lower-case in original). This was not merely an ideological proscription, but an enforcement of normativity by economic and legal forces as well. 'In this country', Cherríe Moraga writes of the United States, 'lesbianism is a poverty – as is being brown, as is being a woman, as is being just plain poor' (1983).

The ideal of sexual propriety, women of colour feminists argued, enforces racial hierarchies by making white female innocence the standard of 'respectability' against which black, Native, Latina and Third World women are found lacking.[8] In its universalization of Western domesticity, Hazel Carby observes, 'Colonialism attempted to destroy kinship patterns that were not modeled on nuclear family structures, disrupting, in the process, female organizations that were based upon kinship systems which allowed more power and autonomy to women than those of the colonizing nation' (1982: 224). White, Western feminism can sustain the power of capitalism by treating non-white, non-Western women as requiring rescue from archaic customs so that they could catch up to their liberated, 'modern' Western sisters. In opposition to many second-wave white mainstream and lesbian feminists, who tended to see racial oppression as analogical to gendered and sexual oppression rather than coterminous with it, women of colour feminists sought to imagine a 'differential consciousness' that would, in Chela Sandoval's words, find a means of 'weaving "between and among" oppositional categories' (1991: 16).[9]

To be, in Moraga's and Gloria Anzaldúa's own early uses of the term, 'queer' is the condition of women who are racial as well as sexual minorities. This queerness, Anzaldúa argues, is not a singular identity (like, for instance, white feminism or gay rights) but multiply determined by differently queer relations to both dominant and minoritarian culture. Anticipating the later queer challenge to identitarian movements, Anzaldúa describes the consciousness of the *mestiza* – the mixed-race lesbian who has no single home – as 'a tolerance for contradictions, a tolerance for ambiguity … Not only does she sustain contradictions, she turns the ambivalence into something else … (As a lesbian I have no race, my own people disclaim me; but I am all races because there is the queer of me in all races)' (1987: 79–80). Estranged from movements built on national and racial as well as feminist and lesbian solidarity, women of colour writers and activists helped lay the intellectual groundwork for queer thought premised on self-critique and consciousness of the role that Western sexual norms play in sustaining political and economic hierarchies.

HIV/AIDS activism

Academic and activist responses to the HIV/AIDS pandemic that began in the 1980s were perhaps the most direct and widely acknowledged influence on the development of queer theory and politics. A brief survey of US statistics allows us to appreciate how this public health crisis brought to horrific light the deadly consequences of the silencing of and discrimination against sexual minorities. In 1981, the year that the Center for Disease Control (CDC) released the first study of cases of immunodeficiency in gay men, there were 126 cases of HIV/AIDS in the United States. Five years passed before the National Academy of Sciences (NAS) described AIDS as a 'national health crisis' in 1986, a year in which the total number of US cases of HIV/AIDS rose to 28,712 and the total number of deaths to 24,559. US President Ronald Regan would not publicly mention AIDS until 1987, a year in which there were 50,378 cases and 40,849 total deaths. The US Congress would not create a National Commission on AIDS until 1989, and discrimination against those who had contracted HIV/AIDS was legal in the United States until 1990, when Congress passed the Americans with Disabilities Act, which prohibited discrimination against individuals with disabilities, including

HIV/AIDS. By 1991 there were 206,563 cases of HIV/AIDS and the virus had caused a total of 156,143 deaths.[10]

I offer this snapshot of the HIV/AIDS contraction rate and death toll in order to capture the ghastly reality that laid bare the lethal effects of homophobia and heteronormativity. As numerous activists pointed out, the immediate response of both the government and the popular media was to blame the crisis on the ostensibly immoral and pathological nature of homosexuality itself. Simon Watney, for instance, decried the tendency to use HIV/AIDS as a pretext to 'justify calls for increasing legislation and regulation of those who are considered to be socially unacceptable' (1987). The initial public response to HIV/AIDS ranged from deliberate ignorance and neglect, to calls to shut down gay bars and bathhouses, to proposals that those infected with the virus be quarantined or prominently tattooed. In response, early activists in the United States formed the Gay Men's Health Crisis to raise money for research, establish counselling hotlines and disseminate information about prevention. As the rate of contraction increased, more militant groups – OutRage! in the UK (formed in 1990), and ACT-UP (formed in 1987) and Queer Nation (formed in 1990) in the United States – staged demonstrations and sit-ins to demand a public response commensurate with the scale of the crisis.

Literary, theatrical and political work also called attention to the link between discrimination against homosexuals – which had been codified as US law in *Bowers v. Hardwick*, the 1986 Supreme Court decision upholding anti-sodomy statutes – and the implicit decision to permit the spread of HIV/AIDS.[11] Activism and academic studies converged to oppose what some saw as the conservatism of HIV/AIDS organizers such as Randy Shilts and Larry Kramer, who fought for public recognition and funding but who also assigned responsibility to the promiscuity of the gay community and supported zoning laws and the closure of bathhouses.[12] The 1987 volume of the journal *October* on the special topic of 'AIDS: Cultural Analysis/Cultural Activism' sought to challenge the regulation of sexuality from both within and outside the gay community. In his introduction to this volume, Douglas Crimp maintains that 'AIDS does not exist apart from the practices that conceptualize it, represent it, and respond to it'; rather 'AIDS intersects with and requires a critical rethinking of all of culture: of language and representation, of science and medicine, of health and illness, of sex and death, of the public and private realms' (1987b: 3, 15). Together, the essays in the volume insist that activism must go beyond fundraising or calls for empathy. They stress that only by retheorizing sexuality as such to recognize the reciprocal influence of medical, political and cultural discourse can we dismantle the deadly distinction between the safe, moral, normal sex of the 'general public' and unsafe, immoral, perverse sex of a gay minority.

One influential work in queer theory, Leo Bersani's 'Is the Rectum a Grave?' appears in this volume. Opening with the blunt statement that 'There is a big secret about sex: most people don't like it', Bersani attacks what he calls 'the *redemptive reinvention of sex*', or the insistence that sex is moral and healthy only insofar as it is an expression of love, commitment and self-affirmation (1987: 197, 215; original emphasis). This myth, Bersani charges, inspires the cultural denigration of passivity and self-loss, summarized in an image of gay men who – like syphilitic Victorian prostitutes – 'spread their legs with an unquenchable appetite for destruction' that does not so much invite infection as reveal a diseased psyche (1987: 211). As the carriers of illness, gay men are cast as threats to a general public whose murderous indifference to, disgust at, or violence against persons with HIV/AIDS is legitimated as a form of self-defence. Rather than argue that gay relations can be as loving, innocent and monogamous as their straight counterparts, Bersani rejects these dominant relational ideals: '"Purity" is crucial here: behind the brutalities against gays, against women, and, in the denial of their very nature and autonomy, against children lies the pastoralizing, the idealizing, the redemptive project I have been speaking of. More exactly, the brutality is identical to the idealization'

(1987: 221). An idealization of masculine self-affirmation, he concludes, must be rejected by sexual minorities in favour of the realization that 'The self is a practical convenience; promoted to the status of an ethical ideal, it is a sanction for violence ... Male homosexuality advertises the risk of the sexual itself as the risk of self-dismissal, of *losing sight* of the self, and in so doing it proposes and dangerously represents *jouissance* as a mode of ascesis' (1987: 222; original emphasis). In challenging the imperative for 'healthy' and 'normal' persons to affirm themselves – and the corollary that they are justifiably repelled by male passivity and promiscuity – Bersani also rejects one of the cornerstones of dominant sexual morality.

The 1990s: Butler, Sedgwick and 'classic' queer theory

As the above survey attests, a number of writers and activists had challenged the ethics, politics and logical coherence of dominant sexual culture long before such challenges came to be seen as part of a distinct field called 'queer theory'. This number includes two books often viewed as foundational texts of queer theory, Judith Butler's *Gender Trouble: Feminism and the Subversion of Identity* and Eve Sedgwick's *Epistemology of the Closet*, both published in 1990.

Butler's *Gender Trouble* draws on the work of Freud, Lacan, Wittig, Derrida, Irigaray, Foucault and J. L. Austin to challenge 'the metaphysics of substance', that is, the humanist and universalist conception of the subject that assumes 'a substantive person who is the bearer of various essential and nonessential attributes' (1990: 10). In opposition to a metaphysics of substance, Butler argues for an 'antifoundationalist approach' that views gender as 'a complexity whose totality is permanently deferred, never fully what it is at any given juncture in time' (1990: 15–16). Antifoundationalism entails a decisive break from the venerable feminist maxim that gender is a product of culture, sex a product of nature. Insofar as 'sex is a gendered category' it does not precede but follows from cultural constructions of gender: gender itself is 'the discursive/ cultural means by which "sexed nature" or a "natural sex" is established as "prediscursive", prior to culture, a politically neutral surface *on which* culture acts'. In other words, the anatomical or chromosomal difference that feminists had been calling 'sex' may have been gender all along (1990: 7; original emphasis). Gender is not descriptive but 'proves to be performative – that is, constituting the identity it is purported to be. In this sense, gender is always a doing, though not a doing by a subject who might be said to preexist the deed' (1990: 25).

To understand gender as performative – in the senses of theatricality, action and efficacious language – is not to treat it as entirely a matter of individual play or volition.[13] Rather, Butler argues, performance is itself constrained through legal and cultural administration and prohibition which deem genders 'intelligible' only to the extent that they 'institute and maintain relations of coherence and continuity among sex, gender, sexual practice, and desire'. One of the most powerful 'socially instituted and maintained norms of intelligibility' is heterosexuality (1990: 17). Sexuality, in this analysis, is essential to the construction of gender in that heterosexuality helps create the illusion of men and women as inherently distinct, complementary creatures prior to culture. But the discrepancies between multiple repetitions of 'heterosexual constructs' in both 'non-heterosexual frames' and in straight culture 'brings into relief the utterly constructed status of the so-called heterosexual original', revealing that 'gay is to straight *not* as copy is to original, but, rather, as copy is to copy. The parodic repetition of "the original" ... reveals the original to be nothing other than a parody of the *idea* of the natural and the original' (1990: 31; original emphasis). Or, as Butler clarifies a few years later in *Bodies That Matter*, 'To claim that all gender is like drag, or is drag, is to suggest that "imitation" is at the heart of the *heterosexual* project and its gendered binarism ... that hegemonic heterosexuality is itself a constant and repeated effort to imitate its own idealizations' (1993: 125; original emphasis). Radically undermining the coherence of gendered identity or sexual desire, Butler laid the groundwork for work in queer theory that would reveal the instability of dominant culture's constructions of normal, acceptable life scripts, even as it examined the multitude of concrete effects that these constructions have on queer lives.

Equally pathbreaking was Sedgwick's *Epistemology of the Closet*, which opens with the statement that 'an understanding of virtually any aspect of modern Western culture must be, not merely incomplete, but damaged to the degree that it does not incorporate a critical analysis of modern homo/heterosexual definition' (1990: 1). Western culture, Sedgwick argues, is structured by an epistemology in which deliberate ignorance and silence render homosexuality an open secret, one betrayed in the very assiduousness with which it is repressed. Sedgwick's project, accordingly, is to bring to light contradictions and tensions within dominant views of the relationship between sexuality and culture.

Epistemology of the Closet makes several signal contributions that still influence queer theory's vocabularies and conceptual frameworks. One is Sedgwick's analysis of the contradiction between what she terms the 'minoritizing' and 'universalizing' views of homosexuality. The first of these, the minoritizing view, understands homosexuals as a distinct and discrete population; the second, the universalizing view, understands sexual desire in terms of fluid and unpredictable practices and desires that anyone can have. Sedgwick treats these views not as mutually exclusive but as coterminous, mutually formative and equally useful politically. This viewpoint dovetails with another insight that would prove central to queer theory, that

It is a rather amazing fact that, of the very many dimensions along which the genital activity of one person can be differentiated from that of another (dimensions that include preference for certain acts, certain zones or sensations, certain physical types, a certain frequency, certain symbolic investments, certain relations of age or power, a certain species, a certain number of participants, etc. etc. etc.) precisely one, the gender of object choice, emerged from the turn to the century, and has remained, as *the* dimension denoted by the now ubiquitous category of 'sexual orientation'. (1990: 8; original emphasis)

Rather than see sexuality in static terms, Sedgwick argues, anti-homophobic inquiry must create 'nonce taxonomies' and new conceptual tools capable of reckoning with the 'self-evident fact' that the same practices might have entirely different meanings depending on the context and the persons involved (1990: 23). In remaining open to gay and lesbian self-identification while also acknowledging that 'sexuality extends along so many dimensions that aren't well described in terms of the gender of object-choice at all', anti-homophobic inquiry strives to recognize the 'unrationalized coexistence of different models' of sexuality both historically (that is, before the ostensible paradigm shift between acts and identities) and in the present identitarian regime (1990: 35, 47).

Butler and Sedgwick remain required reading, as do many of the scholars writing in the first decade that 'queer theory' existed as a distinct field. During this time, queer theory challenged both the legitimacy and the coherence of normativity in the many forms it took. One central focus was how the life scripts of straight culture – marriage and family, privacy and property – rendered intertwined sexual, racial and class privileges both natural and invisible. An important work in this vein is Warner's *The Trouble with Normal*, which argues that rather than pursue the 'selective legitimacy' of marriage, queer activists must 'resist the state regulation of sexuality' (1999: 82, 88). To treat marriage as a private bond of love 'is an increasingly powerful way of distracting citizens from the real, conflicted, and unequal conditions governing their lives, and ... it serves to reinforce the privilege of those who already find it easier to imagine their lives as private' (1999: 100). Berlant, Samuel Delany and Lisa Duggan, meanwhile, illuminated the force that an ideal of the white nuclear family exerted on definitions of citizenship, urban space and political practice that revolved around ideals of childlike sexual and political innocence (Berlant 1997); public safety as synonymous with family-friendly streets (Delany 1999); and the coalescence of the black rapist and the homicidal lesbian as threats to respectable white women (Duggan 2000).

In this first decade a number of scholars also turned sharp analytic attention to the limitations, contradictions and exclusions of queer theory's resistance to identity politics. A common charge was that queer theory had implicitly replicated the universal humanist subject as a white, cisgendered man. In response, a growing body of work has called attention to the limitations of an abstract definition of queerness. A 1997 special issue of *Social Text* on 'Queer Transexions of Race, Nation, and Gender', for instance, sought 'to bring the projects of queer, postcolonial, and critical race theories together with each other and with a feminist analytic that itself has been a key factor in the critique of social identity'. The editors explain that

This deployment not only illuminates how various dimensions of social experience – race, sexuality, ethnicity, diaspora, gender – can cut across or transect one another, resulting in their potential mutual transformation; it also 'queers' the status of sexual orientation itself as the authentic and centrally governing category of queer practice, thus freeing up queer theory as a way of reconceiving not just the sexual, but the social in general. (Harper et al. 1997: 1)

The provocation of 'Queer Transexions' would be taken up in several subsequent book-length studies, some of which had published articles in this issue. To take one instance, Muñoz's work on queer 'minority subjects' – those who are 'hailed by more than one minority identity component' – proposes 'disidentification' as a means of decoding cultural fields through the specificities of race, ethnicity and gender: 'To disidentify is to read oneself and one's own life narrative in a moment, object, or subject that is not culturally coded to "connect" with the disidentifying subject ... it is the reworking of those energies that do not elide the harmful or contradictory components of any identity' (1999: 8, 12). Muñoz examines queer of colour performance, which he argues makes available a reality of the embodied experience of a dominant culture – including that of white male privilege within queer thought – that cannot be simply rejected but instead can be recycled and reimagined. Further expanding the purview of queer of colour critique, Halberstam (1998), Eng (2001) and Robert F. Reid-Pharr (2001) published influential studies on the attenuation of masculinity and queerness by female and non-white bodies.

It was also in the 1990s that trans* theory emerged to point out both the uses and limitations of queer theory. The anti-essentialism of queer thought might seem a natural ally to trans* theory and politics insofar as it rejects social prescriptions demanding normative and binary alignment of gender expression, sexual desire, and the anatomical and chromosomal sex assigned at birth. However, while trans* and queer theory may form strategic alliances and coalitions, they also diverge politically and conceptually and therefore cannot automatically be incorporated as a single field. On the one hand, as trans* scholars have observed, when queer theory celebrates gender fluidity and neglects the materiality of gender, it risks erasing those for whom gender reassignment is a matter of survival.[14] On the other, trans* scholars have shown that the effort to establish clear taxonomies of butch, drag, transgender and transsexual diminishes the multitude of identifications – including those of racial difference – that shape trans* experience and sexuality.[15] Understood as strategically allied rather than identical with one another, queer and trans* theory must, as Dean Spade writes, engage in 'constant self-reflection' in order to 'spot traps of co-optation and incorporation that our resistant projects face' (2015: 7).

Indeed, the differences between them may be one source of such necessary self-critique.

What's left? Queer theory after the new millennium

One irony of queer theory is that the work pursued under this rubric has often been less interested in sexual practice as an isolated category than in its saturation by public, social, economic and cultural structures. As Janet Halley and Andrew Parker write, 'The problem is less that queer theory makes "everything about sex" than that it lodges the nonsexual firmly within the sexual' (2011: 5). This includes such 'nonsexual' topics as race, colonialism, affect and temporality. Accordingly, when Eng, Halberstam, and Muñoz affirm that 'some of the most innovative and risky work on globalization, neoliberalism, cultural politics, subjectivity, identity, family, and kinship is happening in the realm of queer studies', they designate not so much a new direction for queer theory as the logical outcome of the field's own commitment to self-critique (2005: 5). This commitment has allowed queer theory continually to address changing political conditions. Roderick A. Ferguson, David Eng, Lisa Duggan and Jasbir Puar, for instance, have all examined how the production of deviant sexualities helps sustain global capital and neo-liberal politics. 'The racialization of Mexican, Asian, Asian American, and African American labor as contrary to gender and sexual normativity positioned such labor outside the image of the American citizen,' Ferguson argues, demonstrating how fictions of hypermasculinity, insufficient masculinity and predatory sexuality have shaped interlocking narratives of race and national belonging (2004: 14). Eng critiques the emergence of 'queer liberalism' that privileges consumerism and privacy as signs of equality and freedom and thereby overlooks the structural hierarchies of race, class and global capitalism (2010). Lisa Duggan has dubbed this queer ideology 'homonormativity' because white and economically privileged queers identify with the neo-liberal values of privacy and consumerism (2003). Taking a similarly transnational scope in her critique of 'homonationalism', Puar argues that Western LGBTQ activism, which casts the West as a safe haven for sexual liberation, has too easily embraced neo-conservative narratives of the war on terror as a clash between the freedom and rationality of secular modernity and the oppression and pathology of religious tradition. To extricate queer theory from imperial ideology, Puar argues, scholars must attend to the regulatory logics of their own ideals of transgression, to acknowledge that 'It is easy, albeit painful, to point to the conservative elements of any political formation; it is less easy, and perhaps much more painful, to point to ourselves as accomplices of certain normativizing violences' (2007: 24).

Alongside the forcefully transnational focus of much recent queer theory, other trends and trajectories have emerged. One of these is affect theory, which emphasizes the non-linguistic forces of emotion, phenomenology and embodied response to the world (Sedgwick 2003). Working in this vein, Sara Ahmed has described queerness as an orientation toward particular objects and emotions (2006); Berlant has analysed the potential of sympathy and optimism both to foment and to replace political action (1998, 2011); Ann Cvetkovich understands depression as a political and cultural phenomenon, rather than a strictly medical one (2012); and Heather Love has proposed that rather than leave behind ambivalent or negative identifications with past manifestations of queer shame and mourning, queer scholars can 'turn grief into grievance' to disrupt the politics of the present (2007: 115).

In her defence of the refusal to let go of the past, Love also engages with queer theory's turn to temporality. Foundational to this turn is the work of scholars who – themselves drawing on postcolonial critiques of a progressive model of history – propose that, as Carolyn Dinshaw put it, 'past lives, texts, and other cultural phenomenon' continue to 'form part of our subjectivities and communities' in the present, thus 'making affective connections ... across time' (1999: 1, 12). Such affective connections require a different approach to history, Carla Freccero argues: queer studies can draw on the resources of psychoanalysis to question the 'empiricism of what qualifies as event itself' and produce 'a fantasmatic historiography that acknowledges ... that history is lived as and through fantasy in the form of ideology' (2006: 4). Further contesting 'a vision of time as seamless, unified, and forward moving', Elizabeth Freeman examines how 'temporal drag', or the adaptation of outmoded dress or manners, can constitute a form of resistance against '*chrononormativity*, or the use of time to organize individual human bodies toward maximum productivity' evinced in 'teleological schemes of events or strategies for living such as marriage, accumulation of health and wealth for the future, reproduction, childrearing, and death and its attendant rituals' (2010: xiii, 3, 4; original emphasis). Rather than simply embrace modernity, this work demonstrates, queer theory may also require the excavation of past alternate social arrangements and political formations.

Queer approaches to temporality can also attune us to alternative life itineraries. Rather than accept a definition of success that 'in a heteronormative, capitalist society equates too easily to specific forms of reproductive maturity combined with wealth accumulation', Halberstam explores the affordances of failure: 'dominant history teems with the remnants of alternative possibilities, and the job of the subversive intellectual is to trace the lines of the worlds they conjured and left behind' (2011: 2, 19). Perhaps most controversially, Edelman maintains that any politics focusing on the future participates in 'reproductive futurism', by which meaning must be deferred in the name of the Child. Not to be understood as identical with actual children, the Child is a figure of innocence and promise that is uniquely threatened by the *sinthomosexual*, a Lacanian portmanteau that Edelman coins to summarize the dominant cultural association of queerness with the senseless *jouissance* of the death drive unconstrained by the rational ego (2004: 33–66). As these examples indicate, when we take for granted the appeal of success and futurity, we overlook those lives and desires that these ideals exclude and pathologize.

Disability and crip theory have also drawn on the methods of queer theory even as they have critiqued some of its blind spots and exclusions. Disability studies resists the dominance of a medical model of disability that understands disability as an individual, biological deficit to be cured; this work instead endorses a social model that reveals how social, cultural, legal and architectural conventions disable certain bodies. Rather than conform to norms of able-bodiedness, disabled persons must demand a radical restructuring of both social norms and built environments. The body of writing often described as 'crip theory' brings together the insights of disability and queer theory, having, in Robert McRuer's words, 'a similar contestatory relationship to disability studies and identity that queer theory has to LGBT studies', with the important difference that 'crip theory does not ... seek to dematerialize identity' but rather 'remaps the public sphere and reimagines and reshapes the limited forms of embodiment and desire proffered by the systems that would contain us' (2006: 35, 31). McRuer argues that 'compulsory able-bodiedness, which in a sense produces disability, is thoroughly interwoven with the system of compulsory heterosexuality that produces queerness: that, in fact, compulsory heterosexuality is contingent on compulsory able-bodiedness, and vice-versa' (2006: 2). Resisting these mutually sustaining compulsions, recent work by Mel Chen (2012) and Alison Kafer (2013) has shown, can help us to notice the racial, environmental and global dimensions of normative notions of health and ability and, even more radically, to reassess conventional definitions of 'human' life in relation to ostensibly inanimate or animal others.

Another recent controversy in queer theory has been the utility of anti-normativity as a conceptual or political stance. In their Introduction to a 2015 special issue of *differences*, Robyn Wiegman and Elizabeth A. Wilson argue that in setting itself against 'norms, normalization, and the normal', queer theory 'turns systemic play into unforgiving rules and regulations and so converts the complexity of moving athwart into the much more anodyne notion of moving against' (2015: 18). Wiegman and Wilson challenge a queer focus on evaluative or prescriptive norms and instead emphasize the statistical meaning of the 'normal'. They cite actuarial models to argue that 'the norm is a dispersed calculation (an average) that enquires into every corner of the world. That is, the measurements, comparisons, adjudications, and regulations that generate the average man do so not in relation to a compulsory, uniform standard, but through an expansive relationality among and within individuals, across and within groups' (2015: 14, 15). From this perspective, 'Averages don't exclude anyone; on the contrary, their power as statistical tools relies on the method of counting or ordering everyone in the group'; because 'the center calls on and is constituted by the periphery', they continue, 'In this [all-inclusive mathematical or statistical] sense, it is not clear what antinormativity would be' (2015: 16–17). By resisting the allure of transgression and anti-normativity, Wiegman and Wilson argue, scholars can formulate analytic methods that are less obviously radical or heroic but also better suited to the complexity of lived experience. In responses to Wiegman and Wilson's provocation, Halberstam contends that 'Most of the theorists assembled under the heading of the antinormative produce the very scholarship that Wiegman and Wilson call for – namely a critique of simple notions of the political as oppositional' (2015). Moreover, Duggan argues, to treat mathematical norms as value neutral is to fail to acknowledge the violences of the ordinary and the status quo – particularly 'the civilizational, imperial history of norms as racial ideals used to measure the "development" of inferior races' (2015).

We can understand this most recent dispute over the definition and utility of that central queer concept, normativity, as evidence of the continued intellectual vitality and political seriousness of the field. As the following chapters argue, queer studies of Shakespeare and early modern culture have a lot to contribute to that collective project.

2

Homoeroticism in Shakespeare Studies

In this chapter, I discuss queer analyses of same-sex desire in early modern moral, legal, medical and literary tracts. Homoeroticism, this work has demonstrated, was neither marginalized nor repressed in the period. Instead, eroticized same-sex friendship, pedagogy, religious devotion and textual production were central to cultural institutions. Two adult men sharing a bed, kissing or embracing one another, or addressing one another with terms of endearment – Jeffrey Masten gives the examples of 'sweet prince' or 'sweet friend' – would have seemed unremarkable, customary behaviour, not a sign of a specific sexual orientation.[1] Because authorized same-sex intimacies between men and between women were ingrained in the social and political structure of early modern England, they could be hard to distinguish from their demonized counterparts, sodomy and tribadism.[2] As Jonathan Goldberg puts it,

> if ... sodomy named sexual acts only in particularly stigmatizing contexts, there is no reason not to believe that such acts went on all the time, unrecognized as sodomy, called, among other things, friendship or patronage, and facilitated by beds shared, for instance, by servants or students, by teachers and pupils, by kings and their minions, or queens and their ladies. ([1992] 2010: 19)

This ambiguity and overlap between idealized and stigmatized homosociality exposes what Alan Sinfield has called our cultural 'faultlines', those 'awkward, unresolved issues' that reveal the lack of harmony in and coherence of a culture's ideology and thereby 'distress the prevailing conditions of plausibility' on which the dominant social order depends (1992: 47). For Sinfield, as for many scholars, Shakespeare's writing provides a lens through which we can discern these faultlines through 'study of cultural apparatuses that arrange writing and theater in early modern England and the modern world, and of their relations with other institutions (such as the church) that tend partly to legitimate state violence but may be bent partly to other purposes' (1992: 9). The opacity and fluidity of sexual categories in early modern England, that is to say, can attune us to the complexities and contradictions of our contemporary sexual mores. Below, I describe some of the frameworks through which scholars have understood homoerotic affections and practices in Shakespeare's England: sodomy, friendship, rivalry, tribadism, religious devotion and humanist pedagogy and poesis. These alternative expressions of same-sex desire and attachment are valuable to queer theory because they attune us not only to forms of homoeroticism before nineteenth-century identity categories, but also to the insufficiency of either simple identification with or distinction between early modern and modern sexuality. Learning more about same-sex intimacies in Shakespeare can compel us to notice the ambiguous, even obscure eroticism of relations – from friendship to pedagogy to collaboration – beyond courtship and marriage today.

Sodomy

It is difficult to overestimate the influence of Foucault's distinction between sexual acts and identities on queer studies of Shakespeare. As we have seen, this distinction hinged on the claim that the emergence of medical psychiatry in the late nineteenth century introduced a profound shift in dominant views of the relationship between what one does and who one is. In Foucault's oft-cited formulation, 'The sodomite had been a temporary aberration; the homosexual was now a species' ([1978] 1990: 43). Sodomy, which Foucault described as an 'utterly confused category', was a temptation to which anyone could succumb. It could denote oral and anal sex, bestiality, mutual masturbation and a whole host of other non-reproductive activities, both same-sex and cross-sex, that threatened marriage, legitimate procreation or sociopolitical order ([1978] 1990: 101). In its widest sense, sodomy could describe any act *except* the one that Henry Abelove has helpfully specified as 'sexual intercourse so-called': 'cross-sex genital intercourse (penis in vagina, vagina around penis, with seminal emission uninterrupted)' (2003: 23).

Most early modern scholars agree with Foucault that there was no early modern identity that was synonymous with that of the modern 'homosexual', but they have differed as to how to interpret the category of sodomy or the figure of the sodomite. Studies of early modern moral, legal, medical and literary writing have borne out the truth of Eve Sedgwick's axiom that 'The historical search for a Great Paradigm Shift may obscure the present conditions of sexual identity.' In emphasizing the alterity of the past, Sedgwick explains, scholars endorse 'a unidirectional narrative of supersession' of one coherent model of same-sex relations by another. Instead, she argues, anti-homophobic inquiry must uncover the 'unexpectedly plural, varied, and contradictory historical understandings whose residual – indeed, whose renewed – force seems most palpable today' in order 'to denaturalize the present' and render the significance of homosexuality 'less destructively presumable' (1990: 44, 46, 48).

Early modern scholars writing both before and after Sedgwick published this axiom have underscored the 'plural, varied and contradictory' perceptions of sodomy in Shakespeare's world. Alan Bray's pathbreaking study emphasizes that sodomy was understood as a threat to cosmic as well as social order: as a 'crime against the order of God and nature' it aroused 'revulsion and violent hostility' (1982: 26, 58). Subsequent work has shown that the charge of sodomy likely had specific enough meaning to be used for legal convictions and for political, religious and colonial propaganda.[3] In most of these usages, sodomy is limited to sexual, usually penetrative, acts between men. Yet scholars have also explored the consequences of the broadness of sodomy as a category. Indeed, one of the ideological contradictions that Bray uncovers is 'the discrepancy between this society's extreme hostility to homosexuality [by which Bray means sex between men] which one comes across when homosexuality was being referred to in the abstract and its reluctance to recognise it in most concrete situations' (1982: 77).[4] Intimacy between men, Bray argues, was part of many dominant cultural institutions: the household, where male masters could have sex with male servants and apprentices; universities, grammar schools and village schools, where male schoolmasters could have sex with male students and male students with one another; street prostitution and all-male brothels (what the playwright John Marston called 'male stews'); political and literary patronage, where male patrons could have sex with the courtiers, actors and writers they supported; and the theatre, an all-male institution with a reputation for what we would now call homosexual activity and for arousing homoerotic appetites and identifications (1982: 43–55). The single-sex composition of the early modern English playhouse also enjoined one of the customs that has most interested feminist and queer Shakespeare scholars: the performance of women's roles by boys. In Stephen Orgel's analysis, part of the allure of having boys play the parts of women was that 'boys were, like women – but unlike men – acknowledged objects of sexual attraction for men ... the homosexual, and particularly the pederastic, component of the Elizabethan erotic imagination is both explicit and for the most part surprisingly unproblematic' (1996: 70).[5] Valerie Traub further emphasizes that the phenomenon of the boy actor makes the stage a site on which 'homoerotic energy is elicited, exchanged, negotiated, and displaced' (1992: 118).

As Bray (1982) and Bruce Smith (1991) discuss at length, anti-sodomy laws instituted under Henry VIII and refined over the following century were at once precise and capacious, and they were rarely enforced. In Edward Coke's *Institutes*, sodomy as a general category of non-procreative acts is hard to distinguish from buggery and bestiality. In a chapter summarizing laws against 'Buggery and Sodomy', Coke explains that 'Buggery is a detestable, and abominable sin, amongst Christians not to be named, committed by carnall knowledge against the ordinance of the Creation and order of nature, by mankind with mankind, or with brute beast, or by womankind with brute beast.' While this statement focuses more on excoriating than defining sodomy, Coke does go on to specify that in legal terms, sodomy (like vaginal rape) requires penetration, not mere sexual contact or ejaculation: '*Emissio feminis* [ejaculation onto the thighs] maketh it not Buggery, but is an evidence in case of buggery of penetration: and so in Rape the wordes be also *carnaliter cognovir*, and therefore must be penetration; and *emissio feminis* without penetration maketh no Rape.' In his definition of rape in the chapter following that on buggery and sodomy, Coke again specifies that 'Although there be *emissio feminis*, yet if there be no penetration, that is, *res in re*, it is no rape, for the words of the Indictment be, *carnaliter cognovit, & c.*' – the legal euphemism of *res in re*, 'thing in the thing' aligns penetration with carnal knowledge as knowledge of the body's interior cavities as opposed to the mere surface contact of friction or ejaculation (1644: 58–60).

Smith argues that Coke's limitation of the legal definition of sodomy to anal penetration (of men, women or animals) works to narrow the more expansive medieval category (1991: 50–1). As Smith also notes, court records from the sixty-eight years that comprised the reigns of Elizabeth I and James I (the monarchs who ruled during Shakespeare's lifetime) show that prosecutions for bestiality outnumbered those for sodomy by six to one. Between 1558 and 1625, there were only six indictments for sodomy; among these, the one man convicted had raped a five-year-old boy (Smith 1991: 48). 'Unless one were famous and had powerful enemies', Smith writes, 'one could be indicted for sodomy only by forcing another male (more likely than not a minor) to be a passive partner in anal sex ... On the larger matter of mutual desire between men as equals the law remains tactfully silent' (1991: 53). This silence did not indicate tolerance but a calculated misrecognition of same-sex sexual contact that did not disrupt social or economic hierarchies. As Goldberg puts it, sodomitical acts 'emerge into visibility only when those who are said to have done them also can be called traitors, heretics, or the like, at the very least, disturbers of the social order that alliance – marriage arrangements – maintained'; as long as such acts did not disturb institutionalized order, they would not be recognized as sodomy, 'especially if, in other social contexts, they could be called something else, or nothing at all' ([1992] 2010: 19). Accordingly, ontological or epistemological inquiries about sodomy (what is it? how do we know?) 'will never deliver the sodomite per se, but only ... sodometries, relational structures precariously available to prevailing discourses' ([1992] 2010: 20).

Research on early modern European culture examines the prominence of explicitly sexual contact between men in this period as well as the cultural centrality of sodomy as a concept. A brief sampling of this body of work reveals its multiple challenges to the Foucauldian distinction between pre-modern acts and modern identities, suggesting instead that there was some consciousness of homoerotic relations as legitimate practices or recognized adult ways of life. N. S. Davidson has uncovered 'a surprisingly self-confident literature available in Venice arguing that sexual preference was a matter of choice, not of law' (2002: 71). Mary Bly proposes that early modern sodomites can be understood as an 'erotic minority' who would have sought out dramatic representations of same-sex eroticism (2000: 16). Daniel Juan Gil understands same-sex sexuality not as a product of social order but as '*a special class of interpersonal relations* that, like modern intimacy, is set apart from conventional modes of sociability' (2006: xi; original emphasis). Mario DiGangi proposes that far from being unrecognizable or invisible, the sodomite was a wholly recognizable 'composite type' in early modern literature, one that 'worked to render theologically and legally demonized same-sex practices intelligible in terms of familiar gender, social, and economic transgressions that could be practiced ... in any street, market, or household' (2011a: 59). Gary Ferguson examines the cultural meaning of a same-sex marriage ceremony that took place in Rome in 1578 and was widely discussed, including in the celebrated work of Michel de Montaigne (2016). (Shakespeare scholars will note that this ceremony offers a literal instance of Arcite's declaration that he and Palamon are 'one another's wife' in *The Two Noble Kinsmen* (2.1.80).)[6] James M. Bromley has found 'alternative life narratives' based on male sexual relations in Shakespeare's *Cymbeline* and *All's Well That Ends Well*; he has also argued that depictions of male sartorial flamboyance and public sex culture in Ben Jonson's plays can be understood as part of 'the transmission of forms of knowledge about being and belonging so necessary to the task of sustaining queer community through time' (2012: 49–78; 2016: 25). Will Stockton demonstrates that the anus as site of excrement is central to representations of sexual pleasure in *The Merry Wives of Windsor* and *All's Well That Ends Well*, comedies that revel in the failure of sublimation (2011). And Masten traces the etymology of 'fundament' – which in Shakespeare's day could mean 'anus' or 'buttocks' but also 'foundation', 'origin' or 'author' – to challenge modern understandings of the rectum or anus as 'a passive recipient or receptacle of dominating penetration' (2016: 181). Attending to constructions of the anus as 'largely outside or unengaged with an active/passive binary', Masten argues, can attune us to alternative experiences of 'the body-in-culture' (2016: 182, 189). As this work demonstrates, same-sex sodomy did not necessarily have to be disavowed as the repellant other of friendship, pedagogy or other socially sanctioned homosocial relations. While it may not have constituted a 'homosexual' identity in modern terms, sodomy may well have been a recognized aspect of early modern life and self-understanding.

Friendship

Along with the category of sodomy, that of friendship has provided a longstanding framework for discussions of same-sex relations in Shakespeare's writing and culture. The cultural veneration of friendship – especially male friendship – over heterosexual romance may be one of the most conspicuous differences between past and present views of gender and sexuality. In the early modern period, friendship was a culturally central model for same-sex love that is absent from a modern relational landscape in which heterosexual marriage and the formation of a nuclear family is assumed to be the most fulfilling and healthy expression of adult sexuality. Indeed, same-sex friendship was so central to early modern ideals of ethics and politics that Laurie Shannon has contrasted modern heteronormativity to Renaissance 'homonormativity,' which she defines as 'an almost philosophical preference for likeness or a structure of thinking based on resemblance' (2002: 94).

Renaissance celebrations of male friendship as a uniquely fulfilling and virtuous relationship find their roots in Aristotle's *Ethics* and *Politics* and Cicero's *De Amicitia*. For Aristotle and Cicero, true friendship is a relationship of perfect equality and similarity. A friend is, as Cicero would famously put it, 'another self (*alter idem*)' (21.80). Heterosexual relations could never achieve such perfection. Because women were deemed men's inferiors in intellect and self-mastery, a man's attachment to a woman was a sign of the effeminate, irrational passion of *eros* – an expression of need, appetite and self-interest that created, in Shannon's words, a 'monstrous form of male subordination' (2002: 65). By contrast, when a man loved a male social equal, this was the masculine, rational affection of *philia*.[7]

In the sixteenth century, Montaigne would enthuse about the unique wonders of male friendship in an elegy for his friend Étienne de La Boétie. Like Aristotle and Cicero, Montaigne contrasts male-male friendship with the inconstancy of heterosexual passion, the social calculation of marriage and the immoderation of 'Grecian license'. Far more than Cicero or Aristotle, however, Montaigne underscores the erotic nature of male friendship, as exemplified by his bond with de La Boétie: 'at our first meeting ... we discovered ourselves to be so seized by each other, so known to each other and so bound together that from then on none was so close as each was to the other' (211–12). We see such language throughout Shakespeare's work, for instance when Valentine in *Two Gentlemen of Verona* says of Proteus, 'I knew him as myself' (2.4.61). In Shakespeare's Sonnets, the speaker's determination to believe that 'my friend and I are one' has provided, for early queer scholars, affirmation of the possibility that male homoeroticism could indeed be celebrated as superior to heterosexual courtship or marriage (42.13).[8] The mutuality and constancy of men's love for one another, in fact, began to provide a pattern for heterosexual companionate marriage (rather than the other way around) by the late sixteenth century, a borrowing acknowledged by Edmund Tilney's conjugal advice book describing marriage as 'the flower of friendship'.[9] In fact, the rise of marriage to its current status as the centre of adult life required that heterosexual relations pattern themselves on the reciprocity and intellectual camaraderie of same-sex friendship. Unfortunately, this ideological appropriation also demoted friendship to an adolescent phase to be outgrown.

In Shakespeare's day, marriage had yet to achieve its modern, uniquely elevated status as the singular locus of affect and voluntary kinship. Rather, as Bray has shown in detail, the institution of sworn brotherhood existed alongside marriage from the eleventh through the seventeenth century. In sworn brotherhood, 'friendship is given a formal and objective character by ritual and oath', publicly forging a kinship that 'could be as indisputable as that formed by marriage' (Bray

2003: 312, 112). Confirmed in the Church and sealed by a kiss and the taking of Communion, ritual brotherhood was manifested during a pair's lifetime by such practices as the kiss and embrace of greeting, the exchange of letters swearing fidelity, and the sharing of meals and beds; after the death of one member of the union, wills passed on property and wardship of children (marriage and sworn brotherhood were not mutually exclusive unions) and sworn brothers were sometimes buried in the same grave with a joint monument. However much official discourse sought to differentiate between the spiritual relation of friends and the physical entanglements of sodomites, such polite fictions could not fully suppress awareness of the 'unacknowledged connection between the unmentionable vice of Sodom and the friendship that all accounted commendable' (Bray 2003: 186). Indeed, as Masten shows, recognition that friendship might include sexual contact appears in the early modern words 'intercourse' and 'conversation'. Until the eighteenth century, 'intercourse' signified 'a mutuality, reciprocality, and two-way transit that is, at least ideologically, largely imagined as possible only within certain male-male contexts'; from the sixteenth century 'conversation' could mean sexual intimacy as well as talking (Masten 2016: 102). Appearing in neutral and positive descriptions of male friendship, Masten concludes, the history of these words attests to the existence of 'culturally sanctioned male-male forms of *conversation* and *intercourse*' (2016: 105; original emphasis). When we come upon representations of male friendship in Shakespeare's plays, we must understand that relationship as signifying affective intensity and physical intimacy often not registered in modern usage.

The same can be said of female friendship. Several queer feminist scholars have refused to take Aristotle, Cicero and Montaigne at their misogynistic word and assume that there was no cultural place for female friendship comparable to that between men. Building on early work on pre-modern female relations by Carol Smith-Rosenberg and Lillian Faderman, Traub argues that a queer focus on exclusively male same-

sex relations can have the same effect as a feminist focus
on marriage and motherhood: 'the erasure in our critical
practice' of Shakespearean representations of women's desire
for women (1992: 93). Correction of this erasure began with
the 1992 publication of Traub's *Desire and Anxiety* and the
1994 publication of Goldberg's *Queering the Renaissance*, an
edited volume which included essays by Traub, Carla Freccero,
Dorothy Stephens and Richard Rambuss that discussed
portrayals of what we would now call lesbian desires and
practices in early modern literature. Within the next decade,
books by Traub, Shannon, Kathryn Schwarz and Denise A.
Walen would demonstrate that female friendship – understood
through a classical philosophical vocabulary and with a
recognizably erotic component – in fact had a prominent place
in early modern culture.

Like representations of male friendship, Traub shows,
'early modern representations of women's desires for intimacy
and physical contact are likewise usefully understood to
exist on the unstable boundary between *philia* and *eros* –
or, to use the terms of some of the texts we will consider, in
the interactions of amity and amour' (2002: 19). Indeed, as
Shannon demonstrates, the veneration of female chastity as an
associative, rather than solitary, virtue allied female with male
friendship as a guard against sexual excess and political tyranny
alike (2002: 57). Shakespeare's *A Midsummer Night's Dream*
is one frequently cited example in which female friendship
and community are not only highly visible, but also directly
resist the naturalization of a heterosexual order based on male
superiority. Examples of women's desire for relations with
other women appear in the figure of the Amazon Hippolyta
and in Titania's memories of her beloved Indian votaress. Most
prominently, Helena describes her relationship with Hermia
in terms of the language of classical friendship and ritual
kinship – they have 'two seeming bodies, but one heart' and
their 'sisters' vows' should secure this 'ancient love' (3.2.212,
199, 215). In Schwarz's words, 'Female separatism, with its
evasions and revisions of patriarchal control, is a powerful

erotic presence' in *A Midsummer Night's Dream*, where 'traces of female exclusivity highlight the sense of something lacking in relationships among men' and 'preoccupation with homosocial and homoerotic bonds makes heterosexuality an awkwardly subjunctive third term' (2000: 219, 221).

Schwarz's reading of female friendship and community is also part of scholarship that builds on Sedgwick's formative theory of the triangulation of desire in *Between Men*. Heterosexual courtship does not undermine bonds between men, Sedgwick argues. Rather, competition over a female love object may facilitate male attraction and attachment. Erotic energies are directed at the competing male suitor, not the woman being wooed, and rivalry keeps men together while also denying that their obsession with one another has anything to do with sex. Sedgwick sees Shakespeare's Sonnets as one canonical instance of the triangulation of desire, and subsequent critics have continued to emphasize the convergence between male hetero- and homoerotic desire in this poetic sequence (1985). Challenging earlier work that deemed heterosexual courtship and marriage the end of women's attachments to one another, queer feminist work has argued that these institutions may coexist with, or even make possible, such attachments. To take just one instance, Jennifer Drouin shows that according to Pierre de Bourdeille, Abbe et Seigneur de Brantome, a woman could not cuckold her husband by having sex with another woman, and some men actually welcomed such practices on the logic that they prevented wives from sleeping with other men. Brantome writes, 'I have never seen any [husbands] who were not right glad their wives should fall in love with their lady friends, and they would like that they should never commit worse adultery than in this fashion; in truth, this kind of cohabitation is very different from that with men, and whatever Martial says, men are not cuckolds for this' (quoted in Drouin 2009: 88). Nor were same-sex relations necessarily monogamous: as John Garrison has shown, same-sex love and friendship often extended to groups of men and women (2014). Queer feminists have traced the complexity and persistence of female homoeroticism alongside heterosexual courtship and marriage in the relations of Rosalind, Celia and Phoebe in *As You Like It*; Viola and Olivia in *Twelfth Night*; Desdemona and Emilia in *Othello*; and Helena and Hermia in *A Midsummer Night's Dream*.[10] Like the modern opposition between homosexuality and heterosexuality, that between cross-sex marriage and same-sex bonds does not accurately describe early modern practice or ideology.

Queer feminism: dildos and tribades

Attention to representations of early modern women constitutes an important contribution to the question of whether feminist and queer theory are necessarily distinct fields, with the former focused on gender and the latter on sexuality. The political and theoretical stakes of this question are made explicit in early work by Gayle Rubin and Sedgwick and, more recently, by Janet Halley's recommendation that scholars invested in sexuality 'take a break from feminism' and the analytic blind spots it brings (Halley 2006). In 'Thinking Sex', Rubin argues that 'Feminism is the theory of gender oppression. To automatically assume that this makes it the theory of sexual oppression is to fail to distinguish between gender, on the one hand, and erotic desire, on the other' and concludes that 'it is essential to separate gender and sexuality analytically to more accurately reflect their separate social existence' ([1984] 1992: 307–8). Sedgwick makes a more provisional distinction, stating as her second axiom for anti-homophobic analysis that 'The study of sexuality is not coextensive with the study of gender; correspondingly, antihomophobic inquiry is not coextensive with feminist inquiry. But we can't know in advance how they will be different' (1990: 27, 29, 31). Considering that 'It may be … that a damaging bias toward heterosocial or heterosexist assumptions inheres unavoidably in the very concept of gender,' Sedgwick proposes that 'in twentieth-century Western culture gender and sexuality represent two analytic axes that may productively be imagined as being as distinct from one another as, say, gender and class, or class and race' (1990: 31, 29).

In a critique of the limitations of this analytic separation, Biddy Martin writes that 'Conceptually ... as well as politically, something called femininity becomes the tacit ground in relation to which other positions become figural and mobile' (1994a: 119), a concern whose theoretical and political implications have been teased out by Judith Butler (1994; 2004: 157–74), Anna Marie Jagose (2009) and Jack Halberstam (2011:109–18). Traub brings this perspective to bear on her discussion of queer studies of early modern literature and culture:

> My resistance to the trend to ignore, despecify, or dispatch gender in the name of queer is theoretically grounded in an appreciation of the multiple vectors (gender, sexuality, race, class) that historically have underpinned and crosshatched embodiment in sometimes congruent, sometimes incongruent ways. It also stems from a historical sense that queer studies misrecognizes its own conditions of emergence when it categorically rejects affiliation with feminism in the name of analytically separating sexuality from gender. (2015: 18)

Indeed, Traub demonstrates, to consider the operations of gender and sexuality together may shed greater light on the specific forms that women's queerness takes.

One norm that feminism has disrupted is the cultural truism that women want love while men want sex. This belief is implied in a good deal of early work on what Smith-Rosenberg named 'the female world of love and ritual', the relations of friendship and sisterhood that were understood as nurturing and spiritual rather than appetitive or sexual (1975). What Traub calls the 'insignificance of *lesbian* desire' – the inability of female-female eroticism to register culturally as either admirable (like male friendship) or criminal (like male sodomy) – was part of the same cultural fantasy that distinguished *philia* from *eros*, one compounded by a modern feminist attachment to a belief in female sexual innocence.[11] Traub traces the 'cultural perversion' of female homoeroticism over the course of the seventeenth century. During this period, idealized chaste friendship came to be challenged by stigmatized tribadism, a process in some ways parallel to the emergence of a male homoerotic sex culture that became visible with the late seventeenth-century advent of the molly house (Traub 2002).[12] As Traub observes, when scholars treat appetite as entirely gender-neutral, the result may be 'that women are subsumed analytically under a historical rubric forged for men' (2002: 30). For instance, the history of the appearance of the clitoris in anatomical and travel writing in the sixteenth century reveals the limitations of queer scholarship that does not acknowledge gender difference. For with the 'discovery' of the clitoris came cultural awareness that women may find sexual pleasures with one another that corresponded to neither vaginal nor anal penetration by a penis – the clitoris, that is, should not be understood as a 'female penis', but as a source of women's pleasures distinct from heterosexual genital sex. By attending to the erotic potential of such non-penetrative activities as kissing and bed-sharing among female friends, as well as understanding representations of tribades and the use of dildos as specifically female practices, Traub argues, scholars can appreciate 'how the rediscovered clitoris upsets prevailing accounts of Renaissance sexuality and the historical narrative of homosexuality derived from them' (2002: 197).

This history is also part of a nascent colonial and imperial imaginary, insofar as it ascribed enlarged clitorises and female homosexual activity to non-European bodies.[13] In perceptive readings of *A Midsummer Night's Dream* and *A Winter's Tale*, DiGangi uncovers the various and unpredictable valences of tribadism as well as its associations with non-European women, witchcraft and female separatism. DiGangi argues that whereas clitoral penetration may signify relations of domination and submission between women, 'Clitoral rubbing less effectively maps on to the ancient binary of active (masculine) and passive (feminine) sexual roles' and blurs the distinction between 'individual aggression' and 'collective pleasure' (2011a: 67, 71). Whereas in her relation to her Indian votaress Titania practices 'domination over a woman who variously fulfills the roles of fertile wife, religious devotee, exotic pet, and domestic servant', Paulina and Hermione's sixteen-year-long exclusive cohabitation with one another is affirmed by the end of the play 'as a legitimate expression of same-sex allegiance, restorative witchcraft, and monarchical service' (2011a: 84, 87). This reading casts tribadism as neither automatically imitative of nor contrary to heterosexual relations under patriarchy, but rather as an ambiguous set of bonds and practices that expands our understanding of the relationship among gender, sexuality and power.

Queer Christianity

Along with the culturally central institution of friendship, the practices of early modern religion encouraged affect and attitudes that complicate heteronormative definitions of gender and sexual normativity. Early modern Christians appear to have taken seriously the biblical figuration of believers – including male believers – as brides of Christ, so that men's prayer takes a form that Rambuss calls 'homodevotion'. Rambuss finds in seventeenth-century metaphysical poetry 'exclamations of devotional affect so intensified that they encroach upon the taboo' and understands this dynamic as the inevitable product of 'a Christian libidinal scheme that both abjects and stimulates same-sex possibilities' – most obviously, 'the queerness of a male Christian devotee offering himself to Christ as his bride or his female beloved' (1998: 18, 19, 70). Rambuss demonstrates that poets such as Donne, Crashaw and Herbert depict their longing for union with Christ in terms of male desire to be wooed, overcome and penetrated by an irresistible, passionate male God. Several other scholars have noted that a literal interpretation of the relationship between Christ and the apostle John was available to the early modern imagination, most notoriously in Richard Baines's allegation that Christopher Marlowe had been known to quip that 'St. John the Evangelist was bedfellow to Christ and leaned always in his bosom, that he used him as the sins of Sodoma.'[14] Though the blasphemous claim attributed to Marlowe was introduced as evidence of the playwright's own sodomitical proclivities, this view of the relation between Christ and John appears to have been commonplace: two decades later, King James I would say of his openly erotic attachment to the Duke of Buckingham, 'Christ had his John and I have my George' (Rambuss 2011b: 562). In early modern metaphors of devotion as well as conceptions of the historical Jesus Christ, the heterodoxy of male same-sex intimacy cannot be separated from the orthodoxy of the conjugal union of Christ and Church as one flesh or of the intense reciprocal devotion of Christ and his apostles.

Citing Butler's discussion of the multitude of kinship possibilities in the present, Rambuss finds a model of nonconsanguineous, voluntary affiliation in both Christ's love for John and in his dying announcement that John and the Virgin Mary will henceforth be as son and mother. Rambuss observes that rather than encourage heterosexual marriage, 'the Christian scriptures are rich in figures and narratives that point the way toward, and even sacralize, other forms of kinship, other ways of intimate belonging' (2011b: 545).[15] Likewise, Will Stockton argues that Shakespeare's plays explore the queer potential of biblical logic by which marriage joins men and women to the body of Christ: in marrying each other, spouses also marry all of Christendom. In this figural logic, the heterosexual monogamy defended by modern evangelical Christians is in fact a polygamous membership in the communal flesh of Christ, a 'union of the multitude that subsumes and exceeds that of mere same-sex coupling' (Stockton 2017: 11). Marriage, in other words, is conceptually queer, if we recognize that the ideal of biblical marriage is haunted by a promiscuous merging of all flesh. Stockton argues that this consolidation appears in the confusions of individual identity and sexual partners in four of Shakespeare's plays in which marriage and adultery are rendered inseparable: *The Comedy of Errors, The Merchant of Venice, Othello* and *The Winter's Tale*. Christianity, Rambuss and Stockton demonstrate, is queer not only because it figures gender transitivity and male homoeroticism, but also because it subordinates the heterosexual couple and the nuclear family to a more expansive, communitarian ideal of intimacy.

Shakespeare's plays depict the non-marital adult life paths that Catholicism made available to early modern men and women. The most prominent of these in the early modern English imagination was that of monasteries and convents. As Bromley argues, 'By suggesting the possible value of intimate content outside marriage, relational forms not governed by the norms of the heterosexual couple, such as communal life in convents, threaten the nation's strategies for asserting sovereignty over its subjects' (2012: 131). Henry VIII and his ministers certainly understood that marriage is not only the model of the subject's relationship to the state – an analogy going back to Aristotle – but also a primary institution for managing property and citizenship. Accordingly, as scholars have long noted, the dissolution of the monasteries was vital to the establishment of Henry VIII's control over the Anglican Church. The break from the Catholic Church that began under Henry VIII and was confirmed under Elizabeth I not only altered forms of worship but also the distribution of property and relational choices of English men and women. In particular, the seizure of monastic lands was justified by the claim that religious institutions were sites of clandestine sodomy and fornication, and the anti-sodomy statutes first published during the Henrician Reforms were directed at reclaiming Church property for the state and at discrediting the sanctity of Catholic communal life (Smith 1991). Read in this context, when Shakespeare in *Love's Labour's Lost* imagines the possibility of single-sex communities that retreat from a public sphere, it also imaginatively incorporates possibilities of kinship and intimacy that no longer had a place in late sixteenth-century England. While the vow of King Ferdinand of Navarre and his courtiers is described in secular terms – they want to shun women so that they can study philosophy without distraction – it nonetheless would have evoked a recent English past in which such retreat from the worldly responsibilities of marriage and family was available as a permanent possibility. At the same time, the emphasis on homoerotic bonds between the King and his men, as well as the announcement that marriage will be deferred for a year beyond the conclusion of *Love's Labour's Lost*, defies both the generic expectations of comedy and the Protestant valourization of marriage in favour of continuing the same-sex communal living that the consolidation of the Anglican Church had rendered foreign and past by the time of the play.

The possibility of lifelong celibacy was at least as disruptive as homoeroticism to conventional marriage and procreation in Shakespeare's England. In a study of twentieth-century celibates, Benjamin Kahan argues that queer scholars should understand celibacy as itself a distinct 'sexual formation', rather than a cover for repressed homosexuality or a rejection of sexuality as such (2013: 1). This view of celibacy contests the religious right's cooptation of that practice, which has been especially prominent in abstinence-only sex education and therapy recommending celibacy as an alternative to homosexuality. Instead, Kahan argues, we can appreciate how celibacy challenges normative developmental timelines that see procreative marriage as the surest evidence of sexual health and emotional maturity. Shakespeare's plays offer a useful archive for such a project, as they attest to a recognition of celibacy as a sexual formation that, in Theodora Jankowski's words, 'represented a queer space within the otherwise very restrictive and binary early modern sex/gender system' (2000: 9–12). Jankowski juxtaposes Martin Luther's view that religious celibates 'vow and swear something which is contrary to God and his ordinance, namely … that you are neither a man nor a woman' with Monique Wittig's statement that in a society in which gendered distinctions are structured by patriarchal privilege and heterosexual institutions of marriage and family, 'lesbians are not women' (Jankowski 2000: 9–12). Reading Luther's attack on the ungendered celibate as a precursor to Wittig's celebration of lesbian nonconformity, Jankowski argues that, particularly for women, 'the condition of virginity, especially during Elizabeth I's reign, could not be anything but queer'. Moreover, the representations of avowed celibate women that aroused anxiety among early modern Protestant audiences continue to trouble modern critics (2000: 15).

Taken as a group, Shakespeare's plays appear ambivalent on the question of the adult female desire for celibacy that they so frequently depict. *The Taming of the Shrew* details the brutality with which Kate is compelled to relinquish her determination to live a celibate life. *A Midsummer Night's Dream* begins with anticipation of the forced marriage of the Amazon warrior Hippolyta, while *The Two Noble Kinsman* concludes in anticipation of the forced marriage of the Amazon Emilia, Hippolyta's sister. Two plays that depict female virginity in specifically Catholic terms treat it as a form of sexual deviance. *Henry VI, Part 1* denies the virginity of Joan of Arc, translating her into a whore who can be condemned in culturally legible terms as foreign, promiscuous and diabolical – in short, her sexuality sums up all that threatens the English nation. *Measure for Measure* depicts the would-be nun Isabella as a masochist, wishing for 'more strict restraint' upon her behaviour in the convent and maintaining that 'Th'impression of keen whips I'd wear as rubies, / And strip myself to death as to a bed / ... ere I'd yield / My body up to shame' (1.4.4, 2.4.101–4). Carolyn E. Brown notes that these lines evoke the Catholic practice of public flagellation in convents, which to Protestant polemicists offered perverse voyeuristic and sadomasochistic enjoyment to the nuns who witnessed it (1994: 191–3). Bromley sees Isabella's character as evidence of a historical moment in which intimacy and pleasure had not yet been interiorized, as in a modern Foucauldian regime. Resisting privacy and interiority, Isabella 'reimagines the body's surfaces as a space for resistance through unabashed pleasure in the face of a state seeking to make political use of its subjects' erotic lives' (Bromley 2012: 140). These queer readings contest the view that Isabella's celibacy is unnatural or prudish and treat it as a refusal of compulsive heteronormativity. More broadly, early modern studies can compel queer scholars to rethink the relationship between religion and normativity.

Pedagogy, pederasty and poetic creation

Religious devotion and community offered one alternative to heterosexual attachment and affiliation in the early modern period, but not the only one. Humanist education and literary creation afforded another form of same-sex kinship and cultural production. The eroticization of intellectual relationships took as its philosophical inspiration Plato's *Symposium*, which distinguishes between physical and spiritual generation. Here, we are told that 'Those whose creative instinct is physical have recourse to women,' with whom they have children, but 'there are some whose creative desire is of the soul, and who long to beget spiritually, not physically, the progeny which it is the nature of the soul to create and bring to birth'. The latter are superior, for 'the partnership between them will be far closer and the bond of affection far stronger than between ordinary parents, because the children that they share surpass human children by being immortal as well as more beautiful. Everyone would prefer children such as these to children after the flesh' (90–1). While Plato's depiction of spiritual generation between male partners resembles the classical philosophy of friendship made famous by Aristotle in its assumption of male intellectual superiority and virtue, it is distinct in that it does not assume that equality is a necessity. In fact, a Platonic conception of eros in this most influential formulation depends on a relation of hierarchy between an older philosopher and his younger pupil. Each have something the other desires: the philosopher has wisdom, while the youth has beauty. Renaissance translators and commentators tended to suppress the specifically sexual dimension of Platonic pedagogy, but, as Smith shows, the writings of Plutarch and Lucian had disseminated this tradition, and its influence is pronounced in a number of literary works of the period (1991: 37–41). Among these are Shakespeare's Sonnets, where the aged poetic speaker surrenders his initial project of persuading the youth he loves to marry and have children in favour of declaring the immortalizing power of his verse: 'So long as men can breathe or eyes can see, / So long lives this, and this gives life to thee' (18.13–14). A sequence that began as an instrument of persuasion to biological 'increase' of 'fairest creatures' from this point on becomes a celebration of a homoerotic love that preserves spiritual immortality (1.1).

Pederasty and pedagogy converge, Masten argues, in literary depictions such as Marlowe's Hero and Leander and Shakespeare's Venus and Adonis in which 'adult figures are always attempting to teach the boy, persuade the boy, to a desire of which they assume him fundamentally to be capable' (2016: 167; original emphasis). The curriculum of early modern grammar schools in which boys came of age began with Ovid, whose poetry is a frequent source of both plots and allusions in Shakespeare's plays. The homoerotic and transgendered desires depicted in the Metamorphoses would have provided the intellectual framework in which boys experienced the sex-segregated schools in which they shared beds and meals with other boys. The tale of Narcissus, the beautiful youth beloved of boys and girls alike, was one locus classicus of same-sex attraction. Even more central to early modern discourses of boy-love was Book 10 of the Metamorphoses. Here Orpheus, himself widely recognized as an emblem of homoeroticism, sings 'of prettie boyes / That were the darlings of the Gods': Ganymede, Adonis, Hyacinth (10.152–3). The myth of Jupiter's ravishment of Ganymede, Smith notes, was 'the best known myth of homoerotic desire in early modern England' in part because 'it articulated the social and political dynamics that complicated male-male desire in the cultural context of sixteenth- and seventeenth-century England' and therefore 'was a particularly eloquent way of putting homosexual desire into discourse' (1991: 192).[16]

These dynamics include the observation of hierarchy that allowed homoeroticism to be recognized as socially acceptable relations of masters and servants, master and pupil, patron and poet, and they attune us to the multiplicity of gender identities and object choices depicted in Shakespeare's plays. 'Ganymede' was early modern slang for what we would now call a homosexual man, a usage whose resonances in *As You Like It*, to take one prominent instance, have been widely remarked.[17] Although this play concludes with heterosexual marriages, these are achieved through a series of both male and female homoerotic encounters: Rosalind tests Orlando's love for her while disguised as a youth named Ganymede, in which persona she is wooed by both Orlando and the shepherdess Phoebe. Nor is *As You Like It* unique. DiGangi traces the prominence of Ovidian material in the plots of many early modern comedies – among them Shakespeare's *Twelfth Night*, in which 'male homoerotic desire actively disrupts marital (hetero)sexuality' – a disruption sustained in Antonio's continued love for Sebastian (1997: 29–62).

The frankly erotic attitude toward boys in early modern comedy reminds us that gender and sexuality are not transhistorical, biological categories but nonce taxonomies particular to given situations in time and space. The convergence of age, gender and social rank appears in the vagueness of the term 'boy', a categorization that had less to do with age than with status and behaviour (Smith 1991: 195–6; Masten 2016: 162). For instance, Smith notes that in one sodomy trial, the 'boy' victim was in fact 29 years old. To be a 'boy' is also to be a particular sexual type defined by passivity and submission. While the instability of the category of the 'boy' – one that could not be decided by legal or cultural designations of having reached majority – appears strange from a modern perspective, it is part of a larger early modern view in which gender itself was thought to be changeable, as much a matter of clothing or prosthetics such as beards or codpieces as it was of anatomical difference.[18] And even anatomical genital difference was not nearly as fixed as modern medical science has sought to make it. As Thomas Laqueur has argued, many believed in a one-sex model in which male and female reproductive organs were inverse versions of one another: if the vagina was an interior penis, the ovaries interior testicles and so forth, then changes of humour or body heat could conceivably relocate these organs, causing them to shrink inside or push out, with the result that spontaneous sex change was a possibility (1990).[19] The transformation of girls into boys and back is sartorial rather than biological in *As You Like It, Twelfth Night* and *The Merchant of Venice*. But in a cultural context that eroticized boys and saw sexual anatomy as potentially labile, Shakespeare's play with gender imbeds homoeroticism in the economies of service, apprenticeship and friendship.

Numerous scholars have demonstrated the centrality of same-sex male intimacy to the structures of early modern education, correspondence, and the production and transmission of literary texts and learning in general. Elizabeth Pittenger, Alan Stewart and Lynn Enterline, for instance, have drawn attention to the climates of grammar schools and universities, where the latent eroticism of punishment, particularly in the form of the flogging of bare buttocks, infused institutional order with pederastic desire (Pittenger 1994; Stewart 1997: xxix, 78, 84–121; Enterline 2012). Goldberg (1990) and Rambuss (1993) have emphasized the close relation between lords and their secretaries (who were always male), noting that the closet in which private – 'secret' – business is conducted is also the space in which secretaries worked. Stewart has argued that humanism itself was closely connected with sodomy in the early modern imagination. Reformers such as John Bale drew connections between monasteries as nests of perversion, on the one hand, and as the original sites of humanist libraries containing classical Greek and Latin texts, on the other. As the young men who were products of a humanist educational system were incorporated into households as tutors and secretaries, the consequent professional intimates signified for many 'an alternative economy of social relations' (Stewart 1997: xxix).

Relations of poets and dramatists to one another and to their patrons constituted another such network of partnership and dependence. As an alternative to biological reproduction, male poetic creation stands outside modern normative views of affect as well as heterosexuality. Stephen Guy-Bray has shown that early modern literary production challenges not only the heterosexual basis of poetic generation as metaphor, but also the teleology implied in a modern focus on a final, triumphant project that is 'not only welcome but socially useful' (2009: 35). Guy-Bray examines a Virgilian tradition counter to that of conquest and redemption, one in which 'poetry comes from abjection, both from those things felt to inspire universal disgust such as dishonoured corpses ... and from shame' (2009: 35). This perspective 'suggests that something that is abject or peripheral or marginal may become not only central but actually indispensable' in that it can 'bring the body in all its messiness, in all its potential for abjection, back into the center of our stories of where things come from' (2009: 40, 41). The male homoeroticism that Bersani so influentially saw as a challenge to the *redemptive reinvention of sex* and its attendant brutality against those whose pleasures could not be redeemed in the name of social utility or romantic love is, in Guy-Bray's analysis, central to what early modern writers understood themselves to be doing (Bersani 1987: 215, original emphasis; Guy-Bray 2002: 15).

These studies of the intense homoeroticism of humanist learning and early modern social structure bear directly on the creation and circulation of literary texts in the period, as Rambuss, Goldberg, Masten and Guy-Bray have shown of early modern letters, poetry and drama. In contrast to modern understandings of the solitary author, this work establishes that the early modern period assumed the centrality of male intimacy and collaboration to writing in nearly all forms. Masten, for instance, examines the presentation of early printed drama, as well as in the later fortunes of co-authored works by Shakespeare, Francis Beaumont and John Fletcher, Thomas Middleton, and Philip Massinger, all of whom collaborated at various points on plays. Masten 'traces the correspondences between, on the one hand, models and rhetorics of sexual relations, intercourse, and reproduction and, on the other, notions of textual production and property' (1997: 4). These correspondences show that the individualized and heterosexual structure of the latter in modernity is a result of the suppression of the homoeroticism of the former, thereby obscuring the fact that 'texts are produced within a particular sex/gender context and that gender and sexuality are themselves in part produced in and by texts' (1997: 5). For Guy-Bray the circulation and adaptation of classical pastoral enables the creation of a public 'homoerotic space: a safe, because carefully demarcated, zone in which homoeroticism can appear' (2002: 15). Less work has been done on women's collaborations with one another, but studies of the sixteenth- and seventeenth-century writers Mary Sidney Herbert, Mary Wroth, Aemelia Lanyer and Katherine Phillips have shown how these women similarly situated themselves in communities of readers, writers and patrons engaged in the intellectual generation idealized by Plato.[20] Women's dedications, verses and letters to one another formed virtual as well as physical communities and challenged classical and early modern relational hierarchies.

Literature in the period, that is to say, makes available a public homoerotic culture. Along with the literal place of the theatre, which physically gathers and represents bodies and desires that exceed conventional gendered and sexual arrangements, the virtual gathering space of manuscript and print is accessible through texts in the imaginary worlds they depict. Communities may also be forged between authors and patrons through such paratextual materials as dedications (as in Shakespeare's dedications of *The Rape of Lucrece* and *Venus and Adonis* to the Earl of Southampton), commendatory verses (as in those accompanying the First Folio), and printers' or editors' prefaces to readers. The 'homoerotic space' of early modern print and manuscript culture may be, as in Guy-Bray's reading, elegiac, mourning its own loss amidst the ascendency of companionate marriage (2002: 211). But the longing they express itself makes visible alternative ways of life, futures that may borrow from the pasts that persist in these records.

3

Queerness Beyond
Homoeroticism

In both the popular and the scholarly imagination, queerness is often treated as synonymous with homosexuality. Accordingly, as the previous chapter demonstrated, early modern historians and literary critics focusing on records and representations of same-sex desire have shown the centrality of homosocial and homoerotic relations to the legal, political, social, religious, pedagogical and literary cultures of Shakespeare's England. This work has made it impossible for the responsible modern critic to argue that because 'homosexuality' was not yet a recognized identity, analysis of same-sex eroticism is anachronistic or inappropriate. To be sure, as Jonathan Ned Katz, Karma Lochrie and Rebecca Ann Bach have argued, there may have been no 'homosexuals' before the nineteenth century, but there were no 'heterosexuals' either (Katz 1995; Lochrie 2005; Bach 2007). Neither term entered the medical, psychological or popular lexicon until 1892.[1]

Yet, as Chapter 1 also made clear, since its emergence in the 1980s, the work that has come to be called queer theory has equally sought to think beyond the gender of object choice as the only marker of sexual normativity.[2] Scholars have cautioned that severing queer theory from LGBTQ politics can lead us to lose sight of, in Eve Sedgwick's words, the 'historical and contemporary force of the prohibitions against *every* same-sex expression' as well as the tacit privacy and privilege accorded to heterosexual relations (1993: 8; original emphasis). Yet

queer theory has also interrogated the normativizing force of
ideals and expectations that cannot be explained by a homo-
hetero binary. As Sedgwick writes,

> the implicit condensation of 'sexual theory' into 'gay/lesbian
> and antihomophobic theory,' which corresponds roughly
> to our by now unquestioned reading of the phrase 'sexual
> orientation' to mean 'gender of object-choice,' is at the very
> least damagingly skewed by the specificity of its historical
> placement. (1990: 35)

To focus only on a modern identity category defined by
same-sex object choice skews our perception of the past in
the direction of present orientations. Rather than begin with
modern categories, queer theorists can look at desires and
practices that counter present ideals of romance, monogamy
and the nuclear family. If queerness is about contesting the
descriptive value of normativity, then we can expand its
lens to an array of norms. In this chapter, I turn to studies
of queerness in Shakespeare's writing and culture that focus
on topics other than same-sex bonds, desires and intimacies.
The first two sections discuss in turn the queer dimensions of
heterosexuality and the relation between emerging categories
of race and colonialism, on the one hand, and early modern
sexual morality, on the other. The following three sections turn
to some broadly applicable methodological and metacritical
topics that have been the subject of early modern queer
debates: epistemology and empiricism; philology, editing and
rhetoric; and historiography and temporality.

Queer heterosexuality

As we have seen, one of the central interventions of queer studies
is to push scholars to re-examine normative assumptions about
healthy, ethical and responsible sexuality and eroticism. Part

of this project has involved questioning what Judith Butler describes as the 'regulatory operation of heterosexual norms' that idealize 'heterosexuality through purifying those desires and practices of their instabilities, crossings, the incoherencies of masculine and feminine through which the borders of those categories are lived' (1998: 227). Medieval and early modern scholars have been central to making available, in Carolyn Dinshaw's words, a 'queer view of heterosexuality', which highlights precisely the instabilities, crossings and incoherencies that Butler remarks (1999: 13). Lochrie argues that 'by disabusing ourselves of this stubbornly intransigent notion of heterosexuality's transhistorical normativity' pre-modern queer scholars can 'begin not only to remap past sexualities more historically but to dismantle heterosexuality's entrenched place in contemporary American culture as a mystifying norm that reaches into the past, permeates the present, and sets the parameters of the future' (2005: xiii–xiv).[3] In our approach to early modern texts, we can resist 'dominant narratives of chastity and lust, virtue and vice, Madonna and whore, object of desire or object of contamination', Carla Freccero maintains, and instead notice those 'queerer intermediate alternatives' that 'the literary, unlike the legislative, is able to touch', however briefly and tentatively (2016: 103). And Mario DiGangi calls our attention to categories that would have been recognizable to early modern theatrical audiences – the narcissistic courtier, the monstrous favourite, the citizen wife and the bawd – which have escaped modern attention as *sexual* types because they do not map onto a homo/hetero divide (2011a).

Transgender performance is one of pre-modern literature's most conspicuous alternatives to modern gendered and sexual norms. Marjorie Garber has argued of crossdressing more generally that it makes legible instances of 'category crisis'. The displacement of a 'failure of definitional distinction' onto the transgender character, Garber contends, is deceptive, for in fact *transvestitism is a space of possibility structuring and confounding culture*: the disruptive element that intervenes, not just a category crisis of male and female, but the crisis of category itself' (1992: 16–17; original emphasis). As we saw in Chapter 2, queer critics have paid a good deal of attention to the homoeroticism of the early modern convention of having boys play women. Feminist critics have also debated the gender politics of the many dramatic plots in which women disguise themselves as men and, in that disguise, attract female desire that the audience knows to 'really' be homoerotic.[4]

Rather than understand these transgender performances as simply enacting binary male/female or homo/hetero desires, we can instead recognize them as resisting precisely the binaries usually understood to structure modern gender, desire and marriage. These comedies, Goldberg argues, flirt not with modern homosexuality but with a discourse of sodomy that encompasses same- and cross-sex erotic acts ([1992] 2010: 143). Transgender performance, whether within plot or performance, does not contrast with or resolve itself into heteronormative romance but attests to the incoherence, even absurdity, of the dominant sexual culture it cites. Simone Chess describes transgender performance in early modern literature as accentuating the queerness of heterosexual desire. Chess explores the phenomenon of 'doublecrossdressing', or the courtships between couples made up of one MTF (male-to-female) and one FTM (female-to-male) crossdresser. Though these relations are technically heterosexual, they are anything but normative. For when a woman dressed as a man and a man dressed as a woman fall in love, the relation decouples 'natural' gender identity from 'naturally' straight sexual desire (2016: 39–71, 103–37). The sense that there is any natural or stable ground for gendered differences repeatedly gives way to a much queerer perspective, one that might even be called 'kinky'. By this Chess means that 'crossdressing has an erotics of its own': dressing in drag, or ambiguous gender presentation more generally, can itself be a turn-on for both parties (2016: 103–4). In the various texts that Chess examines, this desire for gender ambiguity is 'heterosexual' insofar as it involves cross-sex partners, but it is undeniably 'queer' insofar as women are attracted to men who dress as women. Previous scholars, including Valerie Traub and Kathryn Schwarz, have explored how relations between MTF crossdressers and cisgendered women (women whose gender performance matches their anatomical sex assignment) make visible previously unnoticed possibilities of lesbian relations and desires. Chess instead argues that cisgender women know that their objects of attraction are men and that what they perhaps desire are neither women nor cisgendered men, but *men in drag*.

Along with transgender performance, early modern queer scholars have analysed representations of fantasies and practices that take place between men and women but that fit better within the early modern category of sodomy than the modern category of heteronormativity. Goldberg has argued, in light of the puns on 'arse' and the substitutive logic of *Romeo and Juliet*, 'that desire might not be determined by the gender of its object, that the coupling of Romeo and Juliet is not a unique moment of heterosexual perfection and privacy but part of a series whose substitutions do not respect either the uniqueness of individuals or the boundaries of gender difference' (1994a: 222).[5] In my own past work on Spenser's *The Faerie Queene* and Shakespeare's *A Midsummer Night's Dream*, I have traced representations of women whose desires do not tend toward romantic and nurturing coupledom. Rather than treat redemptive models of intimacy, whether homo- or hetero-erotic, as intuitively good, I have drawn on sex-radical feminism to argue that queer feminist critics might consider that 'women's desires for sodomy, group sex, bestiality, and sadomasochism can equally challenge gender hierarchies and sexual norms' (Sanchez 2012: 496). In a discussion of early modern visual culture, Mary Catherine Kinniburgh observes, interspecies eroticism was a common topic of pornographic representation. Citing a text that depicts a man and woman copulating on top of an ejaculating horse, Kinniburgh reveals the inadequacy of modern categories of gay and straight to the variety of sexual fantasies available in early modernity (2016). As this brief sampling of work on queer heterosexuality suggests, if we want to contest the privacy and privilege accorded to heterosexuality, we must consider the broad scope of practices and desires that show normativity to be a fantasy.

Race, empire and colonialism

As we saw in Chapter 1, an early ambition of Anglo-American queer theory was to explore how categories of race, nation, ethnicity and empire helped shape Western conceptions of sexual health, propriety, normativity, deviance and perversion. Early modern queer studies is essential to this work, for it reminds us that racial categories have long been shaped by sexual ones. Pre-modern understandings of 'race', like pre-modern understandings of gender and sexuality, bear an inexact and contingent relation to modern categories. Yet, as Peter Erickson and Kim F. Hall have persuasively argued, when scholars resist discussion of 'race' in Shakespeare on the grounds that the term is anachronistic, they participate in 'reifying a narrative that makes race the regrettable product of modernity' and thereby relieves pre-modern scholars of having to think about the racial and racist dimensions of the literature they study (2016: 9). In fact, for decades scholars of medieval and early modern worlds have demonstrated that what we now understand as racial discrimination is evident by the thirteenth century, that many non-white and non-Christian persons lived in Shakespeare's England, and that the English participated in the Atlantic slave trade from at least the late sixteenth century.[6] In the realm of sexuality in particular, travel writing habitually associated sodomy with dark-skinned bodies and with such foreign locales as Spain, Italy, Russia, Turkey, North Africa, India, Persia, East Asia and the Americas.[7] Rather than insist that the term 'race' must register the persistence of the concept across different periods as an unchanging category, queer scholars can instead adopt Geraldine Heng's definition of race as '*a structural relationship for the articulation and management of human differences, rather than a substantive content*' (2011: 319; original emphasis).

Questions of sexual propriety and perversion in Shakespeare's plays may have as much to do with the perceived races and ethnicities of those involved as with their gender or sexual practice. If we treat representations of normativity and perversion apart from their racial, national and colonial contexts, we fail to notice, as Dollimore puts it, that 'the work of policing boundaries crucial to the maintaining of social domination – boundaries of country, race, and class – is effaced, dissolved into the a priori internal regulation of nature' (1991: 165). In particular, a race-blind queer theory overlooks the projection of perverse enjoyment onto racialized figures of Saracens, Jews and Africans that Jeffery Jerome Cohen has traced and that is central to such plays as *Othello, Titus Andronicus* and *The Merchant of Venice*, along with the contrary association of 'fairness' with sexual health and innocence that Hall has noted (Hall 1995; Cohen 2001). An association between sodomy and foreign invasion is legally codified in Edward Coke's *Institutes*, which claims that '*Bugeria* is an Italian word, and signifies so much, as is before described, *Paederastes* or *Paiderestes* is a Greek word, *Amator puerorum*, which is but a Species of Buggery, and it was complained of in Parliament, that the Lumbards had brought into the Realm the shamefull sin of Sodomy, that is not to be named, as there it is said' (58). Whereas for Coke buggery is Greek or Italian in origin, for travel and medical writers sexual and gendered deviance were the properties of non-European peoples whose oversized penises and clitorises gave anatomical expression to their excessive appetites. John Bulwer's *Anthropometapmorphesis*, for instance, repeats a popular legend that the curse of Noah on Ham is not only blackness or servitude, but also an enormous penis. Similarly, accounts of oversized clitorises and labia, both associated with the 'unnatural' practice of tribadism and excessive female pleasure, were common in travel writing describing Asia, Africa and the New World.[8]

As in queer theory more generally, attention to race, empire and colonialism was characteristic of some of the field's earliest and most influential work. To take two examples, we might consider Bray's *Homosexuality in Renaissance England* and Jonathan Goldberg's *Sodometries*. Discussing a 1647 Assize record of an accusation of 'buggery' against 'Domingo Cassedon Drago, a negro', by 'a poor boy named William Wraxall', Bray briefly calls attention to the role that race might have played in bringing this particular case to the court's attention. Along with the 'frustrating' paucity of information in the record, Bray comments,

> There is also perhaps something else about this document to unsettle us: of all the figures we might expect to see in seventeenth-century England, is it not surprising that the prisoner in the county gaol should have been black? A black face would have been an unusual sight indeed in England in 1647; did that, one might well wonder, have something to do with why Drago found himself in court? (1982: 40–1)

Answering his own question, Bray argues that 'there is good reason to think that it was the colour of his skin' that 'marked Drago out for such treatment', for 'A member of a non-European race was more than a merely unusual sight in mid seventeenth-century England: he specifically brought to mind the image of the sodomite, which was linked in the literature of the time with non-European races' (1982: 72).

In *Sodometries*, Goldberg analyses the colonial implications of the European association of sodomy with racial and religious otherness. He excavates a 'history of sodomy in the New World' that emerges not from Puritan repression, but from a more general European projection of effeminization and sodomitical desire onto indigenous Americans. Summed up in a 1519 letter written by Hernán Cortés, the claim that 'they are all sodomites' justified European colonial dominance as the defence of a gendered and sexual order grounded in both nature and Christianity (Goldberg [1992] 2010: 193). This ideology justified a notorious incident in which 'after killing the leader of the Indians of Quarequa and six hundred of his warriors', Vasco Núñez de Balboa 'fed to his dogs forty more Indians accused of sodomitical practices' (Goldberg [1992] 2010: 180). This story, Goldberg contends, is not merely part of a Black Legend documenting Spanish brutality in service of Protestant propaganda. Retold throughout Europe, including in the English travel writings of Richard Hakluyt and Samuel Purchas, the account is also part of the history of an English defence of colonization as a moral imperative. European descriptions of Native piercing and cross-gender dress depict New World sodomy (also analogized by Columbus to the practices attributed to Moors and Jews) as 'a life practice, routinized, ritualized, differentiated by locale' from which indigenous peoples must be saved by Christianity ([1992] 2010: 195, 196). Yet, as Goldberg shows, the logic of conversion as well as ethnography requires identification that disturbs conjoined racial and sexual categories ([1992] 2010: 219–22). Indeed, to recognize the erotic dynamic of colonial domination and incorporation of otherness, Freccero also argues, is also to be able to detect a counterimpulse of the desire to be penetrated, objectified or haunted. This queer receptivity has the potential to dissolve precisely the gendered and racialized borders that justify aggression as self-defence (Freccero 2006).

In more recent work, Shakespeare scholars have continued to demonstrate the mutual pressure that racial, gendered and sexual identifications exert on one another. Some early scholars tended to pit race against sexuality, a tactic exemplified in Margreta de Grazia's claim that 'the scandal in the Sonnets has been misidentified. It is not Shakespeare's desire for a boy ... It is Shakespeare's gynerastic longings for a black mistress that are perverse and menacing' ([1994] 1999: 106). As Traub has observed, the 'theoretical insistence' that race or class 'displace homosexuality from its position as the "real scandal" bespeaks a competitive logic that may have more to do with the agon of contemporary identity politics than the knotty relations among sex, race, and class in these poems' (2015: 234). For the most part, however, studies of race have been remarkably attentive to its intersections with gender, sex and economic hierarchies.

Arthur L. Little Jr. designates ascriptions of chastity and perversion 'technologies of racism', and many scholars have studied the intersections of gender, race, desire, religion and sexuality in early modern prose, poetry and drama (2000: 1).[9] This work has continued to uncover the historical presence of non-European, non-Christian persons in early modern England as well as the significance of Shakespeare's prevalent racialized language, topics that I will address more fully through readings of *Othello* and *The Merchant of Venice* in Chapter 4. Virginia Mason Vaughan (2005), Celia Daileader (2005) and Ayanna Thompson (2011) have forcefully argued for the continued impact of early modern culture on twentieth- and twenty-first-century views, largely but not only by examining modern cinematic and theatrical performances of Shakespeare's plays. Insofar as Shakespearean performance is mediated through a history of race, colonialism and chattel slavery that was only beginning to unfold when the plays and poems were written, decisions about casting, costumes and setting can put in relief the normalizing work of an association of somatic whiteness with morality and romance.

Epistemology and empiricism

As the discussions of queer heterosexuality, race and colonialism indicate, the charge of anachronism has long been the default objection to analysis of Shakespeare's writing that does not assume a transhistorical whiteness and heteronormativity. The notion that sex is heteroerotic unless proven otherwise, Traub notes, is a singular instance of the presumptive knowingness critiqued by Sedgwick, and in early modern studies it has prevented many critics from asking 'how do we know what is erotic?' in the first place (2002: 11). The claim that a text represents queer sex – both homoeroticism and non-normative, non-reproductive practices such as masturbation, oral and anal sex, bestiality, what we would now call BDSM and intercrural (sex rubbing the penis or clitoris between or against the partner's thighs) – requires a heavier burden of proof than the assumption that it depicts straight sex.[10] Stanley Wells encapsulates this logic when he distinguishes between 'legitimate readings-between-the-lines' and 'over-readings that are ahistorical and sometimes untheatrical in imposing upon the texts meanings that must originate rather in the minds of the interpreters than of the dramatist'. He compares those critics he deems 'lewd interpreters' to 'naughty boys and girls [who] would sit at the back of the classroom sniggering and giggling amongst themselves whenever the teacher said anything that might be remotely open to lewdness of interpretation' (2004: 2, 36). As numerous critics have pointed out, the presumption that we can fully distinguish between (to use Wells's words) 'gratuitous imposition' and 'authentic interpretation' of what is erotic in a text must ignore the fact that non-reproductive, non-penetrative sex acts may have been as, if not more, common than Abelove's 'sexual intercourse so-called' in the early modern period (Abelove 2003; Wells 2004: 31). Indeed, as I noted in my discussion of sodomy in Chapter 2, Edward Coke's definition of sodomy and rape both required penetration: '*Emissio feminis* maketh it not Buggery, but is an evidence in case of buggery of penetration: and so in Rape the wordes be also *carnaliter cognovir*, and therefore must be penetration; and *emissio feminis* without penetration maketh no Rape' (1644: 58–60). In Coke's explicit exclusion of '*emissio feminis*' from his definitions of carnal knowledge, ejaculation onto the thighs serves as a synecdoche for all acts that do not involve the penetration of the anus or vagina by the penis. The need for this specification to be codified in the law indicates an awareness that a wide range of practices were part of the early modern imagination of sex and eroticism.

Rather than assume that only penile penetration of the vagina – Coke's *res in re* – counts as sex in Shakespeare's writing, queer critics have instead urged us to interrogate our own empirical, hermeneutic and epistemological procedures. What constitutes empirical evidence of sex? How do we interpret what Christine Varnado has called 'invisible sex', that sex which happens offstage and appears in plays only through euphemism and innuendo? Given that many acts that we would now understand as unquestionably sexual – penetration of the anus or vagina by the penis, oral sex, and solitary or mutual masturbation – do not appear in the stage directions of any early modern plays and are only described through slang, puns and euphemisms in the plays' lines, how do we define what it would mean to 'know' whether sex has happened? Varnado offers the instance of the offstage intimacy of Romeo and Juliet on their wedding night: in the absence of stage directions or spoken lines that explicitly indicate that Romeo has inserted his erect penis into Juliet's vagina, Varnado compels us to recognize, there is no more empirical evidence for a 'straight' reading than for a queer one. It is only our modern presumptions and prejudices about what two teenagers *must* want that have excluded the possibility of other acts as (to recall Wells) 'gratuitous imposition' (2013).

We modern readers may be limited in our imagination about what really might happen offstage not only by a modern heteronormativity, but also by our historical situation in which many of the erotic practices that might have been familiar to Elizabethan and Jacobean audiences are no longer part of common sexual consciousness. We may not even have thought of acts that would have been regarded as sexual in Shakespeare's day. As James M. Bromley and Will Stockton argue in their introduction to *Sex Before Sex*, 'sex' has no clear or stable definition (2013). They point out that the word 'sex' is itself as anachronistic as those other conceptual categories that have been more widely challenged and defended: 'race' and 'homosexuality'. In fact, the word 'sex' was not used to describe erotic contact until sometime between the eighteenth and twentieth century.[11] Essays in this volume by Melissa J. Jones, Will Fisher, Stephen Guy-Bray and Will Stockton examine acts and fantasies that may not register as sexual now but that were saturated with erotic significance in early modern culture: erectile dysfunction, chin-chucking, the practice of botany, the pleasure of drinking alcohol.[12] As these essays demonstrate, the project of 'understanding sexual practices in their historical specificity and complexity' requires 'reading what isn't there', as Hall writes of the work required for studies of race in early modern texts that obscure the presence of racial knowledge and non-white persons (1993). While studies of early modern representations of race and of queerness converge and diverge in unpredictable ways, these (sometimes intersecting) topics both require, as Varnado points out, attention to what José Esteban Muñoz characterizes as 'ephemera', or the 'trace, the remains, the things that are left, hanging in the air like a rumor'. As Muñoz recognizes, such 'ephemeral evidence is rarely obvious because it is needed to stand against the harsh lights of mainstream visibility and the potential tyranny of the fact. (Not that all facts are harmful, but the discourse of the fact has often cast antinormative desire as the bad object.)' (2009: 65).[13] Rather than deny that such 'bad objects' as analingus and fantasies of animal rape could have been part of early modern literary culture, Bromley and Holly Dugan argue, early modern queer critics must grapple with their structuring force on conceptions of patriarchy, intimacy and 'human' eroticism more largely (Bromley 2013; Dugan 2013).

Neither the empirical evidence we study nor the ephemera with which we supplement the literary and cultural archive can be treated as transparent. Instead, as the brief examples above indicate, queer scholars must continue to question whether we really know what a given Shakespearean line means. Traub, focusing on sexual slang, euphemism and double-entendre in early modern writing more generally, points out that 'this language is curiously devoid of specific corporeal information, gesturing vaguely toward nebulous behaviors (which scholars fill in presumptively) or referring the meaning of sex to the social relations it underpins, expresses, and creates' (2015: 180). Rather than rush to fill in the blanks, Traub urges scholars to linger with opacity and ask, for instance, 'To what *specific* sexual activity does "tapping a beer keg" or "ladling a pot" actually refer?' or what are we to make of the 'dildos and fadings' that Autolycus peddles in *The Winter's Tale* (2015: 183; original emphasis)? Scholars have never been able to gloss these terms with certainty, and this undecidability 'implicates all of us in the cluelessness that seems to be part and parcel of the desire to sexually know' (2015: 222). But the possibility that we may never know for sure is not so much a lack or failure of scholarship, Traub argues, as itself a form of information about the limitations of sexual epistemology: 'An epistemological approach – asking *what* can be known as well as *how* it is known – recasts the dynamics among sex, representation, signification, and historiography as a problem of knowledge relations: constituted not only by social interchange but by implicit understandings of what counts as knowledge and what eludes or baffles as ignorance' (2015: 5; original emphasis).

The willingness to ask what Traub calls 'the stupid question', as well as the willingness to accept opacity and frustration in response, can be invaluable to a project of queering Shakespeare studies. Instead of aspiring to the smug and tweedy mastery of an Oxbridge professor, queer scholars can 'devise new strategies to confront some of the ways it is possible *not to know*' and thereby develop more experimental and curious forms of pedagogy and scholarship (Traub 2015: 25; original emphasis). Rethinking our interpretive and epistemological procedures is a way to fulfill the potential that Michael Warner in 1993 attributed to queer theory to 'mess up the desexualized spaces of the academy, exude some rut, reimagine the publics from and for which academic intellectuals write, dress, and perform' (1993: xxvi). Over twenty years later, Traub remarks, professional scholarship continues to expect a certain degree of respectability: 'When I have said words such as "cunt," "fuck," or even "clitoris" in academic venues, the room tends to go strangely quiet' (2015: 214). Assumptions about what we as scholars and teachers can say are also assumptions about the proper objects of research and knowledge that may replicate the norms of propriety and modesty that queer theory is dedicated to questioning.[14]

Queer language and literature: editing, philology, rhetoric

From early on, feminist and queer studies of the early modern period have pointed out that when scholars and editors seek to standardize Shakespeare's texts, spellings and meanings, they not only suppress alternate, perhaps perverse readings, but also perpetuate what Stephanie Jed calls 'chaste thinking', the humanist philological practice that expunges textual corruption and variation as well as the excessive passions deemed antithetical to intellectual and politically responsible behaviour (1989). Topics that would appear to be the province of dusty antiquarians – philology, editing and rhetorical analysis – in fact have important implications for queer scholarship. These practices bear on the production of the scholarly apparatus itself, permitting and foreclosing readings in the editions of texts that are available to students and scholars. Accordingly, queer studies of Shakespeare's texts at the level of etymology, spelling, glosses, and rhetorical and figural convention have demonstrated the necessity of contesting practices that assume or establish single, authoritative texts, meanings or audiences.

A reassessment of philology – the study of linguistic history, or etymology, as well as the reconstruction of written works' original forms and authentic meanings – is central to queer theory. The impulse of humanist philology to trace words' origins and to distinguish between valid and spurious readings, Freccero argues, is also 'phallology' by which the 'constitution of the citizen-subjectry – as masculine and as "straight" – is reenacted' (1994: 112). Freccero argues that 'It is a ruse of modern and Western phallocentrism ... that passion, emotion, lust, desire – incestuous, homosexual – cluster on the side of tyranny', while chastity and restraint enable republican self-rule. Nonetheless, attentive critics can detect queer 'disturbances' within texts themselves, and these disturbances afford 'shadows of (utopian) doubt' that resist a normatively castigating, straightening approach to pre-modern literature

(Freccero 1994: 120). Reading Shakespeare 'from the margins' – of society, of traditional philological and editing practices – as Patricia Parker and Leah H. Marcus have also emphasized, disrupts precisely the stable and monolithic view of the centre that traditional critics drew from Jacob Burkhardt's celebratory picture of Renaissance individualism or from E. M. W. Tillyard's comprehensive 'Elizabethan world picture'.[15] Queer critics in particular, Traub argues, must resist the 'bid to stabilize sexual language' by dismissing euphemisms and stock phrases, 'relying on and enforcing a kind of studied imprecision' that preserves the critic's own chastity and interpretive authority (2015: 190–1).

More comprehensively, Jeffrey Masten has argued that a method of queer philology can 'draw critical attention ... to the ways in which philology's manifold methods and rhetorics of investigation are often themselves thoroughly implicated in the languages of sex, gender, and the body' (2016: 18). Queer philology, Masten proposes, 'will exert a double action, signifying both a philology *of the queer* (that is, of sexual practices, bodies, affects, and identities that seem nonnormative, whether in their own time or from this historical distance) and a *queer* philology (the traditional and once-hegemonic discipline of philology read and practiced in a way that will highlight its own normativizing categories and elisions)' (2016: 214; original emphasis). Queer philology reveals how modern politics of sexuality may influence editorial and philological work and vice versa. For instance, Masten sets the editorial project to authenticate Shakespeare's spelling in the framework of the Lavender Scare to show that 'the language of mid-twentieth-century compositorial study, in its search for essences/identities that can be read out from spelling habits, behaviors, tendencies, and practices, bears resemblance to, and is startlingly contemporaneous with, other mid-twentieth-century attempts to monitor and detect identities – *sexual* identities – on the basis of visible physical signs and behaviors' (2016: 53; original emphasis). Such 'a historicized – even queered – sense of identity in relation to the spelling and printing habitus', he proposes, 'might help us to rethink the complex problem of agency in and around Shakespeare's texts': the pursuit of a single, authentic authorial intention when it comes to spelling may itself shore up modern notions of stable and knowable sexual identity that, in the mid-twentieth century were evoked by the US government and by a number of US universities to root out the 'perverse' and 'unpatriotic' influence of homosexuals (Masten 2016: 61). The sexual politics of the Shakespearean oeuvre are not limited to their early modern contexts but persist into modern constructions of national belonging.

The queer approach to language endorsed by Freccero, Traub and Masten is also explored by Parker and by Madhavi Menon in what we might call a queer rhetoricism. Attention to the place of rhetoric in naturalizing social order extends into anti-homophobic analysis the insights of *Literary Fat Ladies*, Parker's feminist study of how humanist writing produces 'motivated rhetorics', or an 'interpenetration between the rhetorical and the ideological' (1987: 113). Parker influentially examines the 'Shakespearean preposterous', understood as the plays' 'pervasive network of wordplay and structural play' that resists the prescriptions of humanist rhetoric (1992: 187). Shakespeare's unwieldy use of puns, metaphors, repetitions and inversions 'functions as a marker of the disruption of orders based on linearity, sequence, and place' and 'reveals the language of order as obscuring the logic of its own construction' (Parker 1992: 188, 209). Similarly, Parker traces the sexual implications of rhetorical elevations of the spare, 'virile style' (*virilitas*) associated with the force of the *nervus*, or erect penis, and the effeminacy of ornamental and extravagant prose deemed *molles* – a word that not only meant soft or flaccid, but that also was associated with the classical *cinaedus*, or effeminate man who enjoyed being penetrated (Parker 1996b: 202–6). As Parker demonstrates, the requirements of rhetorical order and discipline are also vehicles for social control.

Explicitly engaging queer theory, Menon argues that 'a discussion of "sexuality" in the Renaissance, far from being anachronistic, is strongly marked by theoretical ideas about language that were in circulation at the time' (2004: 4). Because

Shakespeare's rhetoric depends on eroticized association and confusion, rhetorical treatises – classical and Renaissance manuals teaching the art of poetry and persuasion – are also theoretical guides to pre-modern sexuality. Examining the tropes of metaphor, metonymy, catachresis and allegory, Menon argues that 'the material of rhetoric undermines its own investment in coherence by being linguistically and sexually wanton' (2004: 7). Metonymy, or what the rhetorical theorist George Puttenham calls 'the misnamer', in which a term is named by that with which it is associated ('crown' for 'king'), is one particularly trenchant example. As Menon maintains, 'Metonymy's constitutive tendency is to merge into other tropes so as to itself remain unmarked in the realm of signification' (2004: 39). Insofar as it depends on 'an *affinity* between two things rather than an *innate* link between two terms', metonymy disrupts expectation of proper and stable linguistic and sexual identities: 'The shadowy nature of Renaissance (homo)sexuality and its potentially corrupting influence is distinctly reflected by the textual use of an indistinguishable metonymy in which it is impossible to tell one trope and one sexuality from the partner that "[lies] alongside" it' (2004: 39; original emphasis). Attention to the sexual dimension of rhetoric, Menon shows, alters our perception of many familiar scenes in Shakespeare's plays. Rhetoric draws attention to ambiguous desires that are unspeakable not because they are forbidden, but because they have no proper, singular name or identity. Accordingly, they can only appear in nonce terms that are inexact, premature, retrospective or improper, and therefore resist the clear-cut categories and meanings that modern critics and editors often look for.

History and temporality

Since the inception of gay, lesbian and queer studies, scholars examining Shakespeare's plays have seen their work as having direct relevance to the politics and culture of their present moment. Yet the precise relationship between, as Bruce Smith categorized them, 'literary, historical, and political' concerns has been a longstanding topic of debate (1991: 28). Given the break that Foucault posited between the sodomitical acts of the past and the homosexual identities of the present, is queer theory an anachronistic lens through which to view the past? To what extent are similarities with or differences from the past a product of empirically verifiable history, and to what extent are they products of modern, Western ideology? How does temporality (the experience of time) relate to history (the record of times past)? When we study the past, are we doing historical or theoretical work? Early modern queer scholars have offered a variety of answers to these questions; below, I trace some of the more influential arguments and debates that have shaped the field.

Over the past few decades, queer studies of Shakespeare and pre-modern literature have both engaged in careful historical and archival research *and* challenged new historicist prohibitions against anachronism.[16] In particular, queer early modern scholars have defied Stephen Greenblatt's oft-cited denunciation of psychoanalysis as a product of twentieth-century bourgeois culture and therefore an inappropriate framework through which to view early modern subjects.[17] As Freccero sums up this objection, 'psychoanalytic interpretation therefore performs a metalepsis on early modernity, belatedly attributing a cause (subjectivity) to what is, in fact, an effect (of culture)'. Noting that 'objections of belatedness' can and have also been directed at queer theory and poststructuralism, Freccero offers the rejoinder that

> One equally materialist response to the observation that psychoanalysis seems causally belated with respect to early modernity has been to dispute, on historical grounds, a certain conception of the modern subject as the subject that serves as one of psychoanalysis's foundational categories. If early modern European textuality foregrounds the status of the subject as linguistically constructed, contingent, textual,

and fragmented, then early modern subjectivity has more in common with psychoanalytic and poststructuralist notions of the subject than it does with the modernity that appears in the intervening period of Western European philosophical and literary discourse. (2006: 1)

Against new historicist strictures, Traub, Cynthia Marshall and Graham Hammill have joined Freccero in asserting the analytical value of such concepts as the unconscious, projection, transference and narcissism. These concepts can illuminate past desires that cannot be empirically and unquestionably verified insofar as they appear in euphemism, stock phrases, double entendre and literary representations rather than factual documents.[18]

The queer rejection of a historicist common sense about chronology, anachronism and method with regards to psychoanalysis was one piece of a more general defiance of a prohibition against finding the present in the past. Addressing the charge that identification with the past constituted a narcissistic self-indulgence, Louise Fradenburg and Carla Freccero contend that an 'opposition between transhistorical perspectives and historicist perspectives that "accept" difference is itself ideological' rather than empirical (1996a: viii). This ideology, they further suggest, serves to uphold a 'fantasmatic figure of modernity symmetrically and absolutely opposed to premodernity' (1996b: xix). Fradenburg and Freccero urge queer critics instead to strive to 'write a history of the way the past works to define its future, or a history of the ways in which the past is in us' (1996b: xix). The affirmation that history encompasses not just objective facts or punctual events, but also fantasies, affective connections, and repetitive structures of feeling has encouraged queer analysis of the relationship between temporality (the experiential relationship to time) and historiography (the principles by which we narrate the past). Much of this work adopts a poststructuralist and postcolonial critique of a Western historiographic tradition that represents time as a linear, forward movement, assumes cumulative progress, and therefore depicts non-Western peoples as belatedly catching up to the enlightenment of Western modernity.[19] These challenges to historicist temporality, particularly as formulated by new historicism, can be understood as falling into several analytical frameworks which tend to overlap: presentist, multi-temporal, and unhistorical or homohistorical.

The first of these emphasizes the presentism of any reading of past texts and sees this presentism as a positive quality. This view, as summarized by Evelyn Gajowski, entails 'a heightened degree of self-awareness' that 'constitutes the theoretical stance' that 'all our knowledge of Shakespeare, including that of his historical context, is shaped by the ideologies and discourses of the cultural present. Far from being impediments to our knowledge, this understanding is its enabling foundation' (Gajowski 2009: 12).[20] Drawing on work from feminist and critical race studies of early modern literature, presentist methods underscore the affinity between interpretations of the past and political investments in the present. This work has allowed us to see that the effort to purify the past of present perspectives – especially those focused on race, gender, class, sexuality and global politics – itself obscures the ideological and political investments of critics in a particular ideal of early modern England as a time untroubled by racism or homophobia. Nor is presentism limited to 'our' (twentieth- and twenty-first-century) present. It is part of earlier sexology and historiography as well. As Fisher shows, Victorian writers like Havelock Ellis, Walter Pater and John Addington Symonds – whose myth of Renaissance sexual freedom Bray critiques as unhistorical – are key figures in the history of sexuality insofar as they sought to legitimate the category of the homosexual which was being formed contemporaneously (Fisher 2009).[21] Contesting traditional versions of past events and values is a way of intervening in present and future politics.

A second methodological perspective draws on new materialist critiques of modernity and traditional historiography by Bruno Latour, Michel Serres and Hayden White. Rather than emphasizing the critic's own presentism, these studies stress the multiple temporalities of literary and material artefacts. Attention to multitemporality allows us to see that these artefacts encode different moments in their content and construction. One ready example is the triple temporal location of *Pericles*: this play, written by Shakespeare and Wilkens in the seventeenth century, is based on a third-century Greek romance and framed by the summaries of the medieval author John Gower, who acts as Chorus. Along with its attention to the different historical moments that explicitly appear in cultural artefacts, a multitemporal perspective acknowledges that literary and material works are palimpsests that have accrued different meanings across different moments in time through archival discoveries, editorial influence, different material presentation, and changing interpretive frameworks. These meanings come to coexist, recede, reappear, and influence different situations and readers.[22] Literary objects thus attest to the 'non-self-identity of any historical moment', as Goldberg argues, including our own (2011: 502–3).

A third perspective that opposes traditional historicism is homohistory or unhistoricism. Advocating for this method, Goldberg and Menon contend that 'the challenge for queer Renaissance studies today is twofold: one, to resist mapping sexual difference onto chronological difference such that the difference between past and present becomes also the difference between sexual regimes; and two, to challenge the notion of a determinate and knowable identity, past and present' (2005: 1609). Further elaborating this position, Menon elsewhere argues that the view that the past and the present are two different sexual regimes (one based on acts and one on identities), leads even those critics with a strong anti-homophobic agenda to enforce the stable identification that queer theory should disrupt. Because Shakespeare's writing and cultural legacy are a paradigmatic instance of the 'past-in-the-present', 'Shakespeare' militates against chronological fixity and 'reveals as a symptom' institutionalized periods and field boundaries as 'our desire to keep things clean in the messiest of texts' (Menon 2008: 5). Against 'compulsory heterotemporality', which divides literature into distinct periods and reserves 'theory' for modern writers, Menon argues, queer Shakespeare studies must understand Shakespeare *himself* as a queer theorist, 'not because he has written essays with the word "queer" in the title, but because his work already inhabits the queer theory we occupy today' (2011a: 12).

Although presentist, multitemporal and unhistorical work has been interpreted as operating in a synchronous mode that focuses on discrete moments and thereby excludes diachronous difference and change over time, it would be more accurate to understand it as challenging the distinction between synchrony and diachrony altogether.[23] The queer critique of historicism is a rejection of singular temporality, whether past or present, as Guy-Bray, Vin Nardizzi and Will Stockton frame it, that seeks to avoid 'fetishizing' either 'historical accuracy', on the one hand, or 'the needs of contemporary gays and lesbians', on the other (2009: 2). Hammill, to take another perspective, distinguishes between the '*un*historical' and the '*a*historical' (2000: 173; my emphasis). Far from being ahistorical, or outside history altogether, the unhistorical designates 'particular forms of thinking that emerge through the aesthetic at the limits of social thought'. Aesthetic objects, that is, indirectly and incidentally make available modes of cogitation and desire that have not been systematically articulated in their own historical moment. Queer scholars' attentiveness to the possibility of the 'untimely meditations' to be found in literary artefacts that 'stand against the dominant form of the civilizing process' allows us to 'develop modes of interpretation that variously frustrate seemingly sound distinctions between past, present, and future in the space between work and reader or spectator' (2000: 174–5).

A resistance to the assumption of difference to past and present is also an affective stance. It builds on John Boswell's recommendation that we understand community as a fractured and polytemporal set of connections and recognitions (1980, 1994). Recognizing that the past is not over, queer history is, in Carolyn Dinshaw's words, engaged in 'making relations with the past, relations that form part of our subjectivities and communities' (1999: 11–12). The effort to make 'affective connections across time' centres not on the assumption of identity, but on the recognition of a shared, though still historically contingent, queerness. Dinshaw explains what this means through the example of her own attachment to the medieval woman Margery Kempe: 'Queerness denotes a relation that can be specified in a given time and place (Margery is queer in relation to her neighbors) and can be traced across time … (Margery and I are both queer – in different ways, in relation to our very different surroundings – and are thus queerly related to one another)' (1999: 158). Like Dinshaw, Freccero urges not rejection of the past but a redefinition of our approach to it (2006: 4–5). Rather than the active and ideological formation of narratives that White has designated the actual work of even the most purportedly objective historiography, Freccero writes, queer scholars can cultivate 'passivity – which is also a form of patience and passion' that manifests itself not as 'quietism' but as 'a suspension, a waiting, an attending to the world's arrivals (though, in part, its returns), not as guarantee or security for action in the present, but as the very force from the past that moves us into the future' (2006: 104).

Although the project of queering history has had significant impact on Shakespeare studies, its propositions have not gone unquestioned. One of the chief critiques is that queer dismissals of historicism have the potential to play precisely the policing role that they seek to resist. DiGangi, for instance, worries that Freccero's formulations of alternatives to empirical and altericist groundings of queerness 'reflect a certain canon-forming tendency in Renaissance sexuality studies – a drawing of sharp distinctions between properly "queer" and "non-queer" approaches' (2007: 131). Similarly, in a review essay on Menon's *Shakesqueer*, Stockton cautions against the construction of a 'false dichotomy between queerness and historicism' (2012: 226). Given the reality of historical and embodied specificity that shapes both sexuality and its social rewards and penalties, Stockton wonders 'whether queerness, or the field of queer studies, actually needs some of the limitations against which Menon militates' and notes the 'potentially obfuscating and universalizing consequences' of unhistorical claims (2012: 233, 235).

Most expansively, Traub critiques Freccero, Dinshaw, Goldberg and Menon, whom she groups under the category of 'teleoskepticism', on two main grounds. The first is that in focusing only on a single period (medieval or early modern) in relation to modernity, they 'bracket the question of any intervening time span' and thereby 'avoid all matters associated with chronology, including how to explain the endurance or recurrence of some of the very similarities that interest them' (Traub 2015: 64). The second problem that Traub diagnoses inheres in the 'rhetorical maneuvers and conceptual conflations that underlie their indictments of difference, chronology, and periodization' (2015: 71). Traub identifies an 'associative logic' and 'analogical argumentation', whereby 'historical difference, chronology, periodization, and empirical facts are positioned in an endlessly self-incriminating and disqualifying feedback loop' that is designated straight, normative or heterotemporal (2015: 71). Such analogical reasoning obscures the truth, Traub argues, that 'A scholar's adherence to chronological time does not, in and of itself, have any necessary relationship to sexuality, much less to sexual normativity' (2015: 73). Rather than reject historical alterity and change altogether, Traub proposes, queer historians might attend instead to 'cycles of salience', or those 'forms of intelligibility whose meanings recur, intermittently and with a difference, across time' (2015: 85). Traub argues that 'recognition of these periodic cycles of salience – flaring up and abating – could provide us with a means to collectively write ... a transnational, culturally specific, and comparative history of lesbianism over the *longue durée*' (2015: 85–6). Similarly, Masten maintains that connection across time is not the only queer game in town. Historical alterity may itself be 'potentially queer – though not necessarily always so'. In response to this possibility, scholars must ask 'What queerness can be mobilized and deployed by and through – not *despite* – recognizing and analyzing alterity?' (2016: 35; original emphasis).

If, as Masten pithily reminds us, 'there is more than one way to queer a Renaissance', then the contentions about what queering history would look like may not be an unfortunate squabble to get past so much as an enabling examination of assumptions about queerness, identity, difference, theory and history. Addressing queer debates about history, Ari Friedlander argues that while 'It might seem more productive to agree that different methods serve different disciplinary agendas, and that the academic world is large enough to support all different kinds of work', a liberal discourse of tolerant coexistence might 'make it too easy to foreclose the possibility of transgressing methodological boundaries' and 'discourage ... self-reflexivity rather than encourage it'. This would be unfortunate, for 'theoretical difference can help sharpen ... methodological practices' (Friedlander 2016: 10). Rather than seek premature reconciliation, I have previously proposed that we see our disagreements as 'attempts at persuasion' whose end is not the conversion of our interlocutors but rather refinement of our own positions and continued, more nuanced debate (Sanchez 2016: 143). If Sedgwick's analysis of homosocial rivalry teaches us anything, it is that rivalry is not a relationship of indifference. It is one of ambivalent identification and desire, in which the disagreement and competition that can be sources of discomfort are also sources of inspiration and pleasure. Queer scholars are rivals, rather than enemies, precisely because we are ultimately on the same side.

4

How Queer Is the Shakespearean Canon?

I turn in this chapter to several of Shakespeare's poems and plays to consider their potential to queer normative conceptions of race, gender, friendship, love, marriage, desire and even what counts as sex itself. I begin with an examination of the mobility of desire across multiple categories (gender, age, species, acts) in *A Midsummer Night's Dream* and *Venus and Adonis*, which feature cross-generational, cross-species, homoerotic desires. These plays depict what Freud called 'polymorphous perversity' – the aptitude to find sexual gratification in a range of practices – and thereby expand the domain of 'sex' itself ([1905] 1975: 57). I then discuss the shaping force that race, religion and ethnicity exert on sexual categories and desires in *The Merchant of Venice* and *Othello*. In these plays, racial and religious specificity disrupt convergent discourses of universal sameness, one ancient and one emergent at the time of the play's composition: Pauline universalism and global capitalism.[1] Finally, I trace the queer perspective on temporality, memory and historiography offered by *Henry V* and *Hamlet*, the former on the level of narrative sequence, the latter on that of cultural standing. I hope this small sampling of plays and analytical paths will illuminate two of the many reasons that Shakespeare's oeuvre provides a valuable archive for queer studies. First, it features a number of characters whose desires, practices and fantasies challenge us to formulate nonce terms and taxonomies. Second, in its self-conscious moments of anachronism, preposterous sequencing and resistance to humanist optimism, Shakespeare's oeuvre is itself structurally and conceptually queer. Long the centrepiece of Western literary culture, Shakespeare may in fact offer what Lee Edelman calls a 'bad education' – preserving memory of ambivalences, aggressions and perversities at the core of the master canon (2011: 169).

The limits of polymorphous perversity: *A Midsummer Night's Dream* and *Venus and Adonis*

For sheer range of sexual possibilities, there are few plays to match *A Midsummer Night's Dream*, which evokes fantasies of incest, BDSM and cross-species eroticism, both homo- and heterosexual. This variety has sometimes been overlooked because the two central plots of the play – the four Athenian lovers' quadrangulated desires and the conflict between Titania and Oberon – appear to end in the cliché of heterosexual coupledom summarized by Puck's 'Jack shall have Jill' (3.2.461). In Louis Montrose's influential description of this plot, 'the Amazons have been defeated before the play begins; and nuptial rites are to be celebrated when it ends'; together, Hippolyta's forced marriage, Titania's loss of her votaress, and the dissolution of Hermia and Helena's friendship reveal that 'the dramatic process that forges marital couplings simultaneously weakens the bonds of sisterhood and strengthens the bonds of brotherhood' (1983: 69). But Montrose's spare reading, in which ending trumps experience, performs its own normalizing exclusions. In fact, as Bruce Boehrer has argued, the play's prevalent references to bestiality and to same-sex communities form parallel discursive patterns that constitute 'nervous projections of tendencies intrinsic' to the play's understanding of gender difference and love between human men and human women (2004: 99). These intrinsic tendencies can be summed up, Richard Rambuss has argued, in the play's interest in 'anality', which 'is the play's chief strategy for shaming, even as it supplies its erotic core' (2011a: 240). In Rambuss's analysis, the convergence of proscribed acts at the centre of the play's plotlines can be seen in Titania's and Oberon's competing desires for the Indian boy; in Titania's incestuous role-play with a bestial object; in Helena's wish to be 'used' as a spaniel; in Puck's 'prepost'rously' fluid multitude of shapes; and in the Rude Mechanicals' play, in which the male Flute, as the female Thisbe, kisses the 'hole' of the Wall (played by the male Snout), in lieu of the 'lips' of Pyramus/Bottom (5.1.199; Rambuss 2011a). The play's most memorable scenes, that is, depict sexual impulses that are not only homoerotic but also cross the borders of generation, race and species (humans, Rambuss points out, are a different species than fairies as well as animals (2011a: 236)).

The love potion by which Oberon manipulates the plot metaphorically condenses a larger dynamic of *A Midsummer Night's Dream*: the patriarchal and heteronormative effort to reproduce the orderly structures of marriage and procreation as voluntary itself relies on inciting desires whose objects and effects are unruly and unpredictable. Oberon's 'love juice' is extracted from a flower that was accidently hit when Cupid aimed an arrow at an 'imperial votress' (2.1.163).[2] Although the votaress 'passed on / In maiden meditation, fancy-free', Oberon explains, the 'little western flower' on which 'the bolt of Cupid fell' was transformed, 'Before milk-white, now purple with love's wound: / And maidens call it "love-in-idleness"' (2.1.164–5, 167–8). This would seem a pretty literal image of heterosexual penetration as a simultaneous deflowering and fertilization, particularly when we remember that 'flowers' was also slang for menstruation in early modern England. As Montrose has cogently argued,

> Oberon's maddening love-juice is also a sublimation of vaginal blood. It conflates menstrual blood with the

blood of defloration: The former is the ambivalent sign of women's generative power and of their sexual pollution, of the dangers they pose to men's potency, to their reason, and to their honor; the latter is the sign of men's assertion of control over women's bodies, the sign of masculine mastery over potentially dangerous feminine generative and erotic powers. (1996: 174–5)

But this is not just any flower. It is a specific type, and if we trace its resonance both in early modern and later culture, the eroticism that it represents begins to look less amenable to the heteropatriarchal ideology that Montrose traces. The bud that 'maidens call ... "love-in-idleness"' is the Viola tricolour, or wild pansy. Its name is derived from the French *pensée* ('thought'), an etymology that Ophelia notes in *Hamlet*: 'There is pansies, that's / for thoughts' (4.5.174–5). The thoughts from which the pansy takes its name are the mark of the lovesickness that, as Carol Thomas Neely has shown, was understood as 'a somatic disease of inflamed and congested genitals leading to disordered fantasy' that 'drive[s] sufferers to resist or disrupt status roles, gender hierarchies, and binary constructions of sexual desire and object choice' (2004: 99, 100). No mere metaphor, lovesickness was taken seriously by medical tracts whose 'emphasis on the extremes to which lovesickness drives its victims ... overrides sharp distinctions between normative and transgressive desires and between heteroeroticism and homoerotism' (Neely 2004: 112).[3]

By designating the source of the potion a flower called 'love in idleness', *A Midsummer Night's Dream* also questions distinctions between romantic love that can be directed toward marriage and polymorphous perversion that is not organized according to socially useful ends. Lysander's and Demetrius's shifting attractions, and Helena's and Hermia's change of allegiance from one another to their male lovers, may structurally lead to procreative heterosexual unions, but this very logic of substitutability undermines any sense that those unions are inevitable or permanent. Titania's 'hateful fantasies' are but one instance of the 'fond pageant' in which all who are struck by desire participate (2.1.258, 3.2.114). In the play's first scene, Egeus claims that Lysander has 'bewitch'd' Hermia (1.1.27). Helena, more expansively, muses that 'Things base and vile, holding no quantity, / Love can transpose to form and dignity: / Love looks not with the eyes, but with the mind' (1.1.232–4). These lines' emphasis on the subjective quality of the 'vile' – that which arouses disgust – anticipate Oberon's incantatory hope that Titania will desire 'some vile thing' and thereby connect it to the other, seemingly more conventional, plot strands (2.2.33). Along with Lysander and Demetrius, Titania is also influenced by the love potion and she, as Neely rightly notes, 'desires everything in sight including a woman, a boy, and an ass' (2004: 114, n. 14). These objects are themselves connected by an associative logic that reveals desire to circle back on itself. The 'vile thing' Titania dotes on turns out to be Bottom, whose head has been 'translated' into that of an ass and whose name, numerous critics have noted, evokes anal eroticism. Gail Kern Paster, most influentially, has described the scenes between Titania and Bottom as an incest fantasy in which Titania administers erotic laxatives to 'purge' Bottom's 'mortal grossness', so that the 'differences between heterosexual intercourse and anal cathexes of maternal nurture become blurred' (*MND* 3.1.152; Paster 1993: 126). Titania's maternal relation to the asinine Bottom also makes him a surrogate for the changeling child, that 'lovely boy, stol'n from an Indian king' (2.1.22), who is himself, as Titania recounts, a surrogate for the 'votress of my order' who died bearing him (2.1.123). Read amidst the 'fond pageants' of promiscuous homo- and heteroerotic attachment, incest, cross-species contact and anal eroticism, the marriages anticipated at the end of *A Midsummer Night's Dream* are not desire's final resting place, but one among many fantasies that give desire an object and shape.

The inexplicable, perverse, and sometimes violent nature of both hetero- and homoerotic desire is equally on display in Shakespeare's 1593 Ovidian epyllion *Venus and Adonis*.

This poem departs from its model, Ovid's *Metamorphoses*, in its emphasis on Adonis's adamant resistance to heterosexual consummation, a revision which, Catherine Belsey and Madhavi Menon have argued, figures Shakespeare's corresponding rejection of teleology (Belsey 1995; Menon 2008: 34–44). Whereas Ovid's Venus is Adonis's 'companion' (*huic comes est* (10.533)), Shakespeare's Venus is helpless to interest him. A number of critics have seen this rejection as a sign of Adonis's effeminacy, immaturity, and even pathology. William Keach claims that 'there is something mean and perverse in Adonis's aversion to love as such' (1977: 70); Coppélia Kahn writes that when Adonis 'sternly rejects an enviable chance to prove his manhood' with the goddess of love herself, he 'meets death in the boar hunt, and metamorphosed into a flower, ends up as a child again, sheltered in Venus's bosom' (1981: 22); Maurice Evans describes Adonis as 'callow, petulant ... above all, narcissistic' (Evans 1989: 13); Mario DiGangi describes Adonis as a 'passively "feminine" boy' (1997: 136). What these interpretations share, as Goran Stanivukovic and Richard Rambuss have argued, is a perspective in which normative masculinity expresses itself in heterosexual object choice. Rather than understand Adonis's rejection of Venus as immaturity or effeminacy, as Stanivukovic puts it, we would do better to recognize that 'signs of Adonis's queerness are numerous' (2000: 90). Once we see Adonis as queer, Rambuss argues, Adonis's rejection of Venus need not signify effeminacy, immaturity, or narcissism, 'at least not to those who can conceive of masculinity and male sexuality apart from heterosexuality ... to those, in other words, who can grasp that a boy *as a boy* may desire something else' and that 'a man may refuse, may turn away from the love of women – and that refusal be neither deviant nor necessarily tantamount to an expression of misogyny' (2003: 244, 251; original emphasis). In this light, the poem reads as a meditation on 'male initiation or coming of age, male homoeroticism, and hypermasculinity' signified in the hairy and brutal male boar's penetration of Adonis (Rambuss 2003: 242).

Although the poem emphasizes Adonis's youthful appearance – he is a 'Rose-cheek'd' 'tender boy' with a 'hairless face' (*VA* 3, 32, 487) – it also retains the Ovidian assurance of Adonis's masculinity. In the *Metamorphoses*, Adonis is 'now man' (*iam vir*) when he first encounters Venus, and he chooses to hunt the boar out of 'manly courage' (*virtus*) (10.522). Shakespeare emphasizes, perhaps even more than Stanivukovic or Rambuss recognize, Adonis's masculine gender and penetrative sexuality. One of the first things we learn is that 'Hunting he lov'd, but love he laugh'd to scorn', and this rejection of romance and preference for hunting with male friends would, in a Renaissance context that saw excessive love for women as effeminate and deemed hunting a manly activity, have signalled his masculinity (*VA* 4). Adonis's repeated affirmation of his preference for male companionship – 'tomorrow he intends / To hunt the boar with certain of his friends'; '"I am," quoth he, "expected of my friends"' – would have made perfect sense to Plato, Aristotle, Cicero and Montaigne (587–8, 718). Adonis also illuminates the erotic dimension of philosophical ideals of male friendship, for he describes the hunt not as the rejection of eroticism but as an alternative form of it when he rebuffs Venus by insisting that 'I know not love ... nor will not know it, / Unless it be a boar, and then I chase it' and, having affirmed that 'Love surfeits not, lust like a glutton dies', departs for what Venus recognizes is 'no gentle chase, / But the blunt boar, rough bear, or lion proud' (409–10, 803, 883–4). Venus herself describes his choice as one of masculine aggression: however much she tries to warn Adonis that the boar is 'Like to a mortal butcher, bent to kill', she understands Adonis to have a similarly violent desire to penetrate the boar, 'With javelin's point a churlish swine to gore' (618, 616). Adonis in this view is not passive or receptive, qualities associated with femininity. He wants to be on top.

The explicitly male boar, as critics have pointed out, is also hyperbolically masculine, indeed phallic, and he also wants to be on top.[4] He has 'bristly pikes' and 'crooked tushes', Venus tells Adonis, and 'His brawny sides with hairy bristles armed / Are better proof than thy spear's point can enter' (620, 624, 625–6). The boar's physical armour, in Venus's eyes, also signals emotional impenetrability: 'he naught esteems that face of thine', Venus warns (631). This would seem to distinguish the boar from the infatuated Venus and align him with the unmoved Adonis. But according to Venus, it is not only Adonis whose defences have been overcome, as we see in her response to 'the wide wound that the boar had trench'd / In his soft flank' (1052–3). The boar is also susceptible to Adonis's beauty, but his desire appears not as tender care but as insatiable drive. Venus, the poem has already informed us, is dangerous in her appetite for Adonis: she is like 'an empty eagle, sharp by fast', who 'Tires with her beak on feathers, flesh and bone / … devouring all in haste, / Till either gorge be stuff'd or prey be gone' (55–8). She projects similar desires onto the boar, interpreting Adonis's death as an accidental effect of passion that got out of control:

If he did see his face, why then I know
He thought to kiss him, and hath kill'd him so.

'Tis true, 'tis true; thus was Adonis slain:
He ran upon the boar with his sharp spear,
Who did not whet his teeth at him again,
But by a kiss thought to persuade him there;
          And, nuzzling in his flank, the loving swine
          Sheath'd unaware the tusk in his soft groin.

(1109–16)

Although the rapacity of desire is not gendered in the poem, sexual positioning definitively is. The most telling difference between Venus, on the one hand, and Adonis and the boar, on the other, is that Venus desires to be penetrated, but Adonis and the boar wish to penetrate. Venus begs Adonis to treat her body as a park in which he can 'Stray lower, where the pleasant fountains lie'; but when she pulls him on top of her,

'He will not manage her, although he mount her' (234, 598). By contrast, Adonis *does* want to take the active, dominant role with the boar. In his own words, he will 'know' love with the boar and 'chase it'; Venus laments his desire to 'enter' and 'spear' the boar (626, 1112).

The poem, I am arguing, presents the encounter between Adonis and the boar as one driven by a mutual desire to penetrate. It is neither an imitation of heterosexual coitus nor a pederastic union in which who will be on top is determined in advance by age or status. Adonis and the boar are the same not only in gender but also in desired act and position. Their mutual desire to dominate perhaps crystalizes Leo Bersani's argument that 'Human bodies are constructed in such a way that it is, or at least has been, almost impossible not to associate mastery and subordination with the experience of our most intense pleasures' (1987: 216). For Bersani, understanding this association is a 'question of positioning' – who's on top? – and a 'question of the penis'– who penetrates whom? (1987: 216). Because positioning and penetration are culturally constructed in terms of mastery and subordination, activity and passivity, 'A reflection on the fantasmatic potential of the human body – the fantasies engendered by its sexual anatomy and the specific moves it makes in taking sexual pleasure' are ripe for 'ideological exploitations' that deny the appeal and '*value* of powerlessness in both men and women', by which Bersani does not 'mean the value of gentleness, or nonaggressiveness, or even of passivity, but rather of a more radical disintegration and humiliation of the self' (1987: 217; original emphasis).

Bersani's analysis is useful in allowing us to see the continuity between desire and aggression, kissing and killing, in *Venus and Adonis*. But the 'anatomical considerations' he analyses too easily equate possession of a penis with penetration, mastery and masculinity. Shakespeare's epyllion acknowledges that you do not need an actual penis in order to penetrate. A spear or a tusk will do just as well. This acknowledgment makes it all the more curious that the poem limits the desire to penetrate to those born with penises.

In accentuating Venus's helpless desire to be penetrated by Adonis's penis, the poem treats anatomy as destiny, foreclosing the possibility of other acts between them, and thereby retains domination as a masculine property. Jonathan Crewe is right to describe Venus's forceful abduction of Adonis as a form of sexual assault (1999: xxxv–xxxvii). But the poem stops short of imagining that assault as taking the form of penetration, despite the fact that it depicts Adonis's spear and the boar's tusk as alternatives to an erect penis. *Venus and Adonis* excludes the possibility that a woman might enjoy penetrating a man or a woman with tongue, fingers, other body parts, or instruments like the 'dildos' that Autolycus advertises in *The Winter's Tale*. Venus may dwarf Adonis in size and strength, carrying Adonis under her arm and forcing him to lie on top of her. But because 'He will not manage her' she remains unsatisfied in her desires (598).

Read in conjunction with *A Midsummer Night's Dream*, we can understand *Venus and Adonis* as both queerer and more normative. *Venus and Adonis* is queerer in that it is a more explicitly 'proto-gay text', in Rambuss's words (2003: 252). But it is more normative in that it defines both gender and sexual desire according to a conventional interpretation of bodily morphology. Venus's desire for sex in the missionary position is strikingly pedestrian, particularly in contrast to Adonis's much kinkier agon with the boar. Titania's administration of enemas puts her and her fairies in the position of penetrating Bottom's orifices, even as Bottom's pleasure appears to inhere at least as much in this infantile receptivity as in any offstage penetration of Titania we might imagine. The relation between fairy queen and asinine mortal in *A Midsummer Night's Dream* is queer not only because it is cross-species and cross-generational, but also because it does not conflate the penis with the phallus and thereby confine desire to acts associated with anatomical sex assignment. The relation between Adonis and the boar – imagined as penetration of side by spear, groin by tusk – equally resists treating anatomy as destiny, even as it naturalizes Venus's female desire to be 'managed'. Gender in *Venus and Adonis* poses a curious limit to the forms of queer desire that the poem can imagine.

The erotic life of racism in *The Merchant of Venice* and *Othello*

In this section, I turn to another topic that, along with gender, has a complicated relation to queer theory: race. Sharon Holland has argued that 'the boundary-breaking futurity in which queer studies finds its subject would balk if such a subject were held to a *transhistorical* view of time', for such a view would reveal that erotic desire is not an autonomous individual drive but itself conditioned by a long history of racial, ethnic, religious and colonial hierarchy (2012: 62; original emphasis). When queer theory romanticizes lust as spontaneous and inherently transgressive of dominant culture, it fails to confront the 'erotic life of racism', or the material history that has produced desire and desirability (Holland 2012). The difference that a history of interlocking ethnic, racial and religious categories makes to taxonomies of desire appears starkly in two plays whose plots explicitly address both homoerotic desire and racial difference: *The Merchant of Venice* and *Othello*. Both are structured by a logic of substitution that would appear to render all objects of desire homologous.

The Merchant of Venice seeks to naturalize the legal dominance of Christians over Jews by aligning racial and religious identities with a series of binaries in which the first term transcends a logic of bargaining and exchange that the second assumes: faith versus works, grace versus law, mercy versus justice, spirit versus body, love versus money. This structure pits Antonio against Shylock. Antonio freely offers 'My purse, my person, my extremest means' to Bassanio, the 'bosom lover' for whom, Solanio reports, Antonio 'only loves the world' and on whose behalf he would gladly leave it; Shylock values his daughter and his ducats equally and demands that his bond be fulfilled to the letter (1.1.138–9, 3.4.17, 2.8.50). Accordingly, queer critics have frequently seen Bassanio's relationship to Antonio as the ultimate refuge from the corruptions of self-interest and material accumulation that the play associates overtly with Shylock and, more subtly, with Portia and heterosexual marriage. *The Merchant of Venice*, that is, adopts a classical idealization of male friendship as the only relationship immune to material interest, as against the ultimately worldly institution of heterosexual marriage, and thereby aligns marriage with works, law and money. As Arthur L. Little Jr. argues, for instance, 'The commodifying of Portia through gold, silver, and lead caskets links her to the capitalism of Venice and, especially, to its raison d'etre, the (re)production of wealth' (2011: 219). Bruce Smith notes that Bassanio himself describes his courtship of Portia as the quest of a merchant adventurer, a description borne out by Bassanio and Gratiano's comparison of themselves to 'Jasons' seeking the 'golden fleece' that is also likened to Portia's hair (3.2.240, 1.1.170; Smith 1991: 57–8). In *The Merchant of Venice*, Antonio himself explicitly associates heterosexual marriage with conditional (Jewish) law and works, male homoeroticism with unconditional (Christian) grace and faith. He pleads that Balthasar's 'deservings and my love withal / Be valued 'gainst your wife's commandment', and he reconciles Portia to Bassanio by promising 'My soul upon the forfeit, that your lord / Will never more break faith advisedly' (4.1.448–9, 5.1.252–3). A queer reading could see Antonio's self-sacrificial desire as challenging the longstanding connection between sodomy and Jewish practices of usury and idolatry, on the one hand, and procreative sex with Christian charity and faith, on the other. By asserting the spiritual nature of male homoerotic love as against the worldly practice of marriage, Antonio's pronounced anti-Semitism can thereby be understood as part of a bid to distance himself from the legal association of sodomy with heresy and witchcraft.[5]

In general, queer critics have tended to imagine queerness as disrupting the Venetian world of exchange, whether by exposing the perverse logic of marriage or by demonstrating the hypocrisy of Christian values. As Will Stockton argues, Portia's acceptance of Antonio as Bassanio's 'surety' constitutes a three-way marriage 'in which husband and wife, husband and friend, and friend and wife, are all one flesh' – thus exposing the perversely logical end of a queer Pauline universalism that dissolves all flesh into a single, Christian body (*MV* 5.1.254; Stockton 2017: 56, 60). Yet as numerous feminist, historicist and Marxist critics have detailed, *The Merchant of Venice* makes visible the early ideological foundations of capitalism.[6] Queer theory helps us to notice the role of liberatory models of sexuality in this ideology. In championing any private relation on the ground that it is uncontaminated by market considerations, queer criticism inadvertently perpetuates the logic of what Lisa Duggan has called 'the new homonormativity' and what David Eng has called 'queer liberalism' (Duggan 2003: 50; Eng 2010). This neo-liberal logic, as 'a ruse that obscures the intricate imbrications of relations of race, gender, sexuality, and class in the institutions of capitalist modernity', works in two ways (Duggan 2003: 83). First, it erects a firm barrier between public and private and thereby renders intimate relations a refuge from the dehumanizing operations of the marketplace rather than a necessary part of them. Second, it cordons off economic from cultural concerns, so that racial, ethnic and religious hierarchies appear immaterial to finance.

The ideological division of public from private, finance from culture, appears structurally in the play's treatment of Venice as a city whose 'trade and profit ... / Consisteth of all nations' in contrast to Belmont as a pastoral refuge that frees affection from commerce. The contrast, as Little puts it, imaginatively 'solves Venice's global quandary, its desire to have the world but not belong to it' (*MV* 3.3.30–1; Little 2000: 71). Alan Stewart points out that 'instead of portraying neatly opposed systems – usury versus charity, Judaism versus Christianity, contractual literalism versus merciful equity – all the relationships of the play are better understood on a sliding scale of credit relationships' (2008: 189). I would add that racial distinctions also delimit which credit relations are desirable, or even imaginable. Even as the 'infidel' Jessica's conversion to Christianity affirms the possibility of her incorporation into the privatized world of Belmont, that world is introduced as the site not only of a 'lott'ry' for the chance to marry Portia but also of systematic racial discrimination (3.2.217, 1.2.29). Portia, as has been frequently noted, is repelled by the Prince of Morocco for no reason other than his skin colour, averring that 'If he have the condition of a / saint and the complexion of a devil, I had rather he / should shrive me than wive me' and hoping that 'all of his complexion' will choose the wrong casket (1.2.127–9, 2.7.79). And Lorenzo, responding to Launcelot's jibe that, as Jessica summarizes it, 'in converting Jews to Christians, you raise the / price of pork' hints at anti-miscegenation laws that seek formally to direct desire along racialized lines: 'I shall answer that better to the / commonwealth than you can the getting up of the / negro's belly: the Moor is with child by you / Launcelot' (3.5.33–8). Set in a context in which, as Loomba puts it, 'English anxieties about commerce, race, and sexuality' overlap, we must understand the love between Antonio and Bassanio, no less than the marriage between Portia and Bassanio, as a product of interwoven racial, religious and economic hierarchies, not an escape from or transgression of them (Loomba 2002: 137). Antonio and Bassanio's bond upholds the religious, economic and ethnic hierarchies of Venice – made material in the compulsory transfer of Shylock's money to the state and to his daughter, a newly converted Christian. Read in the context of the history of sodomy laws and their uneven enforcement, we might also notice that their relation enjoys the privileges of privacy because of their status as Christians. *The Merchant of Venice* confronts us with a homoerotic relationship that is nurtured by the conjunction of religious and racial privilege. Accordingly, we must ask: how are we as queer readers to respond to representations of same-sex desire that conform to a larger structure in which attraction is a response to racial sameness and disgust to racial difference?

The Shakespearean play that confronts racism in the form most legible to modern audiences is, of course, *Othello*. The play is replete with racial venom: Roderigo calls Othello 'the thicklips'; and Iago describes him as an 'old black ram', a 'devil' (proverbially black) and a 'Barbary horse'; Othello describes his own face as 'begrimed and black'; Emilia calls Othello 'the blacker devil' (1.1.65; 1.1.87, 90, 110; 3.3.390; 5.2.131). In his analysis of *Othello*, Dollimore demonstrates how 'misogyny and xenophobia are rampant in the accusation of perversion, and so too is racism'. Set in the context of the Turkish invasion of the Venetian territory of Cyprus, what Iago calls Desdemona's 'thoughts unnatural' displace and condense an external threat into an 'internal deviation' (Dollimore 1991: 152, 155; *Oth* 3.3.237). This also naturalizes European sexuality as innocent and proper while treating both the desires of non-Europeans and the desire for them as pathological and destructive. In this context, an interracial relationship can be understood only through the lens of racism that, as Little has argued, exonerates Desdemona by deeming Othello 'the first black rapist of a white woman in early modern drama', or that of misogyny, which, as Stockton has argued, treats Desdemona's desire for a black husband as itself adulterous in the etymological sense of contaminating desire (Little 2000: 4; Stockton 2017). Religious conversion, Loomba has shown, is imagined as a form of contamination, and Othello's marriage to Desdemona expresses English anxieties about the appeal of Islam and the vulnerability of Christian religion and Western power (2002: 91–111).

As this brief survey suggests, most scholars have understood the erotic dimension of racism in *Othello* primarily in heterosexual terms.[7] However, several queer critics have pointed out that the language of race is as inseparable from a discourse of sodomy as from that of misogyny. Little demonstrates that Iago's notorious announcement to Brabantio that 'an old black ram / Is tupping your white ewe' (1.1.87–8) uses the language of bestiality to connect the union of a white woman and a black man to sodomy, which was bestiality's legal cognate (2000: 83–5). Othello's blackness may be threatening because, as Robert Matz (1999) and Ben Saunders (2004) have observed, he, not Desdemona, is the play's primary object of desire. Iago, Cassio and Desdemona all explicitly seek his love and employ one another as go-betweens in its pursuit. Indeed, the word 'love' expresses the bonds between Cassio, Iago and Othello at least as insistently as that between Othello and Desdemona. Iago makes good his oath to 'show out a flag and sign of love' for Othello throughout the play, protesting 'My lord, you know I love you' and vowing, in their much-discussed espousal, 'I am your own for ever' (1.1.154, 3.3.119, 482). He also professes his love for Cassio: 'good lieutenant, I think you think I love you' (2.3.301). Even as Othello himself dismisses Cassio, Othello assures him, 'Cassio, I love thee', a feeling he apparently confirms to Emilia, who reports that 'he protests he loves you' (2.3.240, 3.1.48). Othello demands proof of Iago's love: 'If thou dost love me / Show me thy thought' (3.3.118–19). Cassio, likewise, seeks to 'be a member of [Othello's] love' (3.4.113). Indeed, the stock explanation of Iago's motivation as repressed homosexuality might more accurately describe the structure of the play as a whole.[8]

The multiple triangulations of desire that Matz has seen as structuring the play extends interracial bonds beyond the straight or dyadic couple. Male homoeroticism is the love that speaks its name insistently through structures of alliance and enmity. In the play's opening lines, Roderigo describes Desdemona's elopement as a betrayal of the bond he thought he had with Iago, in that Iago kept Othello's secret rather than sharing it with Rodrigo:

Tush, never tell me, I take it much unkindly
That thou, Iago, who hast had my purse
As if the strings were thine, shouldst know of this.
…

> Thou told'st me
> Thou didst hold him in thy hate.

$$(1.1.1–3, 5–6)$$

Anticipating the later scene in which Iago proves his love for Othello by promising to murder Cassio, Iago here responds to Roderigo's charge of infidelity by instructing him to 'Despise me / If I do not' hate Othello and swearing that 'I follow him to serve my turn upon him' (1.1.7–8, 41). And Iago espouses himself not only to Othello but also to Roderigo: 'Give me thy hand, Roderigo' (4.2.208). This triangulation appears in Emilia's own final choice of Desdemona over Iago. Her last request is 'O lay me by my mistress' side' in the marriage bed, in Othello's place (5.2.237).

This intricate web of desires is also a competition over who can substitute for whom. Iago complains that Othello has failed to 'make me his lieutenant' (literally, place-holder) and claims to 'suspect the lusty Moor / Hath leaped into my seat' and to 'fear Cassio with my night-cap too' (1.1.8, 2.1.293–4, 304). Othello bows to the news of letters that 'command him home / Deputing Cassio in his government' by stating that 'Cassio shall have my place' (4.1.235–6, 261). The fungibility of persons that allows Cassio to be deputy for Othello in governing Cyprus also allows Iago to substitute for Cassio as lieutenant or Desdemona as spouse and Cassio and Emilia to substitute for Othello in Desdemona's bed. This structure, Matz has argued, also makes the signs of proper socio-sexual order infinitely interpretable as something else. In the wake of so many possible substitutions, there is a systematic motility and lack of precision that makes interpretation and knowledge itself inexact and subject to failure. Just as Cassio's courtesy to Desdemona might be retrospectively revealed as the sign of adultery, the male love and loyalty that characterized friendship could prove the signs of sodomy (Matz 1999: 266–70). This chain of substitutions appears most explicitly in Iago's fictional report of Cassio's dream:

I lay with Cassio lately
And being troubled with a raging tooth
I could not sleep. There are a kind of men
So loose of soul that in their sleeps will mutter
Their affairs – one of this kind is Cassio.
In sleep I heard him say 'Sweet Desdemona,
Let us be wary, let us hide our loves',
And then, sir, would he gripe and wring my hand,
Cry 'O sweet creature!' and then kiss me hard
As if he plucked up kisses by the roots
That grew upon my lips, lay his leg o'er my thigh,
And sigh, and kiss, and then cry 'Cursed fate
That gave thee to the Moor!'

                                                    (3.3.416–428)

Matz reads this scene, the play's 'most extended representation of sex', as a fantasy of access: 'Cassio fantasizes that he had the same access to Desdemona that he now has to Iago. Yet … the dream itself reflects a situation in which Desdemona herself serves as a means of access to Othello' and it is really *Iago's* fantasy 'to displace Desdemona as Othello's "bedfellow," an intimacy that is both personal and political' (1999: 265, 264). In Iago's fabricated memory of sharing a bed with Cassio, if Cassio is displacing Othello, Iago is also displacing Desdemona. I would add to Matz's reading the observation that Iago's story of the dream does not only narrate an event but serves as a promise of his fidelity to Othello: rather than wake Cassio up, he has learned his secrets by enduring rough kisses and intercrural sex. In betraying Cassio, in serving as virtual spy on him, Iago proves that he deserves to be in Desdemona's place by casting her as treacherously agreeing to 'be wary' and 'hide our loves'. The accusation of misplaced secrecy voiced in Roderigo's 'Tush, never tell me' returns here in Iago's self-situation as an agent provocateur.

Like the 'love' professed throughout the play, the term 'friend' can designate both sexual and non-sexual ties, and there is no objective rubric by which to tell the difference.

Although, as Masten has shown, editors try to standardize such distinctions by glossing 'friend' differently in different contexts in Shakespeare's plays, the word can be synonymous with 'lover' in each of these instances (2016: 69–82).[9] In *Othello*, Iago fuses friendship with sodomy when he asks Othello to imagine Desdemona in the same place he claimed to be – sharing a bed with Cassio – then asks if it is possible 'to be naked with her friend in bed / An hour or more, not meaning any harm?' (4.1.3–4); Bianca employs the same usage when she accuses Cassio of acquiring the handkerchief 'from a newer friend!' (3.4.181). Accordingly, when Iago affirms that 'I have professed me thy friend', when Desdemona seeks to make Othello and Cassio 'as friendly as you were', or when Othello calls Iago 'My friend', to take just a few instances, we cannot rule out the same sexual contact that Iago details in the fictional scene between himself and Cassio (1.3.338, 3.3.7, 5.2.152). This ambiguity, as Matz points out, means that the precise nature of relations between men as well as between men and women are subject to interpretation as sodomitical (2004: 262–4). It is impossible by any objective criteria to distinguish between lover, friend and enemy. And while queer readings have generally focused on men, we can say the same of relations between women if we recall the similar ambiguity of the word 'mistress': Cassio assures Bianca that the handkerchief is not 'from some mistress' while Emilia calls Desdemona by this term rather than her proper name: 'The Moor hath killed my mistress!'; 'My mistress here lies murdered in her bed'; 'Ay ay; O lay me by my mistress' side' (5.2.165, 183, 237). To fully distinguish the paramour from the employer, the lover from the friend – to read as though we *know* the true nature of the play's complex and promiscuous intimacies – is to impose upon the play a presumption that 'we know what that means' whose ignorance effects, as Sedgwick so effectively demonstrates, sustain heterosexual privilege.

It is precisely because sexuality is obscure in *Othello* that race becomes such a focal point. The widespread desire for Othello among the principle characters also draws attention to the instability of Christian identity that Loomba has traced in so many of Shakespeare's plays (2002). The prominence of male physical intimacy in *Othello* allows us to consider, with Daniel Boyarin, the 'open secret' of 'Othello's ambiguously circumcised penis' and, more broadly, that of Islam's seductive presence within Christian Europe (2011: 254). The problem posed by Othello is that he is too much an object of Venetian desire – too easily mixed up with Venetians – and thereby threatens the religious, racial and sexual boundaries between the proper and the improper. When Iago resorts to racist language, Menon argues, he deploys catachresis to construct an unrepresentable, unnamable sexuality by means of the visible medium of race: 'Blackness is used as a tool to fill up a discursive void created by sexuality, and as such, never functions as itself since its self is referenced by a discourse on sexuality that does not exist in this play as an accessible category' (2004: 113). What the play constructs as Othello's hypervisibility, as in the case of Drago cited by Bray (discussed in Chapter 3 above), marshals, in Little's words, 'Some kind of horrific history' that 'is already in place, deeply embedded or suspected to exist in the very physicality of black bodies' (2000: 76). And this history is, as Parker and Saunders allow us to see, a fiction connected to a civilizing narrative centred on the suppression of the anal pleasures of penetration and defecation. These pleasures' backwards and overlapping appeal is conspicuously suppressed by a demand for vigilant hygiene in the service of literally and figuratively forward-looking procreative, dynastic marriage among Christians (Parker 1992; Saunders 2004).

If all of the characters in *Othello* 'can turn, and turn, and yet go on / And turn again', then racism and heteronormativity sustain one another by facilitating what Cohen has described as the disavowal of perverse enjoyment through its projection onto the composite figure of the Saracen (4.1.253–4; Cohen 2001). As in *The Merchant of Venice*, the interlocking discourses of sex and race in *Othello* are an essential feature of economic discourses of inheritance that appear to see money and property as abstract goods that anyone can acquire. In fact, the restriction of inheritance to Christians in these plays reveals that the open market of Venice shares the exclusions that Julia Lupton has noted in Christian humanist discourse, which operates 'as a universalism minus one: minus the circumcised' (2005: 78). Portia's redirection of Shylock's property to Lorenzo as his 'son' in *The Merchant of Venice* and Lodovico's decree that Gratiano, as Desdemona's uncle, may 'seize upon the fortunes of the Moor / For they succeed to you' naturalize racial and religious domination as the smooth succession of property (*MV* 4.1.385, *Oth* 5.2.367–8). Governed by male relations that are filial rather than sexual, these relations are made possible by excluding sexual desire as a consideration, thereby permitting eroticism to occupy a private realm that escapes a history of racialized dominance and dispossession.

Using Shakespeare: history, memory and futurity in *Henry V* and *Hamlet*

This linear view of inheritance and social hierarchy, as Patricia Parker argues, must exclude those 'preposterous' desires, relations and practices that threaten it. The operations of such exclusions are particularly noticeable in the history plays, whose explicitly inverted composition and performance history 'exposes the relentless appeal to "linear honor" (*2H4* 4.5.46) and "lineal descent" (*1H4* 3.1.165)' as 'a retroactively constructed narrative not "natural" but forged, and hence not that different from the preposterous estate of a son who creates for a father, and hence for himself, the genealogy of an authorizing "pedigree"' as Shakespeare himself had done for his father (Parker 1992: 202). This appears in the composition of the two tetralogies. The first tetralogy relates the chronologically later events of roughly 1422 to 1485 (the Wars of the Roses that shape the turbulent reign of Henry VI, the usurpation of Richard III, and the triumph of Henry

VII and the Tudor line). These events frame the historically
prior episodes of 1398 to 1421, which are staged in the second
tetralogy (the political decline and death of Richard II and the
reigns of Henry IV and Henry V).

The action of *Henry V*, the history play that was composed
and performed last, concludes on a triumphant note of military
and dynastic victory, with Henry's marriage to Katherine,
princess of France, cementing his descendants' claim to the
French throne. Henry V's marriage makes him the symbolic
son and political heir of the King of France, a filial relation
asserted in the play both in the language of the conquered
France ('*Notre très cher fils Henri, roi / d'Angleterre, héritier
de France*') and in the lingua franca of Latin ('*Praeclarissimus
filius noster Henricus, rex Angliae et / haeres Franciae*') (*HS*
5.2.331–4). This marriage is not only between Henry and
Katherine, but, more importantly, between former male
political rivals. The French King, offering his daughter, hopes
that 'from her blood raise up / Issue to me' in which France and
England will be reconciled (5.2.340–1). His wife, Queen Isabel,
more expansively prays for a marriage between kingdoms:

> God, the best maker of all marriages,
> Combine your hearts in one, your realms in one!
> As man and wife, being two, are one in love,
> So be there 'twixt your kingdoms such a spousal
> That never may ill office or fell jealousy,
> Which troubles oft the bed of blessed marriage,
> Thrust in between the paction of these kingdoms
> To make divorce of their incorporate league.
>
> (5.2.351–8)

What begins as a hope that Katherine and Henry's 'hearts'
will become 'one' quickly extends to include their 'realms':
the syntactic parallelism obscures any distinction between the
union of private and political bodies. But in the subsequent
lines, the rhetorical sleight of hand is immediately accentuated
with the conspicuous simile. Isabel is not talking about Henry

and Katherine at all, for they will in actuality be 'man and wife'. She is talking about the King and Henry, whose 'hearts' and 'realms' that will be '*As* man and wife'. Isabel's hope is that this male political 'spousal' will be uniquely firm, free of the 'ill office or fell jealousy, / Which troubles oft the bed of blessed marriage'. In the preposterous figural logic that Parker has designated, vehicle and tenor are reversed, so that male homosocial union is the ideal to which heterosexual marriage aspires.

Isabel's hope can only be ironic in light of an impending history in which 'ill office and fell jealousy' will indeed 'Thrust in between the paction of these kingdoms.' This 'divorce' between England and France is first led by Joan the Pucelle, who inverts gender order to lead the French invasions in *1 Henry VI*. 'Thrust'-ing herself not only between the 'incorporate leagues' but also at the front of male military endeavours, Joan is just one of many scheming women, effeminate men and lower-class rebels who challenge proper hierarchy and thereby threaten the English state.[10] The Chorus's final lines in *Henry V* look both backward (to plays that have already been staged and written) and forward (to a history yet to come) when they temper the news of Henry V's victory over France with the sobering reminder that we have already seen the 'divorce' of England and France both historically and theatrically. The seemingly natural order of primogeniture claimed by the language of filiation, heritage and issue has already been exposed as a weak fiction. In fact, the Chorus reminds us, there is nothing natural at all about the dynastic order that Tudor propaganda continues to attribute to 'God, the best maker of all marriages':

> Thus far, with rough and all-unable pen
> Our bending author hath pursued the story,
> In little room confining mighty men,
> Mangling by starts the full course of their glory.
> Small time, but in that small most greatly lived
> This star of England. Fortune made his sword

By which the world's best garden he achieved,
And of it left his son imperial lord.
        Henry the Sixth, in infant bands crowned King
Of France and England, did this king succeed,
Whose state so many had the managing
That they lost France and made his England bleed,
                Which oft our stage hath shown; and for their sake
                In your fair minds let this acceptance take.
                                                (H5 Epilogue.1–14)

Formally, this Epilogue is a sonnet, a lyric form whose causal
connection to a larger sequence is a matter of projection
and conjecture rather than coherent linear narrative. This
form is an apt one for Prince Hal, the betrothed king who
has overcome a past association with England's criminal
underclass and the soft, indulgent eroticism of Falstaff. Yet,
as Drew Daniel has pointed out, Hal's previous, chameleon-
like inhabitation of multiple identities also renders suspect his
ultimate role as the manly King Henry, urging on a 'band of
brothers' against the effete French (H5 4.3.60). Rather than
find his 'true' self as soldier, husband and father, 'convolving
a self out of Hal and Henry Plantagenet and Harry Le Roy',
Henry V 'is an identity sampler, a "queer assemblage" who
speaks "what pleases" to whoever happens to be in earshot'
(Daniel 2011: 127). Like the young man of Shakespeare's
Sonnets, to whom William Empson and Jonathan Goldberg
have likened him, Hal provokes desire despite his proclivity
to disappoint (Empson [1935] 1950: 102–9; Goldberg 2003:
233–5). Rather than exemplify integrity, Henry V reveals the
ease with which the convention of growing up and setting
oneself straight itself depends on a conspicuously strained
narrative: if the marriage of Henry to Katherine and his
anticipated paternity is the triumphant highpoint of the
two tetralogies, its optimistic heteronormativity is not only
thwarted by the actual events that follow but also undercut
by the homosocial terms in which it is presented, by Henry's
own homoerotic past, and by the queerness of the past and

future kings (Richard II, Henry VI, Richard III) evoked by the Epilogue.

To appreciate what it means for Henry V to have 'achieved' the 'world's best garden', the Epilogue states, audiences must *remember* what a poor gardener was that previous king, Richard II, whose deposition is historically first but comes *in media res* at the start of the second tetralogy. Richard's downfall sets the stage for Henry V, 'This star of England' to rise, becoming in Goldberg's estimation a figure for the heteronormative masculinity of traditional critical desire ([1992] 2010: 145–78). This history looks back at its own performance, evoked in the Epilogue as both the events of the first tetralogy and those of the place where the second tetralogy starts, *Richard II*. As Menon has shown, Richard is an unfit king not only because of his fiscal and political mismanagement of the kingdom, but also because 'he is not metaphoric enough and has allowed caterpillars to feed on his own body, reducing king from active gardener to passive garden' through intimacies whose 'lack of precision' constitutes the source of their horror (2004: 50, 52). Bolingbroke begins the task of judiciously ridding England of 'too fast growing sprays', 'noisome weeds', and 'Swarming … caterpillars' that represent the disordered sexuality of Bushy, Bagot and Green, the men that Richard has inappropriately favoured (*R2* 3.4.34, 38, 47). Living up to this paternal example, Hal banishes the parasitic Falstaff and rids himself of his youthful folly so that, as synecdoche for England, he can restore the 'soil's fertility' whose loss Richard's Queen Isabella weeps in the second tetralogy's first play (*R2* 3.4.39) and whose return Queen Isabella of France celebrates in its last.

Yet the recalcitrance of political history to the narrative of 'reproductive futurism' as the language of politics reveals the limitations of a model of history as progressive or linear. The historiographic position summed up in the Choral Epilogue that concludes not just *Henry V* but also the composite effort of the two tetralogies is that what we call 'history' is the belated reproduction of the past by the present. In this light, the maturation of the effete Hal into the resolute Harry so lauded by early critics follows what Daniel calls a 'functional imperative' rather than an organic one. For not only *Henry V* but the two tetralogies as a whole 'articulate an alternative history' in which Hal's ability to 'phallicize himself' in fact questions normative narratives of psychosexual development through an Oedipal adjustment to masculinity and heterosexuality (Corum 1996: 74–5).[11] In political as well as psychic terms, Shakespeare's alternative history is less a series of punctual events organized in a causal chain than an enactment of the queer temporality that Annamarie Jagose has influentially described as 'a mode of inhabiting time that is attentive to the recursive eddies and back-to-the-future loops that often pass undetected or uncherished beneath the official narrations of the linear sequence that is taken to structure normative life' (2009: 157–8). What Stephen Guy-Bray has said of *2 Henry VI* also furnishes a guide to reading the Chorus's qualification of the optimism with which the second tetralogy concludes: 'The substitutions and instabilities of the play recall (or anticipate) our contemporary idea of queerness, but the play's ultimate focus on the limits of substitutions and instabilities should remind us that performance is not action' and in that very pessimism may 'lead us to question both our sense of how politics does and should work' (2011: 145). With their thematic and formal attention to the centrality of usurpation, disinheritance and contested legitimacy in English history, the two tetralogies render preposterous the ideal of divine order that upholds both past and present politics based on what Edelman names 'reproductive futurism'.

In a published conversation on *Hamlet*, Edelman (2011), Carla Freccero (2011a) and Kathryn Schwarz (2011) practice a queer infidelity to literary criticism as such. They present not so much readings of plots or language as a meditation on the ethical and political implications of 'Shakespeare' as the paradigmatic figure of humanist education. As Edelman makes clear, the queer critique of reproductive futurism does not address the generation of children per se. Rather, it examines the logic of political investment in the figure of the Child as a fantasmatic emblem of a future in which a lost sense of freedom, wholeness and comprehension will be restored. Reproductive futurism, that is, seeks the revival of a past plenitude and certainty that is dimly sensed but not fully grasped. In the Western philosophical tradition, this fantasy is articulated in Plato's claim that philosophy is not the acquisition of external knowledge by a mind that begins as a tabula rasa, but a re-collection, re-covery or re-membering of an originary knowledge of Truth that has been lost in the trauma of birth. Plato calls this recollection *anamnesis* in the dialogues *Meno* and *Phaedo*. The Socratic method of drawing out knowledge through questions, rather than imposing lessons from the outside, strives to teach students to re-cognize a truth beyond the distractions of sensory experience.

As Edelman points out, at the same time that it imagines cultural memory as anamnesis, reproductive futurism assumes that memory is preserved in material archives. For Jacques Derrida, the archive is conceptually antithetical to a definition of 'memory or anamnesis as spontaneous, alive and internal experience'. This is because the creation of an archive at once anticipates and seeks to forestall 'the breakdown of the said memory' by stabilizing it into the material form from which Platonic anamnesis endeavours to free human thought.[12] Writing more specifically on the relationship between memory and reproductive futurism, Edelman analyses Derrida's writing on *Hamlet* as emblematic of the 'function of the specter ... as it bears on just these questions of futurity, the death drive, and cultural transmission' (2011: 154). Edelman, like Derrida, focuses on the Ghost's command to 'Remember me', 'Swear', 'Do not forget', and Hamlet's own response: 'Remember thee? ... thy commandment all alone shall live / Within the book and volume of my brain, / Unmix'd with baser matter' (*Ham* 1.5.91, 189, 3.4.110, 1.5.97, 102–4).[13] Here, Edelman writes, Hamlet 'assumes the status of an archive that keeps his father's word "alive" by becoming the agent of his father's will, the instrument of a vital force to which he must cede his own' (2011: 155).[14] This promise to become the conduit of paternal law, Edelman

further argues, makes Hamlet 'the prototype of the modern
subject as Child' who perpetuates a reproductive futurism that
structures not only political but also pedagogical ideals:

> He establishes thereby the contours of a reproductive
> futurism bringing archive and anamnesis together in an
> ideology whose complicity with aesthetic education and
> therefore with the *violence* of aesthetic education not
> only shapes the text of *Hamlet* but also contributes to its
> privileged position as the paradigmatic literary work of
> modern Western culture. (2011: 167, 155; original emphasis)

'Queerness' names the rejection of symbolic survival in favour
of the *jouissance* of a death drive that remembers and repeats
'the inarticulable loss that accompanies and makes possible
signification' (Edelman 2011: 158). Put another way, queerness
seeks neither recollection nor preservation, but 'creation *ex
nihilo*, refusing the instinct of conservation that by anticipating
the future prevents it, allowing it recognition only in a form
already known' (2011: 158, 163). The spectre haunts *Hamlet*
– understood as synecdoche for the materials of humanist
education more broadly – with an unbearable recognition of the
loss and ambivalence that Hamlet obediently labours to suppress.

A queer education, Edelman argues, would refuse the
conservative logic whereby anamnesis and archive converge in
canonical literary texts like *Hamlet*, whose words are believed
to contain transcendent truths that exceed the ink, paper or
parchment on which they are recorded. As Edelman puts
it, paraphrasing Oscar Wilde, 'education as (and in) fiction'
means 'compulsory and routinized sublimation'. Consequently,
'However we read it, *Hamlet* must sublimate the impossible
Thing, the unthinkability at its core, so long as we bestow on
its specter, and so on its always ungraspable queerness, the
marketable value of a domesticated and domesticating good,
of a faith in the power of literature to make us better, more
fully human'. And because to read *Hamlet* is to preserve the
fantasy of something that survives beyond death, to entertain

the fantasy of reproductive futurism, 'What *Hamlet* does not and cannot teach, and what we can never know, is how to escape the will-to-be-taught, the desire for a lesson,' the desire for sense and meaning (2011: 169).

In their responses to Edelman's essay, Schwarz and Freccero take Edelman's argument to its logical end, for they suggest, in different ways, that the very desire to 'escape the will-to-be-taught' may inevitably replicate the larger ideological structures of cultural authority and gender hierarchy that the queer pursuit of a radical rebeginning strives to resist. The questioning of cultural reproduction, Schwarz shows, is itself a revival of past scholarly concerns, rather than a break from them. Edelman, Schwarz observes, 'returns us to the questions of ideology and canonicity that preoccupied, or more aptly haunted, the professional self-interrogations of the 1980s', particularly with regards to the centrality of Shakespeare to the humanities curriculum (2011: 174).[15] Schwarz asks 'what would it mean for "us," with brazen infidelity to that pronoun of survivors, to say "no" to Hamlet: to refuse not just an inheritance but the very idea of inheritance, to see neither a web nor a line nor a mirror, but a historical artifact that retains a certain dated charm?' (2011: 176). Saying 'no', Schwarz demonstrates, would itself suppress an ambivalent and ambiguous relation to the past as much as the piety of loving commemoration. Whereas Edelman maintains that the 'or' of that famous 'To be or not to be' voices the 'reification of differences' that make signification possible, Schwarz argues instead that 'the 1603 text – disreputable "bad quarto" that it is – gets it right. "To be, or not to be, I there's the point," Hamlet begins. There's the point, indeed' (2011: 178). Despite his endorsement of a radical politics of demolition and rupture as against a liberal politics of expansion and repair, Edelman himself, Schwarz observes, is not immune to the piety of preservation: his treatment of Hamlet as 'the prototype of the modern subject as Child' accepts the spectral presence of *Hamlet* in order to gesture toward a queer refusal that, as Edelman concedes, 'we can never know' (Edelman 2011:

167, 169). Instead, we might return to an archive that makes ambivalence and indeterminacy the 'point', which might permit us to refuse 'the spectral mandate of legacy' to which Hamlet suicidally accedes (Schwarz 2011: 179).

Also addressing the decision proposed in 'to be or not to be', Freccero designates *Hamlet* a text of a 'sacrificial culture, where the injunction is to sacrifice the meat of oneself – and one's *jouissance*, Edelman would add – in exchange for transcendence, subjectification, entry into the order of the Symbolic and so signification' (2011a: 171). Yet, Freccero observes, to say 'no' to this injunction is not necessarily to choose radical creation from nothing:

> If Hamlet can be said to inaugurate something, I would venture that it is the order of brothers, the 'fratriarchy' that dreams the demise of patriarchy and thus conceals its own patriarchal dream of rule. Here is a kingdom purged of the fathers, purged too of the one who was charged with extirpating and obeying them and thus of the guilty predicament that accompanies such purges. The rational order of Horatian oratory instrumentalizes the spectral injunctions of father and son and, in enjoining the dead to rest, erects a fraternal order in place of the paternal one. Perhaps.
>
> But what are all those female bodies doing littering the scene? (2011a: 173)

Freccero's attention to the gender politics both of *Hamlet* and of the queer rejection of reproductive futurism turns us to the question of what fathers and sons, whether obedient or rebellions, 'attempt to extirpate': 'the inhuman mattering of nonsymbolic reproduction … for which female embodiment is – at least in this tradition – a horrifying reminder/remainder. Literature would then be the sign of an effort to eliminate matter … from the books that carry previous coded inscriptions of a history and a living on that is not human at all' (2011a: 173).[16] Freccero here evokes a long association of women with the bodily material from which education promises to free us. Margaret W. Ferguson provides a succinct statement: 'As we hear or see in the word "matter" the Latin term for mother, we may surmise that the common Renaissance association between female nature in general and the "lower" realm of matter is here being deployed in the service of Hamlet's complex oedipal struggle' which his 'disgust at female flesh' renders irresolvable through exogamous marriage (1985: 250, 252). In this context, Freccero's designation of the lesson of *Hamlet* as 'you must submit, dedicate yourself with filial piety to furthering the parental aim or off yourself' and 'off the others, too' may also be summarized as deciding to 'Refuse to be a son, or a brother' (2011a: 171, 173). If we entertain the possibility that '*Hamlet* teaches suicide' but only 'Sort of. For certain special readers' then we can see suicide as a refusal of the sacrificial, sublimating culture it is often read, by humanist and queer scholars alike, as endorsing (2011a: 171). Instead, 'In its very staging of the ideology of the specter as a figure for (non)survival, at least in the minds of some of its readers, perhaps *Hamlet* can open something up to a terrifying futurity' (Freccero 2011a: 173). Or a queer one. For, as Kate Chedgzoy has shown, 'Shakespeare's queer children' – a group of interpreters and adapters that includes Oscar Wilde, Angela Carter, Virginia Woolf and Derek Jarman – have long disturbed a humanist ideal of education as cultural preservation (1995).

In focusing on the pedagogical and cultural uses of *Hamlet* rather than the content of its plot, Edelman, Freccero and Schwarz demonstrate that the queerness of the Shakespearean canon more broadly goes beyond its representations of characters who deviate from norms of heteroeroticism, monogamy or procreation. They compel us to ask: Can we say no to the pieties of the humanist education often summed up in the name 'Shakespeare'? And would our desire for refusal itself signal our participation in an Oedipal struggle that can only reproduce a phallic economy of privilege, exclusion and dominance? Or can we find in Shakespeare what Edelman calls a 'bad' education, one that teaches us to reassess the screen memory of a humanist past?

5

The Politics of Form

Queer Shakespearean Film

This chapter begins with the observation that the director whom B. Ruby Rich called the 'king of queer' – Derek Jarman – was also an amateur early modernist (Rich [1992] 2013a: 49–52). In five of the twelve full-length films that Jarman made, early modern artists, historical personages and literary characters inhabit multi-temporal landscapes that juxtapose past and present mores and politics. These include the title character of *Caravaggio* (1986); Queen Elizabeth I and the sixteenth-century alchemist John Dee in *Jubilee* (1978); the lovers of Shakespeare's Sonnets in *The Angelic Conversation* (1985); and Shakespeare's and Marlowe's characters in *The Tempest* (1979) and Marlowe's *Edward II* (1991).

This chapter's first section discusses Jarman's *The Tempest*, a film whose representation of the past's relation to the present is queer not only because the film features queer characters but also, and more importantly, because its anachronistic staging of Shakespeare expands the forms that political art can take. While, as Anthony Guy Patricia has shown, earlier film versions of Shakespeare's plays had included homoerotic elements (2016: 1–87), *The Tempest*, I suggest, is the first Shakespearean film formally as well as

thematically to depart from a gay liberation project of positive
– that is normative – representation of queer lives. Rather
than seek to recover the presence of queer characters in the
British heritage for which 'Shakespeare' is often shorthand,
Jarman's camp, punk, horror, and postmodern aesthetics seek
to demystify that heritage's nostalgic appeal. In this chapter's
second section, I turn to two canonical works of the New
Queer Cinema whose explicit inclusion of dialogue and plot
from early modern drama resists recuperative as well as
progressive views of the relation between past and present:
Jarman's *Edward II* and Gus Van Sant's *My Own Private
Idaho* (1991) – the latter a loose adaptation of Shakespeare's
second tetralogy. These films bring early modern meditations
on the uses and limits of sovereign authority to bear on the
murderous inadequacy of the Thatcher, Reagan and Bush
governments' responses to the HIV/AIDS pandemic. In
the third section, I discuss two explicitly queer cinematic
renditions of Shakespearean plays that incorporate the
postmodern aesthetics instantiated by Jarman's and Van
Sant's films: Baz Luhrmann's *William Shakespeare's Romeo
+ Juliet* (1996) and Julie Taymor's *Titus* (1999). In these
films, the onslaught of multi-temporal images, fashions,
echoes and allusions functions not to update Shakespeare's
plots to appeal to a new generation but, rather, to situate
the humanist values preserved in 'Shakespeare' as a refuge
from the irrational, overstimulated, degenerate condition of
postmodernity.[1]

I focus throughout this chapter on form rather than
character or content in order to approximate at the
interpretive level a queer political attention to the need
for radical structural change rather than a liberal model of
tolerance, inclusion and privacy. Luhrmann's and Taymor's
films lament the intrusion of, respectively, consumer culture
and global conflict into private lives and strive to imagine
retreat to a pre-political space where love and innocence
can flourish. By contrast, Jarman's and Van Sant's films
brutally remind us that the flip side of a right to privacy

is abandonment by the state and the protections it offers. Reduced to what Giorgio Agamben designates 'bare life', those outside the political community are rendered profoundly vulnerable without claim to the protection of that community (1998: 28). Safety and livelihood becomes a matter of luck rather than right, individual beneficence rather than public responsibility. Jarman's and Van Sant's films remind us of the precarious state of many queer lives, from that of Jarman's Edward II, the king cast as an outlaw by his 'unnatural' desires, to that of Van Sant's Mike Waters, the narcoleptic orphan left to die in the road. In reading the history of queer Shakespearean film in opposition to a narrative of ever-expanding LGBTQ rights and instead attending to the contradictions and exclusions of liberal and humanist politics, I seek to make visible the continued work that queer frameworks can do in attuning us to the discriminatory logic that might undergird and sustain ideals of formal equality and private virtue.

Queer aesthetics in Jarman's *The Tempest*: camp, horror, punk, postmodernism

Reading what is usually regarded as Shakespeare's last romance against the grain of its marriage plot, Jarman deployed *The Tempest* to continue a project that he had begun in the previous year's *Jubilee*: both films present a scathing indictment of present-day England through juxtaposition with the Elizabethan past. In *Jubilee*, Jim Ellis explains, the 'central conceit of mixing the Elizabethan past with an apocalyptic near future is an early example of the postmodernist interest in combining and juxtaposing period styles (one of the first shots in the present is of graffiti reading "post modern"), but it is also part of the punk collage aesthetic' (2009: 50).

This juxtaposition of different historical moments and aesthetic styles resists not only the verisimilitude of previous Shakespeare films but also the norms of gender and sexuality often associated with Shakespeare. It does this not by depicting a plot of homoerotic intimacy, but through the formal cues of dim lighting and barely audible lines, and through (as Ellis notes) the conventions of camp, horror, punk and postmodernism. Jarman's film is set almost entirely indoors in an English country house whose crumbling condition resists the nostalgia of the heritage film and instead evokes the decay of empire.[2] Between the earnest nihilism of punk and the arch sentimentality of camp, as Vincent Canby puts it in his caustic review, 'You can barely see through the production to Shakespeare, so you must rely on memory' (1980). But the point, of course, is that we can never encounter Shakespeare directly. What Canby deems a 'very nearly unbearable' version of *The Tempest* questions what it would mean, in fact, to 'see through the production to Shakespeare' – indeed, it refuses the binary of saying 'yes' or 'no' to cultural tradition by 'intervening in the production of [the play's] past' in order to intervene in England's present (Ellis 2001: 265). Produced in the heyday of gay and lesbian liberation movements, before the HIV/AIDS pandemic, Jarman's film offers a cautionary look at ideals of pride and progress by focusing on characters who refuse assimilation into mainstream values of beauty and innocence.

Jarman's casting choices rewrite the pedagogical, sexual and colonial ideals typically attributed to *The Tempest*. Heathcote Williams, who plays Prospero, is only seven years older than the actor who plays Ariel (Karl Johnson), and he is seven years younger than the drag performer Jack Birkett, who plays Caliban. As Graham Holderness argues, by casting a 'strikingly young Prospero' Jarman rejects traditional readings of the play that naturalize his power as a result of 'patriarchal authority or avuncular benevolence' (1993: 72). Prospero's beneficence, and by extension the beneficence of Shakespeare's art more broadly, is further diminished by the production's Gothic undercurrent. Canby complains that Birkett 'looks and acts as if he had been borrowed from Hammer Films' (1980), that is, the production company whose technicolour representations of blood and gore in *Dracula* and *The Curse of Frankenstein* were instrumental to the genesis of modern horror films. Canby's observation could describe the atmosphere of nearly the entire movie, with its Gothic and punk aesthetic. The actress who plays Miranda, Toyah Wilcox, was a punk singer who, a year earlier, had played the role of the anarchist pyromaniac Mad in Jarman's *Jubilee* (1978). In *Jubilee*, Wilcox sports a bright orange buzzcut as she fights, castrates and kills her way through a dystopian London. In *The Tempest*, Wilcox's Miranda wears her short hair in spikey braids streaked with blue dye and interwoven with straw, beads and feathers; she is not a blushing virgin but a defiant, often barefoot Vivienne Westwood-esque androgyne ill at ease in a ripped and dingy white gown. She knowingly pursues Ferdinand and treats Caliban's sexual advances as a longstanding, mutually sadistic game; more likely to make the ugly faces associated with punk performance than to simper or sigh, Wilcox's Miranda refuses allegorization into an innocent English nation to be protected from barbaric others.[3]

In Shakespeare's play, as numerous scholars have argued, Caliban and Sycorax fill that role, and Caliban's 'You taught me language, and my profit on't / Is I know how to curse' rejects the epistemic violence enacted by Western ideals of education and cultural superiority (1.2.364–5).[4] Jarman has frequently been criticized for casting a white British actor as Caliban and thereby obscuring the explicitly colonial and racial violence captured in Caliban's enslavement.[5] Against this critique, Ellis argues that 'a historical understanding of race might involve more than the specific matter of skin colour' to which modern thought limits it. Instead, 'the film foregrounds the interconnections of racism and misogyny in colonialist discourse and the means by which this discourse constructed racial otherness, without at the same time reforging these links in the film's visual economy' (Ellis 2009: 78). Ellis sets Jarman's film in a longer history in which race was not synonymous with skin colour but instead a name for religious, geographic and cultural otherness that could represent Irish, African, Islamic and indigenous American peoples all as racially inferior to English Protestants. Read in this context, Ellis argues, Jarman's film is an exercise in historical verisimilitude that jars with modern reality in order to denaturalize twentieth-century assumptions about racial difference. The representation of Sycorax is a case in point: she is played by a white actress, Claire Davenport, but conspicuously Orientalized (Ellis 2009: 75–80). As we hear a voiceover of Prospero's demand that Ariel recount the history of the 'foul witch Sycorax', banished from Algiers, we see the corpulent Sycorax, her hair in short, elaborately twisted cornrows dyed silver and gold, sitting nude amidst bales of hay and alternately smoking a hookah and caressing the nude, fully grown Caliban as he avidly suckles her breasts (1.2.258).[6] When Prospero comes to the part of the narrative in which he recalls how Sycorax punished Ariel because he was 'a spirit too delicate / To act her earthy and abhorred commands', Sycorax, smiling, begins to pull a chain that has been lying at her feet (1.2.272–3). As she drags the naked Ariel into the frame, closer to herself and Caliban, we discover that this chain is attached to a collar fixed around Ariel's neck: he has been there all along, witnessing the incestuous tryst, but he is 'too delicate' to join in. While Miranda is androgynous, Ariel is hermaphroditic. He appears in this scene in a shot of full frontal nudity that confirms his possession of a penis; in another scene he is covered in water and sprouting breasts; in still another his legs are twisted so as to obscure his genitalia altogether. Ariel is depicted as an abject, easy target of sexual slavery, his unstable, intersex body removing him from the realm of the human for both female and male captors.

Ariel's style, it turns out, is not punk or BDSM, but camp. It is Ariel, now dressed in a white tuxedo, who opens the final scene of *The Tempest*. Here, a large group of sailors dance an elaborate Busby Berkeley-esque number; then, amidst flurries of rose petals and surrounded by the sailors, the African-American singer Elisabeth Welch performs 'Stormy Weather'. Suddenly, we have moved from the literal and conceptual darkness of Hammer Films to the glittering spectacle of the Golden Age Hollywood musical. Welch's and the sailors' performance is staged as a wedding masque, and one that inspires joy in all present, including not only the previously unfeeling Ariel but, in a striking departure from Shakespeare's play, an enraptured Caliban. Bringing together, Ellis observes, the 'minority aesthetic practices' of blues and camp, this final scene 'combines the two communities continually read as threats to British nationhood in the postwar era, queers and blacks'. Evoking the masque of Shakespeare's *Tempest*, a form that promises political harmony in which the world beyond its performance is incorporated in a dance between actors and spectators, this scene both forges a new community among the characters and invites the audience to join in its redemptive vision (Ellis 2009: 81–7). I would temper Ellis's optimism to attend to the more melancholy elements of the scene. The contrast between what we see and what we hear ironizes what in Shakespeare's play is a triumphant reproductive futurism and reveals that such a happy ending may require us to ignore what is right before our eyes. Or, in this case, ears: the crushing sadness of the lyrics of 'Stormy Weather' is distinctly at odds with Welch's beaming affect and the onscreen audience's enchantment, as well as with an occasion celebrating lifelong commitment. The heteroerotic loss expressed by a female singer pining for her 'man' takes on a broader, more homoerotic valence in the presence of the approving sailors, who stand in pairs and trios leaning on and embracing one another, and in the reaction shots of dreamy-eyed Ariel and Caliban. Love and its inevitable disappointments are extended beyond the heterosexual female persona of Welch's song. This is the work of camp, which, as Jonathan Dollimore explains, 'hollows out sentiments even as it exaggerates and intensifies them' in a perverse pedagogy that teaches us that 'once we have learned to delight in the charade of the sentimental, we can never again be genuinely sentimental' (1990: 488–9). The camp dimension of marriage appears in Miranda's over-the-top makeover in this scene. Paired with Ferdinand all dolled up as Prince Charming, she now sports a stiff blonde updo and wears a fantastical couture wedding dress and hat, both decorated with grass, flowers and perching bird ornaments. The only masque attendees as embellished as the bride are Stephano and Trinculo, one in drag and the other decked out as a Bacchus figure. This is marriage as theatrical lark, not quotidian life.

Jarman's queer politics and aesthetics question the normalizing implications of mining the past for models of pride and instead asserts the value of what, as we have seen, Heather Love calls 'feeling backwards', those past moments of shame and anger, awkwardness and aggression, and desperation and damage that cannot be recuperated into a romantic or redemptive model of love or subjectivity (2007). Jarman's juxtaposition of the subcultural forms of punk, horror and camp in *The Tempest* seeks to broaden the range of forms and feelings associated with queerness. This Shakespearean film thus anticipates on the aesthetic level a critique of political affect that Jack Halberstam addresses on a theoretical level when he contrasts a gay male 'archive of feeling' (Cvetkovich 2003) comprised of 'fatigue, ennui, boredom, indifference, ironic distancing, indirectness, arch dismissal, insincerity, and camp' to a punk archive of 'rage, rudeness, anger, spite, impatience, intensity, mania, sincerity, earnestness, overinvestment, incivility, brutal honesty, and disappointment' (Halberstam 2011: 109–10). Like Love, Halberstam argues for a 'style of failure' that can 'establish queerness as a mode of critique rather than as a new investment in normativity or life or respectability or wholeness or legitimacy' (2011: 110). What Jarman's film allows us to see is that we need not choose: there is a role for irony as well as earnestness, camp as well as punk, spectacle as well as demystification in refusing a normative politics that takes its history and its future straight.

'Intercourse has never occurred in private': *Edward II* and *My Own Private Idaho*

Jarman's work was essential to the development of the cinematic movement of 'New Queer Cinema', the name given in 1992 by B. Ruby Rich to a group of independent, formally experimental arthouse films made in the wake of the HIV/AIDS pandemic ([1992] 2013b).[7] These films were 'doing something new, renegotiating subjectivities, annexing whole genres, revising histories in their images' ([1992] 2013b: 16). They insist on the brutality of mainstream values of heterosexual romance and respectability and take as their subjects same sex relations, sexual subcultures and alternative kinship networks. Formally 'united by a common style: call it "Homo Pomo"', they critique traditional timelines of love, selfhood and family through such postmodern techniques as montage, pastiche, time-lapse photography, anachronism and non-linear narrative ([1992] 2013b). As Ellis writes, though the New Queer Cinema was comprised of a 'fairly disparate group of films' they shared 'an affinity with the new queer activist movement that was identified in the United States with Queer Nation and in Britain with OutRage!' and a 'willingness to abandon positive images and embrace or reclaim negative stereotypes' (2009: 200–1). They often present queer protagonists as abject, damaged, criminal, even homicidal.[8]

Significantly, two of the foundational films of the New Queer Cinema – *Edward II* and *My Own Private Idaho* – make Renaissance plays' plots and dialogue central to their genealogy of the present, in which the HIV/AIDS pandemic had revealed the nauseating truth about Anglo-America: both mainstream culture and national government deemed gay lives disposable.[9] What Rich writes of the effect of *Edward II*'s 'syncretic style that mixed past and present' equally describes *My Own Private Idaho*'s adaptation of Shakespeare's second tetralogy: 'Homophobia is stripped bare as a timeless occupation, tracked across centuries but never lacking in historical specificity. Obsessive love, meanwhile, is enlarged to include queer desire as a legitimate source of tragedy, entitled to inhabit center stage' ([1992] 2013a: 21). Though very different in form and affect, *Edward II* and *My Own Private Idaho* deploy the cultural tradition of the English Renaissance to engage with queer movements protesting the decimation of the welfare state and the neglect of the HIV/AIDs crisis that characterized the 1980s and early 1990s in Britain and America. Together, Jarman's and Van Sant's film resurrect early modern meditations on the limits of sovereignty to offer a scathing view of modern biopolitics, which (as I discussed in Chapter 1) Foucault defines as the political calculus that distinguishes lives that matter from those that do not: 'One might say that the ancient right to *take* life or *let* live was replaced by a power to *foster* life or to *disallow* it to the point of death' ([1978] 1990: 138; original emphasis). *Edward II* and *My Own Private Idaho* take the sovereign figures of Edward and Henry V to consider alternate strategies for interrogating the devaluation of queer life during the HIV/AIDS pandemic. Jarman retells Edward II's deposition and murder as an allegory of the denial of political voice to sexual minorities. Van Sant juxtaposes Scott, a modern version of Shakespeare's Prince Hal, whose political and theatrical life is worth seeing and recording, to Mike, a homeless hustler whose life is apolitical and so has no direct Shakespearean analogue – he is part of the faceless, forsaken masses who have disappeared from historical memory.

Perhaps even more than *The Tempest*, Jarman's *Edward II* imagines a politics that incorporates camp and irony as well as queer rage, earnestness, vengeance and disappointment. Like *The Tempest, Edward II* is set in a multi-temporal world. Yet its precursor in taking Renaissance England as a site of cultural memory by which to frame contemporary politics might be understood less as *Jubilee* or *The Tempest* than Jarman's 1985 *The Angelic Conversation*. Here Judi Dench reads Shakespeare's Sonnets, accompanied by the music of Benjamin

Britten and the experimental group Coil; the action, Jarman's stage direction tells us, consist of 'A series of slow-moving sequences through a landscape seen from the windows of an Elizabethan house. Two young men find and lose each other' ([1987] 2010: 133). *The Angelic Conversation* punctures the delusion that art provides refuge from the wreckage of history. As Jarman recounts,

> *The Angelic Conversation* is a dream world, a world of magic and ritual, yet there are images there of the burning cars and radar systems, which remind you there is a price to be paid in order to gain this dream in the face of a world of violence.
>
> Destruction hovers in the background of *The Angelic Conversation*; the radar, the surveillance, the feeling one is under psychic attack; of course we are under attack at the moment. ([1987] 2010: 133, italics inverted)

Like the lovers in *The Angelic Conversation*, the titular king of *Edward II* lives under surveillance and psychic attack. Yet in this later film destruction does not just hover in the background. The physical attack on gay lives is inescapable and ongoing.

Edward II treats the deposition and murder of Edward and his lover Gaveston as part of the contemporary history of government inaction on the HIV/AIDS crisis, intercutting scenes of political protest by the British gay-rights group OutRage! with the film's narrative action. Some scenes take place in what appears to be an austere stone castle, and the actors sometimes appear in period costumes that evoke the play's original Elizabethan moment. Other scenes take place in 1980s offices or bedrooms and feature male bureaucrats in business suits, women who could be Thatcher's clones, and prostitutes in modern BDSM regalia. The film reveals the omnipresence of discrimination that allows, as José Arroyo argues, 'socially transgressive sexual practices' to become 'the excuse for stripping away class privileges' (1993: 85). Even

more significantly, by making Edward and Gaveston's downfall
a matter of state intervention, Ellis argues, 'The function of the
political story is to move the film out of the realm of private
romantic intrigue,' to utilize a history of the politicization of
sex to illustrate the truth of the activist slogan that appears in
Jarman's *Queer Edward II*, the published script of the film:
'Intercourse has never occurred in private' (Ellis 2009: 211,
213; Jarman 1991: 90).

Three scenes of *Edward II* illustrate formally and
thematically the deadly effects of denying the role of the state
in regulating private lives by materially supporting some forms
of intimacy and sexuality and disallowing others. In the first of
these, Gaveston and Edward dance while Annie Lennox, who
is physically present in the scene, sings 'Ev'ry time we say goodbye'. As Gaveston and Edward say goodbye, we are reminded
that they are set in the space of tragedy between two deaths,
the one that history and literature tell us has already happened
and its yet-to-come realization in the present moment of the
film. This elegiac scene performs the same work that Ellis has
attributed to the scenes of Edward in the dungeon after his
deposition: they render visually 'the psychological landscape
of a person with AIDS: How does one live in the face of a
death that is uncertain but likely imminent? What new horrors
lie in wait before the end?' (2009: 215). *Edward II* emphasizes
that this is not just individual but communal terror. Lennox,
as Rich writes, had recorded this song the year before for the
Red Hot and Blue CD, the first AIDS benefit collection ([1992]
2013b: 6). Lennox's presence at, even participation in, the
couple's leavetaking, allows us to appreciate the implications
of the view that 'intercourse has never been private'. This
song's history and context and its prominence here reconfigure
a torch song about a couple's private parting into a requiem
for a community decimated by a pandemic – a community for
whom saying goodbye, forever, had become a way of life. That
pandemic was itself nurtured by a private/public split that
had treated HIV/AIDS, in its early days, as the consequence
of individual perversion. This split, like Coke's Latin legal

circumlocution that deemed sodomy a 'crime not to be named among Christians' (Coke 1644: 10.59), made HIV/AIDS unspeakable in political discourse and, therefore, denied its status as a public medical emergency to be addressed by state-funded research and education.

The second scene is really a set of scenes: the double ending which stages Marlowe's notorious depiction of Edward's murder by sodomy with a hot poker first as reality then as a nightmare from which Edward awakes, only to be kissed instead of killed by Lightborne. On the one hand, this double ending equates the active persecution of Edward with the passive neglect that allowed HIV/AIDS to spread. The uncertainty as to whether Edward's death 'really' took this particular form, as Ellis writes,

> acknowledges that history cannot simply be wished away. As the rest of the film has argued, the state is involved in the clandestine murder of many queers, either through police harassment or government inaction on HIV/AIDS. This desire for violence is echoed in society at large either literally through gay bashing or, more psychologically, in the pronouncements of the media and the pulpit. (2009: 217)[10]

Was Edward really murdered in this grotesque parody of poetic justice in which sodomy becomes punishment as well as crime? Or did he simply waste away in a dank cesspool? On the other hand, the alternate ending with Lightborne's kiss recasts the legend of Edward's death-by-sodomy as itself a myth of heterohistory. In imagining a history in which Edward survives, Jarman suggests that the myth of the poker may not so much describe the past as work to proscribe queer life in the future. It does so by threatening homosexual desire with a venerable punishment of state-sponsored death, dispossession and torture. What we cannot know about the precise events of the past in which we cannot intervene is also what we choose not to know about the present: that neglect has the same results as brutality.

The third scene is the film's final one, in which Edward's prepubescent son, the future Edward III, points the way to a counterfactual future that is queer not only because it is more inclusive of homosexuals but, more radically, because it reimagines the intersecting structures of gender, sexuality and political participation. Here, Edward III refuses to perform gender according to conventional binaries: he wears his father's suit and his mother's earrings, heels and makeup. He dances atop a dusty cage, imprisoning Isabella and Mortimer in the past rather than allow their vicious homophobia to perpetuate itself in the present, an image that reimagines the historical defeat of Isabella and Mortimer as not just a change in who has sovereign power but a revision of what sovereignty itself means. Dancing to that saccharine ode to bourgeois youth, Tchaikovsky's 'Dance of the Sugar Plum Fairy', which plays on his Walkman, Edward III is an emblem of queer childhood eroticism, not the tabula rasa of sexual innocence projected by normative culture.[11] Nor, we learn as the camera gradually widens its focus, is young Edward alone: the OutRage! protesters who were formerly kept outside the circles of action and power are now in the room with the Elizabethan characters. In Ellis's reading, this scene performs the same work as the masque of *The Tempest*, crossing the line between spectator and performance to encompass us, the audience. The use of Renaissance drama is far from incidental to Jarman's political purpose, Ellis argues:

> The trappings of the past are used to establish the 'once upon a time' space that allows us to ignore temporarily our implication in the events while we absorb the lessons of the story, before being reminded once again that the story is about us. But the film reminds us as well that the past isn't just an elsewhere, where diverting stories can be played out for our amusement, but rather that the past inhabits the present in complex ways and that we ignore it at our peril. (2009: 218)

Understood as part of a genealogy of the present, Jarman's film can be relegated neither to the medieval past of its setting nor to the Elizabethan past of its composition. It is part of a history that we in the present participate in reproducing and for which we are responsible.

Jarman alters the original playtext of *Edward II* by reordering events and cutting and reassigning lines, but the Marlovian provenance is consistent and specific. By contrast, Van Sant is less committed to *Henry IV, Parts 1 and 2*, and the Shakespearean structure and language of *My Own Private Idaho* appears only sporadically. Shakespeare's omnipresence in modern US culture enters the film in the commodified form of a bottle of 'Falstaff' beer, a throwaway image that we realize only retrospectively anticipates one plot line, in which the character Scott, son of the Portland Mayor, is based on that of Prince Hal. The Shakespearean text in the film appears in both original and modernized form. Scott Favor (Keanu Reeves) is a knowing prodigal son, acting out the role in order to reap the celebration that greets that biblical wanderer's return; the gang of street hustlers with whom he slums are mentored by Bob, a Falstaff character; the film stages versions of the Gadhill caper and Hal's eventual repudiation of Falstaff and of his own dissolute youth. These Shakespearean moments, in fact, are what makes the film postmodern rather than realist in form. Along with the time-lapse photography, the presentation of both gay and straight sex scenes as a series of tableaux vivants, and the scene in which models on pornographic magazines suddenly come to life, the Shakespearean dialogue and plot puncture the realist, documentary tone of the film to remind us that the ordinary, even seedy, lives we are following are themselves mediated by art.

Scott's inhabitation of the role of Prince Hal is unsustained and seemingly unrelated to the story of the film's other protagonist, Mike Waters (River Phoenix), a narcoleptic drifter in love with Scott. Reviewers tended to deem the Shakespearean moments at best 'nervy' but irrelevant (Canby 1980), at worst 'labored' (Hinson 1991) or 'squirmingly embarrassing' (Thomas 2015).

I would argue that, read from the vantage of the HIV/AIDS pandemic, and the more general social and economic policies of the Reagan-Bush era, the Shakespearean elements are essential. Whereas Vincent Canby (1980) and David Roman (1994) see *My Own Private Idaho* as avoiding the topic of HIV/AIDS, Arroyo likens it to *Edward II* on the grounds that 'both films depict the context of the [HIV/AIDS] pandemic through their use of style, their romanticism, their representation of sexuality and time, and their dystopic viewpoint' (1993: 80). Building on Arroyo's insight, I argue that the references to the Henriad are critical here, for they introduce a long history of brutal class exploitation that the egalitarian myth of the American dream both obscures and naturalizes. As Hal Hinson observes, 'Scott is merely biding his time, as Shakespeare's young Hal did, waiting to assume his proper place in society, a place that has no room for Bob or for Mike' (1991). Scott, that is to say, *has* a narrative path to security and success, and his ability to plan for a future is a privilege denied society's outcasts. The Henriad's meditation on dynastic power contradicts the myth of equal opportunity encapsulated in the film's gorgeous shots of the open spaces of the American West and musical strains of Eddy Arnold singing 'Cattle Call' and Bill Stafford playing warped versions of 'Home on the Range' and 'America the Beautiful' on the steel guitar. The feudal order of English monarchal history may more accurately describe Reagan-Bush America than the exceptionalist view that the United States is a land of opportunity in which the strong will not only survive, but flourish.

Mike's narcolepsy is essential here, for it literalizes the extraordinary vulnerability of those deemed politically disposable. In the throes of a seizure, Mike is incapable of the individual determination and self-reliance by which the American character distinguishes itself from its Old World counterparts. As Hinson puts it, 'when Mike blacks out, so do we, and we keep waking up in different parts of the story and in different locales. Mike never seems to quite know where he is' (1991). This formal disorientation also captures the power dynamics of a neo-liberal logic by which care and protection are the responsibility of the privatized nuclear family, a view that relieves the state of responsibility for its citizens. At the same time, the state disallows forms of kinship and intimacy beyond the heterosexual couple, as we see in Van Sant's film when the police raid the abandoned hotel in which Mike's alternative family of hustlers has been squatting.[12] In contrast to Scott, heir-apparent to a Portland dynasty, Mike is the progeny of, in Gus Van Sant's words, a 'Sam-Shepherd-like' world – a world, that is, of incest and abandonment.[13] Discarded by biological family and national community, when Mike descends into unconsciousness, he is at the mercy of strangers who may or may not happen to be kind. At one point in the film, he wakes from a seizure and asks Scott, 'how much did you make off me while I was passed out?' The narcoleptic's exposure and powerlessness make palpable the quotidian experience of poverty and homelessness. The effects of this vulnerability are detailed later in the same scene by the matter-of-fact cross-talk where boyish prostitutes share stories of harrowing 'first dates'. One youth, Digger, recalls a man in a 'black Porsche' who, despite the fact that 'I'd already laid down the law' and 'told him what I do and don't do', 'started doing whatever he wanted' and 'basically raped me, put a fucking wine bottle up my butt. It was, like, it was, like, horrible'. Those outside the law cannot lay down the law; they do not even have recourse to it.

The film closes, as it opens, with Mike succumbing to a narcoleptic seizure in the middle of an empty Idaho highway. Watching that first seizure, the most immediate and obvious fear is that Mike will be run over by a car, and it is a relief when the film cuts to a scene of him alive and receiving fellatio from a client in Seattle – his life is not great, but the man treats him fairly (even kindly, giving him $10 extra), and at least he has survived. The closing scene withholds such relief. After Mike passes out, the film lingers silently over his inert body as a truck stops just long enough for two men to hop out and rob him of his shoes and duffle bag. They do not even take the time to push him out of the road before they drive off. 'America the Beautiful' – a song we first heard in the earlier, explicitly Shakespearean scene in which Scott promises his father that he will eventually redeem himself – begins to play as a second car pulls up. The driver gets out and loads Mike's inert body into the car. Is this a Good Samaritan, a Jeffrey Dahmer or someone in between? We'll never know, because the film ends here, with the music shifting to the Pogues's anthem of London destitution, 'The Old Main Drag', as the car draws away and disappears into the horizon. The last two images in *My Own Private Idaho* are an empty ranch house, followed by the words 'have a nice day'. A moment of direct address, this insipid valediction incorporates the viewer into the film in order to pose the moral quandary it summarizes. How can we go forth and have a nice day, knowing that we reside in this landscape of murderous neglect?

These questions compel us to recognize the limitations of the private sympathy and care that Mike has sought throughout the film. Mike's search for the mother who has abandoned him and his appeals for Scott's love are his only hopes for nurture in a nation that has ceased to provide for its citizens. In asking us whether we can go on and have a nice day, the film puts before us the problem inherent to sentimental politics diagnosed by Lauren Berlant, in which 'empathy is mainly directed toward the pain of the privileged for being enslaved by a system of barbarous power in which they were destined, somehow, to be caught' (1998: 641). Fellow-feeling, that is, threatens to erase the true subject of suffering and to focus on the private experience of sadness, with the result that 'the ethical imperative toward social transformation is replaced by a civic-minded but passive ideal of empathy ... Suffering, in this personal-public context, becomes answered by survival, which is then recoded as freedom' (Berlant 1998: 641). Feeling bad for others allows us to feel good about ourselves: even if we are 'enslaved to a system of barbarous power' that we are helpless to change, the very fact that we empathize with those most vulnerable to this system allows us to believe ourselves innocent rather than complicit. Feeling, rather than action, is 'recoded' as evidence of 'freedom', virtue and agency.

In *My Own Private Idaho*, the character who is closest to the audience's position is not the destitute Mike but the privileged Scott. In the film's final twenty minutes, Scott leaves Mike in Rome (that other site of decayed empire) to return home with an Italian bride (a modern version of Hal and his own foreign bride, the French Katherine, as Goldberg points out (2003: 237)). Back in Portland, a trio of scenes depict Scott's cruelty not as active destruction of the disempowered but as a *refusal to see* his former friends and lovers. Scott rides in the back of a limousine, not looking out the window to recognize Mike's unconscious body on the sidewalk. His back turned – literalizing Reagan's refusal publicly to say the word AIDS until 1987 – he answers Bob's affectionate Shakespearean greeting 'God save you, my sweet boy!' with a modernization of Hal's repudiation of Falstaff: 'I don't know you, old man. Please leave me alone'.[14] In the last scene in which Scott appears, at the funeral of his biological father, he averts his eyes from the riotous mosh pit nearby in which the street kids mourn Bob, Scott's symbolic father and their only father. When Scott withholds sympathy, he also withholds the political intervention that, as his father's heir, he will be in the position to make. He chooses instead to sanction the status quo. Scott's heartlessness, however villainized by the film and its critics, may also be the future of the audience: we will momentarily feel bad about what we have seen but eventually go on to have a nice day, just as Scott has gone on to have a nice life.

Yet, as José Esteban Muñoz has argued of the New Queer Cinema more generally, Jarman and Van Sant's queer radicalism has its own blind spots, most obviously with regards to race (1998). Both omit the many persons of colour who died of HIV/AIDS, a percentage that has only grown in the West in the past two decades (Woubshet 2015; Villarosa 2017). In *Edward II*, Jarman's OutRage! protesters are uniformly white. From the vantage point of our current historical moment, 2018, this cinematic focus on white victims of HIV/AIDS is part of a larger cultural neglect of men of colour. Such ongoing disregard has led to the exponential growth of the virus among black and Latino men in the twenty-first century, even as the availability of the preventative drug PrEP has led the mainstream LGBTQ community to declare AIDS a problem of the past and to turn its activist energies to marriage equality. *My Own Private Idaho* is even more explicit in its exclusion of men of colour from its concerns with poverty, homelessness and homophobia. In the same scene in which Digger recounts being sodomized with a wine bottle, another hustler describes a date with 'this big black guy who had a lot of eight-balls with speed, a lot of money ... this black guy, he had a big old fucking cock and shit and it was this totally awful experience'. The hustler addresses an audience (on- and off-screen) expected to sympathize with his casual racism and thereby to overlook the racial exclusions of queer activism and queer cinema. The politics of witnessing, of making visible those who have been left out of history, is ongoing; it may require a critique of queer activism's own past. To retell the history of the recent as well as the distant past – to recover those voices that have been silenced and devalued – may be as difficult as reconstructing the 'truth' of the medieval worlds of the historical Edward II or Henry V.

Not your father's Shakespeare?

The tagline for Baz Luhrmann's *Romeo + Juliet* proclaims that this is 'Not your father's Shakespeare.'[15] The line hails an audience eager to disidentify with the role of the obedient Child who has learned to sit up straight and applaud Shakespeare as staid costume drama spoken in a proper English accent. But this rebellious appeal is marked by two ironies. First, it claims a break from tradition that Shakespearean films had already, as we have seen, been making for decades. It thereby assumes that 'your' father – the 'Father' naming cultural tradition more broadly – is unaware of and unmarked by Jarman's or Van Sant's readings of Renaissance drama through the lenses of punk, camp and postmodernism. At the same time, Luhrmann's film declares *itself* unmarked by its own cinematic predecessors, thereby making precisely the claim to innovation and originality that its postmodern form and ironic emphasis on authorship contests: this is not just *Romeo and Juliet*, but *William Shakespeare's Romeo + Juliet*. But if we understand postmodernism not as mere clever surface but as itself the topic of the film, we can see that *Romeo + Juliet* is *exactly* your father's Shakespeare ideologically. For by contrast to Jarman's or Van Sant's critiques of the ideology of privacy, Luhrmann's film depicts love as the only refuge from the glib and violent world of late-twentieth-century global capital.[16] And the love that performs this task is, just as 'your father' would have it, heteronormative and white – as are the actors who occupy the role of innocent Child, the hope for a better future that is also a nostalgic longing for a purer past. In Luhrmann's film, as in another postmodern Shakespeare, Julie Taymor's *Titus*, the threats to the Child come in the shape of queer, black and brown bodies. Indeed, the queer and multiracial casts of these films validate the myth of Shakespeare's universality by making visible its embodiment in the image of the white, heterosexual Child.

When reviewers sought to convey what they almost unanimously read as the departure of *Romeo + Juliet* from previous film versions of Shakespeare, they invariably pointed to Harold Perrineau's performance of Mercutio, who epitomizes the film's postmodern distractions from the 'real' love story. Describing the film as 'a litmus test for any viewer's willingness to accept extreme stylistic attitudinizing as a substitute for the virtues of traditional storytelling', the *Variety* Staff's review warned that 'anyone unwilling to accept Mercutio as a black disco diva in drag had best stay away' (Variety Staff 1996). Peter Travers's more sympathetic review cites as an example of the film's modernization the casting of 'Romeo's best bud' as 'a black cross-dresser' (1996). Janet Maslin spells out the interlocking racial and sexual categories

that structure mainstream ideals of good art and the good life
when she writes that Luhrmann's film

> nearly turns the Capulets' costume ball into 'Priscilla, Queen
> of Verona'. (Mercutio, played by Harold Perrineau, is now a
> black drag queen in a white wig.) Dressed to ravishing effect
> as a knight and an angel, Romeo and Juliet meet here and
> bring the film to a much-needed mood change.
>
> The frenzy gives way to a tenderness that makes sense in
> any language, or with no language at all, as Mr. Luhrmann
> lets the camera swirl adoringly around the film's young stars.
> Just when 'Romeo and Juliet' has almost fatally pushed
> its luck – with the sight of Paul Sorvino raving in purple
> spangles as Juliet's father, say, or with many comparable
> affronts – it is still able to summon flashes of purity and
> beauty. (1996)

One could not invent a better summary of the idealization of
white, heteronormative romance as the cultural apex to which
healthy individuals are urged to ascend. In Maslin's assessment,
flamboyant black and brown men (god forbid that a 'costume
ball' should include men in wigs or spangles) encapsulate the
film's visual excesses. Loaded with 'many comparable affronts',
the Bacchanalian party expresses the more widespread socio-
sexual disorder of Verona. Indeed, in Luhrmann's telling,
Romeo and Juliet meet because they both flee the sensory
assaults of the ball to find peace contemplating an aquarium,
from either side of which their eyes first meet. Reassuring
us with costumes that reveal their identification with white,
Western clichés of masculine strength and feminine innocence,
Romeo and Juliet not only resist the corruptions that surround
them but also rescue the film from its own self-destructive
indulgence in the nick of time, just when it 'has almost fatally
pushed its luck' and alienated viewers who didn't come for
this. The 'much-needed mood change' from senseless frenzy
to 'a tenderness that makes sense in any language' assumes a
universal desire for 'flashes of purity and beauty'. The white

Children, playing Shakespeare straight amidst irresponsible peers and elders, reassure us that heteronormative romance is still the film's real topic. As Patricia has argued, 'Luhrmann's representation of Mercutio as a drag queen serves to reinforce the strictest of binaries between straight men and gay and/ or queer men' (2016: 112). This visual distinction might be particularly necessary to assure audiences that Romeo is an unambivalent heterosexual, despite the fact that, as Barbara Hodgdon puts it, he is played by Leonardo DiCaprio, whose 'pale androgynous beauty ... makes him a polysexual figure, equally attractive to young women and to gay and straight men' (1999: 93). Childhood is also essential here: Romeo's androgyny is a 'natural' product of his youth and innocence in contrast to Mercutio's 'unnatural', gender-queer adulthood, made visible in the contrast of secondary sex characteristics – facial hair and gym body – to his drag performance in wig and miniskirt.

Luhrmann's formal experimentation does not obscure his conservative racial and sexual politics; it puts them in relief. As Nicholas F. Radel argues, Luhrmann's film uncritically repeats a view that *Romeo and Juliet* shares with *The Tempest*: 'the promise of pure, white marital alliance is defined in distinction to dark-skinned others whose sexuality is conceived as perverse. In short, the play reflects a connection between white purity and sexuality that excludes dark (and implicitly perverse) desires' (2009: 24). In the play this contrast appears in the language by which Romeo and Juliet describe one another: 'Juliet imagines Romeo as "day in night," or "new snow upon a raven's back"' while Romeo sighs that Juliet 'hangs upon the cheek of night / As a rich jewel in an Ethiop's ear' (*RJ* 3.2.17, 18–19, 1.5.45–7; Radel 2009: 26–7). Radel concludes,

the equivocations introduced by the metaphor of the Ethiop reveal how racially problematic it has become for our own age to read Romeo and Juliet's love in distinction to other desires in the play associated with darkness. As we saw with Luhrmann's film, doing so seems to privilege lightness and purity in terms that cannot be separated from the subsequent development of raced thinking in the West. (2009: 27)

Radel's essay focuses on Perrineau's Mercutio as the emblem of such 'raced thinking', but the threats to innocent heterosexual love appear in virtually all of the characters played by black or brown actors. Mercutio's oft-remarked drag performance is, to be sure, the most obvious example: he is accompanied by several men in whiteface and purple spangles that match Capulet's toga. At the same party, John Leguizamo as Tybalt ('a volatile Latino', in Peter Travers's words (1996), who is obsessed with Romeo here and later) French kisses Lady Capulet, his aunt. He wears a devil costume and she is dressed as Cleopatra, costumes that portray their incestuous attraction as both infernal and Oriental. More subtly, the British actress Miriam Margoyles appears in brownface to play, as Travers puts it 'Juliet's bawdy nurse' with 'a broad Hispanic accent (she calls her mistress Wholiette)'. Herself campy enough to verge on drag, Margoyles's mugging and innuendo capture the affective excess that José Esteban Muñoz has dubbed 'feeling brown' to mark her a lewd outsider who can abet but not appreciate the fine and elegant love of the title characters (2000).

By surrounding Romeo and Juliet with these racial and sexual caricatures, Luhrmann makes the young lovers helpless victims of the frenetic postmodern world they would rather escape.[17] He thereby obscures the possibility that Carla Freccero sums up as 'Romeo and Juliet love death' – that they share a suicidal drive that the play refuses to sublimate. Romeo and Juliet 'like teenagers all over the United States, kill themselves and each other, again and again, in the name of a fantasy that wards off the meaninglessness of the void it harbors', and in making this fantasy the cause of their death the play 'indicts, even as it constructs, the modern myth of romantic love' (Freccero 2011b: 304). For Kathryn Schwarz, in *Romeo and Juliet*, the plague that prevents Friar Laurence's letter from reaching Romeo is not just a plot device; it is a literalization of the communal obligations that stymie individual, romantic retreat. Schwarz writes, 'In a play that sequesters its privileged subjects first in a synoptic chorus and finally in an epitaphic couplet, the joint predicament of mortal, sexual bodies activates modes of communion that cause a stutter in social taxonomies. It is on these terms that we might understand infectious communion as queer' (2017: 248). Shakespeare's play, Freccero and Schwarz both notice, sees Romeo and Juliet's deaths as evidence of their own implication in the corrupt world that Lurhmann's visual surfeit creates and that it associates with the camp and violence embodied by Mercutio, Tybalt, Capulet and the Nurse. Luhrmann's film struggles to quarantine sexual drives in black and brown queer bodies, equating whiteness with the hope of transcending the clichés that Romeo and Juliet have become. This is indeed 'your father's Shakespeare' – struggling to carve a space for truth and beauty amidst a world that has ceased to believe in these high ideals.

If Luhrmann hides his humanism under gaudy pastiche, Julie Taymor's *Titus* wears its traditionalism on its sleeve. Shakespeare's *Titus Andronicus* is a revenge tragedy, a genre whose ethos is captured by the Senecan maxim that 'You do not avenge crimes unless you surpass them.'[18] In the Elizabethan revenge tragedies of which *Titus Andronicus* is a part, this one-upmanship not only occurs at the level of plot but also appears as literary competition among playwrights and their classical and contemporary forebears. Much as Titus will outdo his enemies in the play, Shakespeare will outdo Ovid and Seneca. This ethos of rivalry is captured by Titus's words to Chiron and Demetrius: 'worse than Philomel you have used my daughter / And worse than Progne will I be revenged' (5.2.194–5).[19] But the person who indulges a drive to surpass, Shakespeare's contemporary Francis Bacon warns in his essay 'Of Revenge', 'keeps his own wounds green, which otherwise would heal and do well' ([1597] 1994: 11). Refusing to heal and move on, avengers would rather destroy themselves than forgive their enemies. Taymor's film links this devolution of the individual to the decline of civilization, a view spelled out in the tagline: 'The Fall of an Empire. The Descent of Man.' *Titus* has a pedagogical aim: we can save the Western civilization whose line between two millennia stretches from Rome to England to the United States only by resisting the easy adrenaline rush of mindless sex and violence that the film associates with the fall of Rome, the rise of fascism and the decline of American values. If empires fall when 'man' gives into his base instincts, it might be able to rise again if we can get our priorities straight.

This pedagogical aim is made clear by what Stephen Holden deems 'the audacious editorial decision to begin and end the movie with images of children' (1999). The film's first image is of a pair of blue eyes peering through holes in a paper bag; they are those of a white boy who proceeds to stage a bloody war with his action figures before being whisked away to the Coliseum to play the part of Young Lucius, Titus's grandson. The film's final image is of the same boy carrying Aaron's infant son away from the Coliseum and its bloody spectacles. The boy's stricken face tells us that he has learned his lesson: the furious carnage we have just witnessed should arouse horror, not glee. Rejecting his former pleasure in destruction, this Child offers hope for 'our' collective future. These two children will break the cycle of violence that revenge tragedy depicts. The framing device, that is, denies that the action proper provides mindless entertainment and asserts that what we have just seen should prompt the self-reflection of Aristotelian catharsis, teaching us not to emulate what we have seen but to pity and fear it.

Yet the film consistently divides its objects of catharsis between normative gendered and sexual subjects, whom we pity, and perverse gendered and sexual subjects, whom we fear. Among the former is, of course, Titus. He may have initiated the cycle of violence by refusing Tamora's plea to 'spare my first-born son' (1.1.123), but we can understand his merciless desire to avenge the subsequent rape and dismemberment of Lavinia, the murder of her husband Bassianus, and the executions of his own sons. The film encourages a mainstream audience, epitomized by the Everyboy who is its on-screen witness, to identify with and pity the Andronici (whose

scion the boy comes to play). By contrast, the objects of
fear are the Emperor Saturnine and his Gothic and Moorish
compatriots, all of whom are marked as barbaric threats to
Roman civilization.[20] Alan Cummings, who had appeared on
the cover of *Out* magazine in November 1999, shortly before
the premier of *Titus*, plays Saturnine as an effete, flamboyant
manchild. His relationship with the older, Amazonian Tamora
is depicted as a cross-generation, gender-queer perversion of
normal marriage. Tamora's sons Chiron and Demetrius are not
only, as Jonathan Bate puts it, 'Bored young Goths' who 'go
on a killing spree for the sheer fun of it' (2000). They are also
queer and incestuous. The effeminacy of Chiron, especially, is
registered in the casting of Jonathan Rhys Meyers in this role:
Meyers had appeared as a louche glam rock star the previous
year in *Velvet Goldmine*, a film by the New Queer Cinema
director Todd Haynes. In *Titus*, Chiron and Demetrius simulate
sex with one another as they plot Lavinia's rape, exchange long
kisses with Tamora, and appear in drag in a staged masque of
revenge. Aaron the Moor, played by Harry J. Lennix, who had
previously appeared in Spike Lee's *Clockers* and *Get on the
Bus*, is the most terrifying creature of all. The film suggests
that the orgy of rape, incest, mutilation and murder that
Aaron stage-manages is his own revenge against the white race
comprised of Goths and Romans alike. The threat he poses to
white dominance is, as even Chiron and Demetrius recognize,
summed up in the mixed-race child that is the progeny of his
affair with Tamora. Yet, unsurprisingly from a queer point
of view, what redeems Aaron is parenthood. Virginia Mason
Vaughan and Pascale Aebischer agree that the film's portrayal
of Aaron's self-sacrificing love for his son converts him
from racial and religious other to good Christian father – a
conversion signified, Aebischer notes, in the film's images of
Aaron's crucifixion in the Roman Coliseum (Vaughan 2003;
Aebischer 2014: 122). It is the promise that this child will
survive to learn better values than his father with which the
film ends. As in Luhrmann's *Romeo + Juliet*, in Taymor's *Titus*
the innocent white Child is the last, best hope for a future

of renewed innocence, a role the film depicts sartorially when the boy swaps the black T-shirt in which he initially appeared for the white suit in which he rescues Aaron's child. Righting Aaron's political and sexual domination of Tamora, the white boy becomes a new father to the baby, offering a delibidinized, beneficent relation of care to the infant he has removed from his barbarous heritage. This is an alternate form of kinship, but it excludes queerness rather than challenging normativity. It is more like interracial adoption, with all of that institution's implications of assimilation and rescue, than communal experiment.[21]

True to its genre, in which competition is a structural principle, Taymor's film seeks to outdo and rewrite Jarman. To appreciate just how conservative Taymor's lesson is, we might compare the boy of *Titus* with another, far queerer, cinematic boy, the young prince in *Edward II*. In relation to this cinematic forbear, Taymor's own inclusion of a boy doesn't seem so 'audacious' after all. As Jarman writes of young Edward: 'The little boy is always there. He's a witness and survivor' (quoted Ellis 2009: 218). And what he witnesses and survives is the cruelty of a heteronormative cultural tradition that renders vulnerable the queer boys and men who are Jarman's and Van Sant's protagonists. *Edward II*, however briefly, imagines a queer future in which the forces of homophobia will be contained, even as young Edward has caged Isabella and Mortimer. This view is thematized in the published screenplay, *Queer Edward II*, whose inscription states that it is 'dedicated to: the repeal of all anti-gay laws, particularly Section 28', which prohibited 'promoting homosexuality by teaching or by publishing material' (Jarman 1991; n.p.).[22] The view is also stated in one of the many activist slogans that Jarman includes in *Queer Edward II*: 'save queer children from straight parents' (1991: 24). Luhrmann and Taymor, by contrast, seek to save straight children from the corruptions of modern culture.

If for Jarman and Van Sant 'Shakespeare' as metonymy for Western cultural heritage can be disrupted and reimagined, for Luhrmann and Taymor 'Shakespeare' names the better values lost to the MTV generation. Significantly, Jarman, as director of videos for Patti Smyth, the Pet Shop Boys and other 1980s bands, helped form the sensibilities associated with this generation. In this regard, to treat postmodernism as an aesthetic expression of cynicism about traditional humanist values may also signal a rejection of the entirely earnest, indeed enraged, critique of those values in the New Queer Cinema. Jarman was the 'king of queer' or 'grand old man in his fourth decade of queer activity' at the dawn of that movement (Rich [1992] 2013b: 17). We might regard Luhrmann and Taymor as Jarman's (and Van Sant's) Oedipal heirs, rebelling through nostalgia for a time when we could take our Shakespeare straight, and therefore credulously obeying the ironic modernist injunction to 'make it new' with parodic postmodern visuals whose sensory assault made so many of Luhrmann's critics long for the good old days.

Not your father's Shakespeare? Indeed.

Conclusion

Whose Shakespeare?

In its structure and argument, this book has taken up the by now orthodox queer resistance to liberal narratives of progress. Politically, this means eschewing a story of increasing social acceptance and extension of legal rights to the LGBTQ community in the United States, where in less than thirty years the Supreme Court has gone from upholding sodomy laws in *Bowers v. Hardwick* (1986) to striking them down in *Lawrence v. Texas* (2003) to making marriage equality the law of the land in *Obergefell v. Hodges* (2015). Theoretically, this means resisting a depiction of early queer studies as well-meaning but naïve or simplistic, practically begging to have its blind spots addressed and its pronouncements complicated by the work to follow. Culturally, this means noticing that film versions of Shakespeare have gotten less, rather than more, politically radical over the decades. In tracing the major themes and concerns of queer theory and Shakespeare studies, I have attempted to capture the eccentricity and recursivity of these fields of study, to honour the continued relevance of early work at the same time that I trace the productive departures and insights of work that followed. I have also, however, tried to keep in sight queer theory's real and complex engagement with contemporary politics, and to point to ways that queer readings and performances of Shakespeare and the early modern past can contribute to a confrontation with the injustices of the present. In short, I have tried to think about how Shakespeare can be part of what Berlant and Warner call 'queer worldmaking' (1998: 561). In this view of politics and history, it would be misguided to seek a queer theory or politics that lasts, to borrow Ben Jonson's enthusiastic evaluation of Shakespeare's work 'not for an age, but for all time'. Rather, queer theory sees fragility and ephemerality as themselves desirable aspects of utopian worlds that are always on the horizon (Muñoz 2009).

I conclude, therefore, by considering events at my home institution, the University of Pennsylvania, that brought to view the continued political struggle over the place and meaning of 'Shakespeare' in relation to 'queer theory'. In the aftermath of Trump's election in 2016, graduate students at Penn took down a large portrait of Shakespeare, which had long hung over the main staircase in the English Department, and replaced it with a portrait of Audre Lorde. The incident was widely reported in the national press, and it aroused particular ire in the right-wing media. Most headlines offered some variation of 'Shakespeare replaced with black lesbian feminist'.[1] Others announced that 'U-Penn Students Take Down Shakespeare Portrait Because He's Too White And Straight' (Pullman 2016) and 'U Penn Removes Shakespeare Portrait Because He Does Not Represent "Diversity"' (Timpf 2016). The articles themselves expressed outrage with an academic establishment that appeared dead set on attacking the most widely recognized mascot of elite literary culture. Robert Gehl at the *Federalist Papers Project* depicted the act as the epitome of 'leftist, whiny entitlement' whose work 'includes ignoring and wiping out Western history and replacing it' (2016) – anticipating in this local cultural skirmish the cries of the white supremacists who would march in Charlottesville nine months later, in August 2017: 'you will not replace us' and 'Jews will not replace us.' Jonathan Turley's blog called the portrait's removal 'a stereotype of the erosion of academic integrity and principles' and deemed it evidence that 'we are watching a comprehensive attack on classical literature and training' (2016). Katherine Timpf at *The National Review* presented her objections on the same aesthetic grounds that have been used to justify Shakespeare's centrality to Western education, stating that the switch of portraits is especially startling 'considering the fact that the portrait of Shakespeare just looked better in that space than the portrait of Lorde does' and asking, 'Do these kids really hate Shakespeare so much that they couldn't even wait to get an actual portrait of another author to hang up before shoving his portrait in an office somewhere?' (2016). Finally, Joy Pullmann at *The Federalist* treated the physical replacement of Shakespeare by Lorde as a response to a ludicrous and failed theoretical replacement of straight Shakespeare by queer Shakespeare: 'Apparently, attempts to demonstrate William Shakespeare was a gay man despite his fruitful marriage to the female-bodied Anne Hathaway just hasn't been enough to purge his guilt for being born white, male, and a peerless literary genius' (2016). The removal of the portrait, in this analysis, signals the inability of this 'pack of jarring, hell-hated lewdsters' to accept that Shakespeare was a biological father and therefore must be straight. Unable to face facts, these 'lewdsters' have reacted with rage against the 'white, male' 'peerless literary genius' whose superiority they cannot disprove through objective evidence (Pullman 2016).

This consternation at the possibility that Shakespeare would not be the face of an English department reduces graduate students to a rabble practicing leftist identity politics, a view extended to the faculty who supported the removal (in this case, the entire Penn English faculty, who had voted unanimously to replace the portrait years earlier but, through sheer force of inertia, had not figured out what to put up to fill the space). The outrage indicates that Shakespeare for many is still the 'fetish' (Garber 1990) or 'cultural token' (Sinfield [1985] 1994: 177) that he was more than two decades ago. And the implicit contest between Shakespeare and Lorde turns us back to an unsolvable question about education as an ultimately humanist endeavour. On the one hand, as Garber writes, Shakespeare 'has come to stand for a kind of "humanness" that, purporting to be inclusive of race, class, and gender, is in fact the neutralizing (or neutering) of those potent discourses by appropriation and by a metaphysical move to the figure' (1990: 250). White identity politics, that is, become so universalized that we no longer see the whiteness of 'Shakespeare', who has become mere figure for 'the human'. By contrast, Audre Lorde can never become mere figure; she can only be particularized as a 'black lesbian'. On the other hand, as Sinfield argues, however right we are to challenge Shakespeare's role as 'the keystone which guarantees the ultimate stability and rightness of the category of "Literature"', the progressive move to replace canonical with minority literature leaves in place the bourgeois dichotomies that separate the universal from the historical, the individual from the social, in that it preserves a belief in authenticity that 'reproduces in a particularly potent form the bourgeois ideology of individualism, effacing the historical construction ... of individuality itself' ([1985] 1994: 159, 173). In other words, the categories of 'white straight male' and 'black lesbian' are themselves historically constructed as oppressive fantasy and authentic reality, respectively. Just one instance is Pullman's claim that Shakespeare cannot possibly be a married father and a 'gay man' at the same time, thereby relying on just the twentieth-century construction of sexuality as coherent and knowable that queer theory has so assiduously challenged.

The categories of the individual, the private, the present and the authentic do their own ideological work, no less than those of the universal, the public, the past and the derivative. As Roderick Ferguson argues, however much institutional structure may co-opt attempts at radical change from within, and however much academic queer theory is a creature of the university, queer theory has the potential to disrupt dichotomies that would deny the simultaneous existence and ambiguous overlap in the very same textual artefacts of the universal and the historical, the individual and the social (2012: 209–26). Rather than simply dismiss Shakespeare from all that is queer, we must continue to understand his work as a site of contestation and struggle. To recall the observation of Eve Sedgwick discussed in the introduction to this book, to separate Shakespeare as figure of the master canon par excellence from (in this instance) Lorde as figure for 'lesbian and gay literature as a minority canon' is to obscure the 'nonuniversal functions of literacy and the literary' and to suppress a history in which 'not only have there been a gay Socrates, Shakespeare, and Proust, but ... their names are Socrates, Shakespeare, Proust; and, beyond that, legion – dozens or hundreds of the most centrally canonic figures in what the monoculturalists are pleased to consider "our" culture, as indeed, always in different forms and sense, in every other' (1990: 51–2).

Since Sedgwick made this argument in 1990, numerous scholars have demonstrated the manifold insights that come of putting Shakespeare and queer theory in dialogue. Madhavi Menon has sought to re-evaluate the universalism that has tended to have a bad name in leftist (including queer) politics. She argues instead that 'By showcasing a desire that does not allow for any particular identity, universalism not only announces itself as queer – *empty of content, revolutionary, indifferent* – but it also argues that queerness is universal' (Menon 2015: 18; original emphasis). In this light, rather than see Shakespeare as universal in his timelessness, we would understand him as universal in his subjection to time. Valerie Traub argues that engagements with the particular modes of embodiment assumed, obscured and problematized by Shakespeare's plays can illuminate 'the productive difficulty of ascertaining the limits of feminism' – and, I would add, the limits of queer theory (2016: 36).

Methodologically, a queer approach to Shakespeare requires relinquishing a humanist ideal of education and scholarship as the pursuit of mastery and instead lingering with a more tentative, occasional, even amateurish use of his plays and poems.[2] This approach to Shakespeare as well as to queer theory might be illustrated by the following exchange in *The Tempest*:

MIRANDA
   O brave new world!
   That has such people in it!
PROSPERO
                              'Tis new to thee.
                                        (5.184–5)

Over the course of this book, I have endeavoured to make new two fields of study that can, if we let them, become predictable and stale precisely because of their institutional prestige. But there is more to say. I hope and trust that *Shakespeare and Queer Theory* will not be the last word on either topic, but in its very limitations will catalyse newer, stranger theoretical work and political worlds.

APPENDIX

Podcast interviews with the authors of many of the titles in the *Arden Shakespeare and Theory* series are available. Details of both published and forthcoming titles are listed below.

Shakespeare and Cultural Materialist Theory, Christopher Marlow
http://blogs.surrey.ac.uk/shakespeare/2016/11/04/
shakespeare-and-contemporary-theory-31-shakespeare-and-cultural-materialist-theory-with-christopher-marlow/

Shakespeare and Ecocritical Theory, Gabriel Egan
http://blogs.surrey.ac.uk/shakespeare/2016/05/20/
shakespeare-and-contemporary-theory-24-shakespeare-and-ecocritical-theory-with-gabriel-egan/

Shakespeare and Ecofeminist Theory, Rebecca Laroche and Jennifer Munroe
http://blogs.surrey.ac.uk/shakespeare/2016/06/07/
shakespeare-and-contemporary-theory-25-shakespeare-and-ecofeminist-theory-with-rebecca-laroche-and-jennifer-munroe/

Shakespeare and Economic Theory, David Hawkes
http://blogs.surrey.ac.uk/shakespeare/2016/05/05/
shakespeare-and-contemporary-theory-22-shakespeare-and-economic-theory-with-david-hawkes/

Shakespeare and Feminist Theory, Marianne Novy
http://blogs.surrey.ac.uk/shakespeare/2016/05/13/
shakespeare-and-contemporary-theory-23-shakespeare-and-feminist-theory-with-marianne-novy/

Shakespeare and New Historicist Theory, Neema Parvini
http://blogs.surrey.ac.uk/shakespeare/2016/08/29/
shakespeare-and-contemporary-theory-27-shakespeare-and-
new-historicist-theory-with-evelyn-gajowski-and-neema-
parvini/

Shakespeare and Postcolonial Theory, Jyotsna G. Singh
http://blogs.surrey.ac.uk/shakespeare/2016/07/19/
shakespeare-and-contemporary-theory-26-shakespeare-and-
postcolonial-theory-with-jyotsna-singh/

Shakespeare and Posthumanist Theory, Karen Raber
http://blogs.surrey.ac.uk/shakespeare/2016/09/30/
shakespeare-and-contemporary-theory-28-shakespeare-and-
posthumanist-theory-with-karen-raber/

Shakespeare and Presentist Theory, Evelyn Gajowski
http://blogs.surrey.ac.uk/shakespeare/2016/04/29/
shakespeare-and-contemporary-theory-21-the-arden-
shakespeare-and-theory-series-with-evelyn-gajowski/

Shakespeare and Queer Theory, Melissa E. Sanchez
http://blogs.surrey.ac.uk/shakespeare/2016/10/18/
shakespeare-and-contemporary-theory-29-shakespeare-and-
queer-theory-with-melissa-e-sanchez/

NOTES

Introduction

1   Throughout this book, I use the term 'trans*' to include transgender, transsexual, gender queer, non-binary, agender and third-gender persons. As Halberstam has argued, the asterisk calls attention to the open-endedness and instability of the category (2018: 1–21).

2   For an analysis of field formation, see Hemmings (2011).

3   See Martin (1994a, b); Berlant (2001, 2011); Wiegman and Wilson (2015).

4   By 'object choice', queer theorists generally mean the person that one loves or desires, though an object of desire may also be a fantasy, an animal, a group or an inanimate object.

5   To take just a few instances, essays on pre-modern topics were included in *The Gay and Lesbian Studies Reader* (Halperin 1993; Vicinus 1993; Winkler 1993) and *Fear of a Queer Planet: Queer Politics and Social Theory* (Goldberg 1993); likewise, scholars whose work typically focused on contemporary culture were included in *Queering the Renaissance* (Halley 1994; Warner 1994).

6   On the tendency of queer theorists writing on contemporary literature to exclude early modern studies from their theoretical archive, see Stanivukovic (2009: 41–65).

7   See, more expansively, Smith (1991: 1–29).

Chapter 1

1   Derrida ([1972] 1983, [1972] 1985); see also de Man (1986).

2   For Freud, perversion is a broader category than normality: 'the abandonment of the reproductive function is the common

feature of all perversion. We actually describe a sexual activity as perverse if it has given up the aim of reproduction and pursues the attainment of pleasure as an aim independent of it' ([1920] 1966: 392).

3 See 'On Narcissism: An Introduction' (1914), 'Instincts and Their Vicissitudes' (1915) and 'The Economic Problem in Masochism' (1924) all in Freud (1963) and 'A Child Is Being Beaten' (1919) in Freud (1997).

4 See also Freud ([1920] 1990).

5 See, for instance, Katz (1976); Weeks (1977); Boswell (1980); Faderman (1981); Bray (1982); and D'Emilio (1983).

6 On the sex wars, see Vance (1992); Duggan and Hunter (2006); Halley (2006); and Rubin (2010).

7 I use the term 'women of colour feminism' not to name a monolithic or unitary body of thought but to designate the diverse, sometimes irreconcilable, body of insights produced by writers and activists who consider sexual administration in the context of racial and colonial power.

8 For two early instances, see Spillers (1987) and Hammonds (1994).

9 See also Sandoval (2000).

10 For these statistics, AmfAR (2016); on the persistence of HIV/AIDS in the Southern US, see Villarosa (2017).

11 For an overview, see Kaufman (1987).

12 For this critique, see Crimp (1987a) and Bersani (1987).

13 Austin defines performative language as those statements (vows, promises, bequeathals, etc.) that under the right conditions actually change the state of things in the world ([1955] 1962).

14 See Stryker (1994) and Prosser (1998).

15 See Halberstam (1998, 2005, 2018); Salamon ([2008] 2010); Preciado (2013); and Snorton (2017).

Chapter 2

1 Bray (2003: 146–50, 153–4, 167–8); Masten (2016: 69–82).

2 The word 'tribade' comes from the Greek *tribas* and *tribein*, 'to rub'. In early modern England, 'tribade' was an ambiguous

and expansive term: it could designate women who used their enlarged clitorises to rub or penetrate other women, or it could describe any woman who engaged in any sort of same-sex erotic activity (Traub 2002: 17).

3 On legal convictions and religious propaganda, see Bredbeck (1991); Betteridge (2002); Boes (2002); Clarke (2002); Naphy (2002); and Borris (2004). On indigenous sodomy as a justification for colonial violence, see Goldberg ([1992] 2010: 179–246, and 1996).

4 See also Hammond (2002).

5 On transgender performance, see Howard (1988); Jardine (1991); Karen Newman (1991); Goldberg ([1992] 2010); and Chess (2016).

6 Boswell (1994) argues that pre-modern liturgies indicate the possibility of same-sex marriage.

7 On women's incapacity for friendship, see Aristotle (1999: 8.7.1, 8.12.7); Cicero (1923: 13.46).

8 See Pequigney (1985); Sedgwick (1985); Fineman (1986); Smith (1991: 225–50); and Halpern (2002).

9 On the incorporation of classical friendship into companionate marriage, see Luxon (2005) and Sanchez (2011).

10 See Traub (1992: 117–44); Crawford (2009); Menon (2011b); Sanchez (2012); and Drouin (2009).

11 Traub italicizes *lesbian* to foreground its multiple meanings as 'a representational image, a rhetorical figure, a discursive effect, rather than a stable epistemological or historical category' (2002: 15).

12 'Molly house' was the term for male meeting places understood to facilitate homoerotic activities.

13 See Traub (2002: 17); Loomba (2002); and DiGangi (2011a: 67–80).

14 Quoted in Bray (1982: 20). See also Smith (1991: 173); Masten (2016: 86–93); and Goldberg (1991).

15 See also Butler (2000).

16 See also Barkan (1991); Stanivukovic (2000); and Orgel ([2004] 2011).

17 See Smith (1991: 199–200); Traub (1992); DiGangi (1997, 2011a); Masten (2016).

18 See Garber (1992); Traub (1992: 118–22); Orgel (1996); Jones and Stallybrass (2000); Fisher (2006).

19   For a critique of Laqueur's history of anatomy, see Traub (2002: 188–95).
20   On women's writing communities, see Coles (2008); Goldberg (1997); Traub (2002); Andreadis (2001); Lanser (2014); and Crawford (2014).

Chapter 3

1   OED s.v. 'homosexual' and 'heterosexual'.
2   See, for instance, Sedgwick (1990: 8, 31, 35, 45); Warner (1993: xxvi, and 1999: 10, 37–8, 7); Berlant and Warner (1995: 345–6); and Sharon Marcus (2005).
3   See also Traub (1992: 11–14) and Cohen (2003).
4   See Howard (1988), Jardine (1991), Karen Newman (1991), Orgel (1996) and Rackin (2005).
5   See also Goldberg (2000).
6   The scholarship is too copious to list in full; just a few of the works on medieval and early modern race, religion, travel and colonialism include Loomba (1989, 2002, 2007); Hall (1993, 1995); Hendricks and Parker (1995); Singh (2009); Cohen (2001); Little (2000, 2016); Vitkus (2003); Iyengar (2005); Burton (2005); Bartels (2008); Ian Smith (2009); Thompson (2008); and Eliav-Feldon, Isaac and Ziegler (2009). For primary sources on the presence of non-white persons in England and contemporary discussions of race, see Habib (2008); Loomba and Burton (2007); and Kauffman (2017). For discussions of the continued repercussions of early modern literary racial and colonial ideologies in contemporary culture, see Daileader (2005) and Thompson (2006, 2011).
7   Just a few examples include Bray (1982: 75), Parker (1995), Goldberg ([1992] 2010: 179–249) and Traub (1995).
8   See Loomba and Burton (2007), DiGangi (2011a) and Britton (2014).
9   See, for instance, Loomba (1989, 2002), MacDonald (2002), Iyengar (2005), Thompson (2008), Bovilsky (2008), Degenhardt (2010), Britton (2014), and Loomba and Sanchez (2016).
10   Just a few recent discussions of this point include Menon (2009), Varnado (2013), Traub (2016) and Masten (2016).

11 The *OED* is vague on this point, distinguishing without explanation between 'physical contact between individuals involving sexual stimulation; sexual activity or behavior' and acts 'relating to, tending towards, or invoking sexual intercourse, or other forms of physical contact' (Bromley and Stockton 2013: 11–12).

12 See Jones (2013: 89–110), Fisher (2013: 141–70), Guy-Bray (2013: 233–62) and Stockton (2013: 195–212).

13 Quoted by Varnado (2013: 47).

14 See also Goldberg on objections to the MLA talk in which his essay 'The Anus in Coriolanus' originated (Goldberg 2000).

15 See Parker (1996a), Leah Marcus (1996), Burckhardt ([1878] 1990) and Tillyard (1959).

16 New historicism was the dominant method of reading early modern literature in the 1980s and 1990s. While new historicism is not a uniform school of thought, those who practice it share the beliefs that literature cannot be isolated from the social, political and cultural situation in which it was produced and that literary texts are primary sources for the study of history. For overviews of new historicism see Veeser (1989), Gallagher and Greenblatt (2000), and Parvini (2017).

17 See Greenblatt (1986). For a detailed overview of psychoanalysis and Shakespeare studies, see Brown (2015).

18 See Traub (1992: 11–17 and 2015: 25–31), Marshall (2002), and Hammill (2000).

19 See Dinshaw (1999), Bhabha (1994) and Chakrabarty ([2000] 2009).

20 See also Grady and Hawkes (2007).

21 Dinshaw (2012) offers a similar analysis of the cultural productions of medieval studies.

22 See Harris (20109 and Felski (2015).

23 For this characterization, see Traub (2015: 64–5, 73–5) and Friedlander (2016: 4, 8–10).

Chapter 4

1 Pauline universalism purports to make salvation available to anyone who believes in Christ, regardless of ethnic or national background or the practice of particular rituals (such

as circumcision or dietary restrictions); global capitalism also posits a formal equality that claims to make economic opportunity available to all who embrace the gospel of the free market.

2   The imperial votaress is conventionally recognized as a figure for the Virgin Queen, Elizabeth I. For extended discussion, see Montrose (1996: 152–65).

3   Neely here quotes the physician André Du Laurens (1599: 119). Along with Du Laurens, Neely discusses other texts that treat love melancholy as a physical pathology, Jacques Ferrand's 1610 *Treatise on Lovesickness* and Robert Burton's *Anatomy of Melancholy*.

4   For an overview of this argument, see Stanivukovic (2000: 95–6).

5   Sinfield (2006: 67) has argued that Antonio is the character most hostile to Shylock. On the connection between sodomy and usury, see Kleinberg (1983) and Stockton (2017: 45–9). More generally, see Shapiro (1996).

6   There is a large body of work on this topic, but just a few examples are Karen Newman (1987: 19–33); Critchley and McCarthy (2004: 3–17); and Lim (2010: 355–82).

7   See, for instance, Parker (1995); Karen Newman ([1991] 2009: 38–58); Loomba (1989: 38–64, 2002: 91–111); Neill (1989: 383–412); and Callaghan (2000).

8   On this reading, see Smith (1991: 61) and Saunders (2004:151).

9   See also Matz (1999: 268–70).

10   On the relation between gender insubordination and political upheaval in the history plays, see Traub (1992: 50–70); Sinfield and Dollimore (1992: 109–42); Howard and Rackin (1997); and Schwarz (2000: 79–108).

11   On the homoeroticism of the history plays, see Goldberg ([1992] 2010); DiGangi (1997: 100–33, 2011b: 130–8); Howie (2011: 146–51); and Bach (2003: 220–45). The homoerotic valences of Hal's character, as critics have noted, are the foundation of Gus Van Sant's rendition of the play in *My Own Private Idaho*; see especially Goldberg (2003: 222–52), and the following chapter of this book.

12   See Derrida (1996: 3), quoted by Edelman (2011: 155).

13   See also Goldberg (2003: 111).

14   On the proliferation of fathers in *Hamlet*, see Garber (1987).

15   For earlier considerations of the political dilemmas posed by Shakespeare's centrality to humanist pedagogy, see also Sinfield (1985: 134–57) and Garber (1990).
16   As Freccero notes, this matter is literally part of books in the form of the 'animal skins of parchment on which the living dead of language finds its transcendence and for which Hamlet's brain is only, after all, a metaphor' (2011a: 173).

Chapter 5

1   See Lyotard (1979) and Jameson (1991).
2   On Jarman's disruption of the heritage tradition, see MacCabe (1992: 13).
3   On Wilcox's performance, see Ellis (2009: 67, 73–81) and Bennett (1996: 132).
4   For an overview, see Loomba (2002: 161–8).
5   See MacCabe (1992: 11–12); Zabus and Dwyer (1997: 365–6); and Chedgzoy (1995: 202–4).
6   As Menon argues, 'Sycorax has not only had illegitimate sex, but she also spawned an image of illegitimacy in Caliban' (2004: 152). See also Chedgzoy (1995: 202–4).
7   See also Benshoff and Griffin (2004); and Muñoz (1998: 127–38).
8   Rich notes that '"Puts the Homo back in Homicide" is the teaser for Tom Kalin's first feature, Swoon, but it could easily apply to Gregg Araki's newest, The Living End, as well' ([1992] 2013b: 27).
9   Along with Edward II and My Own Private Idaho, critics usually include in this group Todd Haynes' Poison (1990); Isaac Julien's Young Rebel Souls (1991); Jennie Livingston's Paris is Burning (1991); Christopher Munch's The Hours and Times (1991); Laurie Lynd's R.S.V.P. (1991); Tom Kalin's Swoon (1992); and Gregg Araki's The Living End (1992).
10   On critical debates about Edward's historical fortunes, and especially his death, see Haber (2009) and Masten (2016: 152–9).
11   On queer childhood, see Kathryn Bond Stockton (2009).
12   On the film's attempt to imagine queer kinship, see O'Dair (2015). On psychoanalysis and queer kinship more generally, see Butler (2000).

13   Quoted by Fuller (2008).
14   In *2 Henry IV*, the corresponding lines are 'God save thee, my sweet boy!' and 'I know thee not, old man: fall to thy prayers' (5.5.43, 47).
15   On Luhrmann's play with Shakespeare as icon, see Worthen (1998).
16   As Hodgdon observes, 'one of the film's central tropes [is] the desire for a private, utopian space within a threatening social world' forged by 'adult indifference and betrayal, of loss, fragmentation, and despair' (1999: 92).
17   For a more optimist reading of the racial and ethnic multiplicity of the film, see Hodgdon (1999: 96–8).
18   '*Scelera non ulsciceris / nisi uincis*' (Seneca, *Thyestes*, 195–6).
19   Ovid's Tereus raped his sister-in-law Philomela and cut out her tongue; when her sister Procne learned this, she killed the offspring of her marriage to Tereus, her own son Itys, and fed him to his father. Shakespeare's Chiron and Demetrius cut off Lavinia's hands as well as her tongue after raping her; Titus feeds them both to their mother, Tamora, then kills her. On the gender politics of Shakespeare's intertexts, see Jane Newman (1994).
20   On Taymor's use of stereotypes, see McCandless (2002). On the convergence of racial otherness in the Goths and the Moors, see Royster (2000).
21   On this point, see Eng (2010).
22   For the original act, see Local Government Act 1988 c. 9, Part IV, Section 28; available at: www.legislation.gov.uk/ ukpga/1988/9/section/28/enacted (accessed 7 April 2018). On the relation between the representation of young Edward III as queer and Jarman's activism, see Parsons (2014).

Conclusion

1   See *WND* (2016); *The College Fix* (2016); Farberov (2016); and Richardson (2016).
2   For critiques of periodizing and professional approaches to literature, see Hayot (2011); Dinshaw (2012); Underwood (2013); and Felski (2015: 151–85).

REFERENCES

Abelove, Henry (2003), *Deep Gossip*, Minneapolis: University of Minnesota Press.

Abelove, Henry, Michèle Aina Barale and David M. Halperin, eds (1993), *The Gay and Lesbian Studies Reader*, New York: Routledge.

Aebischer, Pascale (2014), *Shakespeare's Violated Bodies: Stage and Screen Performance*, Cambridge: Cambridge University Press.

Agamben, Giorgio (1998), *Homo Sacer: Sovereign Power and Bare Life*, trans. D. Heller-Roazen, Stanford, CA: Stanford University Press.

Ahmed, Sara (2006), *Queer Phenomenology*, Durham, NC: Duke University Press.

AmFAR (2016), 'Thirty Years of HIV/AIDS: Snapshots of an Epidemic', amfAR, The Foundation for AIDS Research. Available online: www.amfar.org/Thirty-Years-of-HIV/AIDS-Snapshots-of-an-Epidemic/ (accessed 2 March 2018).

Andreadis, Harriett (2001), *Sappho in Early Modern England: Female Same-Sex Literary Erotics, 1550–1714*, Chicago: University of Chicago Press.

Anzaldúa, Gloria (1987), *Borderlands/La Frontera: The New Mestiza*, San Francisco, CA: Aunt Lute.

Aristotle (1981), *Politics*, trans. T. A. Sinclair, ed. Trevor J. Saunders, London: Penguin.

Aristotle (1999), *Nichomachean Ethics*, trans. and ed. Terence Irwin, Indianapolis, IN: Hackett.

Arroyo, José (1993), 'Death, Desire, and Identity', in Joseph Wilson and Angelia R. Wilson (eds), *Activating Theory*, 70–96, London: Lawrence and Wishart.

Austin, J. L. ([1955] 1962), *How to Do Things with Words*, eds J. O. Urmson and Marina Sbisà, Oxford: Clarendon Press.

Bach, Rebecca Ann (2003), 'Manliness before Individualism: Masculinity, Effeminacy, and Homoerotics in Shakespeare's History Plays', in Richard Dutton and Jean Elizabeth Howard (eds), *A Companion to Shakespeare's Works*, vol. 2, 220–45, Oxford: Blackwell.

Bach, Rebecca Ann (2007), *Shakespeare and Renaissance Literature Before Heterosexuality*, Basingstoke: Palgrave.

Bacon, Francis ([1597] 1994), *Essays*, ed. Michael J. Hawkins, London: Everyman.

Barkan, Leonard (1991), *Transuming Passion: Ganymede and the Erotics of Humanism*, Stanford, CA: Stanford University Press.

Bartels, Emily C. (2008), *Speaking of the Moor: From Alcazar to Othello*, Philadelphia: University of Pennsylvania Press.

Barthes, Roland ([1967] 1977), 'The Death of the Author', in Roland Barthes, *Image, Music, Text*, 142–8, trans. Stephen Heath, New York: Hill and Wang.

Barthes, Roland ([1973] 1974), *S/Z*, trans. Richard Miller, Malden, MA: Blackwell.

Bate, Jonathan (2000), 'A Shakespeare Tale Whose Time Has Come', *New York Times*, 2 January. Available online: www.nytimes.com/2000/01/02/movies/film-a-shakespeare-tale-whose-time-has-come.html (accessed 18 February 2018).

Belsey, Catherine (1995), 'Love as Trompe-l'oeil: Taxonomies of Desire in *Venus and Adonis*', *Shakespeare Quarterly*, 46 (3): 257–76.

Bennett, Susan (1996), *Performing Nostalgia: Shifting Shakespeare and the Contemporary Past*, London: Routledge.

Benshoff, Harry and Sean Griffin, eds (2004), *Queer Cinema: The Film Reader*, New York: Routledge.

Berlant, Lauren (1997), *The Queen of America Goes to Washington City: Essays on Sex and Citizenship*, Durham, NC: Duke University Press.

Berlant, Lauren (1998), 'Poor Eliza', *American Literature*, 70 (3): 635–68.

Berlant, Lauren (2001), 'Love, A Queer Feeling', in Tim Dean and Christopher Lane (eds), *Homosexuality and Psychoanalysis*, 432–51, Chicago: University of Chicago Press.

Berlant, Lauren (2011), *Cruel Optimism*, Durham, NC: Duke University Press.

Berlant, Lauren and Michael Warner (1995), 'What Does Queer Theory Teach Us about *X*?' *PMLA*, 110 (3): 343–9.

Berlant, Lauren and Michael Warner (1998), 'Sex in Public', *Critical Inquiry*, 24 (2): 547–66.

Bersani, Leo (1987), 'Is the Rectum a Grave?' *October*, 43 (Winter): 197–222.

Bersani, Leo (1995), *Homos*, Cambridge, MA: Harvard University Press.

Betteridge, Tom (2002), 'The Place of Sodomy in the Historical Writings of John Bale and John Foxe', in Tom Betteridge (ed.), *Sodomy in Early Modern Europe*, 11–26, Manchester: Manchester University Press.

Bhabha, Homi (1994), *The Location of Culture*, London: Routledge.

Bly, Mary (2000), *Queer Virgins and Virgin Queans on the Early Modern Stage*, Oxford: Oxford University Press.

Boehrer, Bruce (2004), 'Economies of Desire in *A Midsummer Night's Dream*', *Shakespeare Studies*, 32: 99–117.

Boes, Maria R. (2002), 'On Trial for Sodomy in Early Modern Germany', in Tom Betteridge (ed.), *Sodomy in Early Modern Europe*, 27–45, Manchester: Manchester University Press.

Booth, Stephen (1977), *Shakespeare's Sonnets*, New Haven, CT: Yale University Press.

Borris, Kenneth, ed. (2004), *Same-Sex Desire in the English Renaissance: A Sourcebook of Texts, 1470–1650*, London: Routledge.

Boswell, John (1980), *Christianity, Social Tolerance, and Homosexuality: Gay People in Western Europe from the Beginning of the Christian Era to the Fourteenth Century*, Chicago: University of Chicago Press.

Boswell, John (1994), *Same-Sex Unions in Premodern Europe*, New York: Villiard Books.

Bovilsky, Laura (2008), *Barbarous Play: Race on the English Renaissance Stage*, Minneapolis: University of Minnesota Press.

Boyarin, Daniel (2011), 'Othello's Penis; or, Shakespeare in the Closet', in Madhavi Menon (ed.), *Shakesqueer: A Queer Companion to the Complete Works of Shakespeare*, 254–62, Durham, NC: Duke University Press.

Bray, Alan (1982), *Homosexuality in Renaissance England*, Boston, MA: Gay Men's Press.

Bray, Alan (2003), *The Friend*, Chicago: University of Chicago Press.

Bredbeck, Gregory (1991), *Sodomy and Interpretation*, Ithaca, NY: Cornell University Press.

Britton, Dennis (2014), *Becoming Christian: Race, Reformation, and Early Modern English Romance*, New York: Fordham University Press.

Bromley, James M. (2012), *Intimacy and Sexuality in the Age of Shakespeare*, Cambridge: Cambridge University Press.

Bromley, James M. (2013), 'Rimming the Renaissance', in James M. Bromley and Will Stockton (eds), *Sex Before 'Sex': Figuring the Act in Early Modern England*, 171–94, Minneapolis: University of Minnesota Press.

Bromley, James M. (2016), 'Cruisy Historicism: Sartorial Extravagance and Public Sex Culture in Ben Jonson's *Every Man Out of His Humor*', *Journal for Early Modern Cultural Studies*, 16 (2): 21–58.

Bromley, James M. and Will Stockton (2013), 'Introduction: Figuring Early Modern Sex', in James M. Bromley and Will Stockton (eds), *Sex Before 'Sex': Figuring the Act in Early Modern England*, 1–23, Minneapolis: University of Minnesota Press.

Brown, Carolyn E. (1994), 'The Wooing of Duke Vincentio and Isabella of *Measure for Measure*: "The Image of It Gives [Them] Content"', *Shakespeare Studies*, 22: 189–219.

Brown, Carolyn E. (2015), *Shakespeare and Psycholanalytic Theory*, London: Bloombury.

Burckhardt, Jacob ([1878] 1990), *The Civilization of the Renaissance in Italy*, ed. Peter Murray, London: Penguin.

Burton, Jonathan (2005), *Traffic and Turning: Islam and English Drama, 1579–1624*, Wilmington: University of Delaware Press.

Butler, Judith (1990), *Gender Trouble: Feminism and the Subversion of Identity*, New York: Routledge.

Butler, Judith (1993), *Bodies that Matter: On the Discursive Limits of 'Sex'*, New York: Routledge.

Butler, Judith (1994), 'Against Proper Objects. Introduction', *differences*, 6 (2–3): 1–26.

Butler, Judith (1998), 'Afterword', in Sally R. Munt (ed.), *Butch/Femme: Inside Lesbian Gender*, 225–230, London: Cassell.

Butler, Judith (2000), *Antigone's Claim: Kinship Between Life and Death*, New York: Columbia University Press.

Butler, Judith (2004), *Undoing Gender*, New York: Routledge.

Callaghan, Dympna (2000), *Shakespeare Without Women: Representing Gender and Race on the Renaissance Stage*, London: Routledge.

Canby, Vincent (1980), 'Movie Review: The Tempest', *New York Times*, 22 September. Available online: www.nytimes.com/movie/review?res=9A07EFD81238F931A1575AC0A966948260 (accessed 18 February 2018).

Carby, Hazel V. (1982), 'White Woman Listen!: Black Feminism and the Boundaries of Sisterhood', in Center for Contemporary

Cultural Studies (ed.), *The Empire Strikes Back: Race and Racism in 70's Britain*, 212–15, Hutchinson: Birmingham Centre for Contemporary Cultural Studies.

Chakrabarty, Dipesh ([2000] 2009), *Provincializing Europe: Postcolonial Thought and Historical Difference*, Princeton, NJ: Princeton University Press.

Chedgzoy, Kate (1995), *Shakespeare's Queer Children: Sexual Politics and Renaissance Culture*, Manchester: Manchester University Press.

Chen, Mel (2012), *Animacies: Biopolitics, Racial Mattering, and Queer Affect*, Durham, NC: Duke University Press.

Chess, Simone (2016), *Male to Female Crossdressing in Early Modern English Literature: Gender, Performance, and Queer Relations*, New York: Routledge.

Cicero (1923), *On Old Age. On Friendship. On Divination*, trans. W. A. Falconer, Loeb Classical Library 154, Cambridge, MA: Harvard University Press.

Clarke, Danielle (2002), '"The Sovereign's Vice Begets the Subject's Error": The Duke Of Buckingham, "Sodomy" and Narratives Of Edward II, 1622–28', in Tom Betteridge (ed.), *Sodomy in Early Modern Europe*, 46–64, Manchester: Manchester University Press.

Cohen, Jeffrey J. (2001), 'On Saracen Enjoyment: Some Fantasies of Race in Late Medieval France and England', *Journal of Medieval and Early Modern Studies*, 31 (1): 113–46.

Cohen, Jeffrey J. (2003), *Medieval Identity Machines*, Minneapolis: University of Minnesota Press.

Coke, Edward (1644), *The Third Part of the Institutes of the Laws of England*, London.

Coles, Kimberly Anne (2008), *Religion, Reform, and Women's Writing in Early Modern England*, Cambridge: Cambridge University Press.

College Fix, The (2016), 'U. Penn Students Remove Shakespeare Portrait, Replace It with Black Lesbian Feminist Poet', 12 December. Available online: www.thecollegefix.com/post/30332/ (accessed 28 February 2018).

Combahee River Collective ([1977] 1982), 'A Black Feminist Statement', in Gloria T. Hull, Patricia Bell Scott and Barbara Smith (eds), *All the Women Are White, All the Blacks Are Men, But Some of Us Are Brave*, 13–22, Old Westbury, NY: The Feminist Press.

Corum, Richard (1996), 'Henry's Desires', in Carla Freccero and Louise Fradenberg (eds), *Premodern Sexualities*, 71–98, New York: Routledge.

Crawford, Julie (2009), 'Women's Secretaries', in Stephen Guy-Bray, Vin Nardizzi and Will Stockton (eds), *Queer Renaissance Historiography: Backward Gaze*, 111–34, Burlington, VT: Ashgate.

Crawford, Julie (2014), *Mediatrix: Women, Politics, and Literary Production in Early Modern England*, Oxford: Oxford University Press.

Crewe, Jonathan (1999), 'Introduction', in *William Shakespeare: The Narrative Poems*, xxxv–xxxvii, New York: Pelican.

Crimp, Douglas (1987a), 'How to Have Promiscuity in an Epidemic', *October*, 43 (Winter): 237–71.

Crimp, Douglas (1987b), 'Introduction', *October*, 43 (Winter): 3–16.

Critchley, Simon and Tom McCarthy (2004), 'Universal Shylockery: Money and Morality in *The Merchant of Venice*', *diacritics*, 34 (1): 3–17.

Cvetkovich, Ann (2003), *An Archive of Feelings: Trauma, Sexuality and Lesbian Public Cultures*, Durham, NC: Duke University Press.

Cvetkovich, Ann (2012), *Depression: A Public Feeling*, Durham, NC: Duke University Press.

D'Emilio, John (1983), *Sexual Politics, Sexual Communities: The Making of a Homosexual Minority in the United States, 1940–1970*, Chicago: University of Chicago Press.

Daileader, Celia R. (2005), *Racism, Misogyny, and the Othello Myth: Inter-racial Couples from Shakespeare to Spike Lee*, Cambridge: Cambridge University Press.

Daniel, Drew (2011), 'Scrambling Harry and Sampling Hal', in Madhavi Menon (ed.), *Shakesqueer: A Queer Companion to the Complete Works of Shakespeare*, 121–9, Durham, NC: Duke University Press.

Davidson, N. S. (2002), 'Sodomy in Early Modern Venice', in Tom Betteridge (ed.), *Sodomy in Early Modern Europe*, 65–111, Mancester: Manchester University Press.

De Grazia, Margreta ([1994] 1999), 'The Scandal of Sonnets', in James Schiffer (ed.), *Shakespeare's Sonnets: Critical Essays*, 89–112, New York: Garland.

De Lauretis, Teresa (1991), 'Queer Theory: Lesbian and Gay Sexualities, An Introduction', *differences*, 3 (2): iii–xviii.

De Lauretis, Teresa (1994), 'Habit Changes', *differences*, 6 (2–3): 296–313.

De Man, Paul (1986), *The Resistance to Theory*, Minneapolis: University of Minnesota Press.

Degenhardt, Jane Hwang (2010), *Islamic Conversion and Christian Resistance on the Early Modern Stage*, Edinburgh: Edinburgh University Press.

Delany, Samuel R. (1999), *Times Square Red, Times Square Blue*, New York: New York University Press.

Derrida, Jacques ([1972] 1983), *Dissemination*, trans. Barbara Johnson, Chicago: University of Chicago Press.

Derrida, Jacques ([1972] 1985), *Margins of Philosophy*, trans. Alan Bass, Chicago: University of Chicago Press.

Derrida, Jacques (1996), *Archive Fever: A Freudian Impression*, trans. Eric Penowitz, Chicago: University of Chicago Press.

DiGangi, Mario (1997), *The Homoerotics of Early Modern Drama*, Cambridge: Cambridge University Press.

DiGangi, Mario (2007), 'Queer Theory, Historicism, and Early Modern Sexualities', *Criticism*, 48 (1): 129–42.

DiGangi, Mario (2011a), *Sexual Types: Embodiment, Agency, and Dramatic Character from Shakespeare to Shirley*, Philadelphia: University of Pennsylvania Press.

DiGangi, Mario (2011b), 'Wounded Alpha Bad Boy Soldier', in Madhavi Menon (ed.), *Shakesqueer: A Queer Companion to the Complete Works of Shakespeare*, 130–8, Durham, NC: Duke University Press.

Dinshaw, Carolyn (1999), *Getting Medieval: Sexualities and Communities, Pre- and Postmodern*, Durham, NC: Duke University Press.

Dinshaw, Carolyn (2012), *How Soon Is Now?: Medieval Texts, Amateur Readers, and the Queerness of Time*, Durham, NC: Duke University Press.

Dolan, Frances E. (2017), 'Tracking the Petty Traitor across Genres', in Patricia Fumerton and Anita Guerrini (eds), *Ballads and Broadsides in Britain, 1500–1800*, New York: Routledge.

Dollimore, Jonathan (1990), 'Shakespeare, Cultural Materialism, Feminism and Marxist Humanism', *New Literary History*, 21 (3): 471–93.

Dollimore, Jonathan (1991), *Sexual Dissidence: Augustine to Wilde, Freud to Foucault*, Oxford: Oxford University Press.

Drouin, Jennifer (2009), 'Diana's Band: Safe Spaces, Publics, and Early Modern Lesbianism', in Stephen Guy-Bray, Vin Nardizzi and Will Stockton (eds), *Queer Renaissance Historiography: Backward Gaze*, 85–110, Burlington VT: Ashgate.

Duberman, Martin (1994), *Stonewall*, New York: Plume Books.

Duberman, Martin, Martha Vicinus and George Chauncey (1990), 'Introduction', in Martin Duberman, Martha Vicinus and George Chauncey (eds), *Hidden From History: Reclaiming the Gay and Lesbian Past*, 1–13, New York: Meridian.

Dugan, Holly (2013), 'Aping Rape: Animal Ravishment and Sexual Knowledge in Early Modern England', in James M. Bromley and Will Stockton (eds), *Sex Before 'Sex': Figuring the Act in Early Modern England*, 213–32, Minneapolis: University of Minnesota Press.

Duggan, Lisa (2000), *Sapphic Slashers: Sex, Violence, and American Modernity*, Durham, NC: Duke University Press.

Duggan, Lisa (2003), *The Twilight of Equality: Neoliberalism, Cultural Politics, and the Attack on Democracy*, Boston, MA: Beacon Press.

Duggan, Lisa (2015), 'Queer Complacency without Empire'. Available online: https://bullybloggers.wordpress.com/2015/09/22/queer-complacency-without-empire/ (accessed 1 October 2017).

Duggan, Lisa and Nan D. Hunter (2006), *Sex Wars: Sexual Dissent and Political Culture*, New York: Routledge.

Edelman, Lee (2004), *No Future: Queer Theory and the Death Drive*, Durham, NC: Duke University Press.

Edelman, Lee (2011), 'Against Survival: Queerness in a Time That's Out of Joint', *Shakespeare Quarterly*, 62 (2): 148–69.

Edward II (1991), [Film] Dir. Derek Jarman, UK: BBC Films.

Eliav-Feldon, Miriam, Benjamin Isaac and Joseph Ziegler, eds (2009), *The Origins of Racism in the West*, Cambridge: Cambridge University Press.

Ellis, Jim (2001), 'Conjuring *The Tempest*: Derek Jarman and the Spectacle of Redemption', *GLQ*, 7 (2): 265–84.

Ellis, Jim (2009), *Derek Jarman's Angelic Conversations*, Minneapolis: University of Minnesota Press.

Empson, William ([1935] 1950), *Some Versions of Pastoral*, London: New Impressions.

Eng, David (2001), *Racial Castration: Managing Masculinity in Asian America*, Durham, NC: Duke University Press.

Eng, David (2010), *The Feeling of Kinship: Queer Liberalism and the Racialization of Intimacy*, Durham, NC: Duke University Press.

Eng, David, Jack (Judith) Halberstam, and José Esteban Muñoz (2005), 'What's Queer about Queer Studies Now?' *Social Text*, 23 (3–4): 1–17.

Enterline, Lynn (2012), *Shakespeare's Schoolroom: Rhetoric, Discipline, Emotion*, Philadelphia: University of Pennsylvania Press.

Epps, Brad (2001), 'The Fetish of Fluidity', in Tim Dean and Christopher Lane (eds), *Homosexuality and Psychoanalysis*, 412–31, Chicago: University of Chicago Press.

Erickson, Peter and Kim F. Hall (2016), '"A New Scholarly Song": Rereading Early Modern Race', *Shakespeare Quarterly*, 67 (1): 1–13.

Evans, Maurice (1989), 'Introduction', in Maurice Evans (ed.), *The Narrative Poems by William Shakespeare*, London: Penguin.

Faderman, Lillian (1981), *Surpassing the Love of Men: Romantic Friendship and Love Between Women from the Renaissance to the Present*, New York: Morrow.

Farberov, Snejana (2016), 'Students Remove Shakespeare Portrait at UPenn and Replace It with Photo of Black Lesbian Writer Amid Push for Diversity at English Department', *The Daily Mail*, 12 December. Available online: www.dailymail.co.uk/news/article-4026576/Students-remove-Shakespeare-portrait-UPenn-replace-photo-black-lesbian-writer-amid-push-diversity-English-department.html (accessed 28 February 2018).

Felski, Rita (2015), *The Limits of Critique*, Chicago: University of Chicago Press.

Ferguson, Gary (2016), *Same-Sex Marriage in Renaissance Rome: Sexuality, Identity, and Community in Early Modern Europe*, Ithaca, NY: Cornell University Press.

Ferguson, Margaret W. (1985), '*Hamlet*: Letters and Spirits', in Patricia Parker and Geoffrey Hartman (eds), *Shakespeare and the Question of Theory*, 292–309, London: Methuen.

Ferguson, Roderick A. (2004), *Aberrations in Black: Toward a Queer of Color Critique*, Minneapolis: University of Minnesota Press.

Ferguson, Roderick A. (2012), *The Reorder of Things: The University and Its Pedagogies of Minority Difference*, Minneapolis: University of Minnesota Press.

Fineman, Joel (1986), *Shakespeare's Perjur'd Eye: The Invention of Poetic Subjectivity in the Sonnets*, Berkeley: University of California Press.

Fisher, Will (2006), *Materializing Gender in Early Modern Literature and Culture*, Cambridge: Cambridge University Press.

Fisher, Will (2009), 'A Hundred Years of Queering the Renaissance', in Stephen Guy-Bray, Vin Nardizzi and Will Stockton (eds), *Queer Renaissance Historiography: Backward Gaze*, 13–40, Burlington, VT: Ashgate.

Fisher, Will (2013), 'The Erotics of Chin Chucking in Seventeenth-Century England', in James M. Bromley and Will Stockton (eds), *Sex Before 'Sex': Figuring the Act in Early Modern England*, 141–70, Minneapolis: University of Minnesota Press.

Foucault, Michel ([1969] 1977), 'What is an Author?' in Donald F. Bouchard (ed.), *Language, Counter-Memory, Practice*, 113–38, trans. Donald F. Bouchard and Sherry Simon, Ithaca, NY: Cornell University Press.

Foucault, Michel ([1972] 1980), 'Truth and Power', in Colin Gordon (ed.), *Power/Knowledge*, 109–33, New York: Pantheon.

Foucault, Michel ([1978] 1990), *The History of Sexuality, Volume 1: An Introduction*, New York: Vintage.

Foucault, Michel (2003), *Abnormal: Lectures at the Collège de France, 1974–1975*, trans. Graham Burchell, New York: Picador.

Fradenburg, Louise and Carla Freccero (1996a), 'Preface', in Louise Fradenburg and Carla Freccero (eds), *Premodern Sexualities*, vii–xii, New York: Routledge.

Fradenburg, Louise and Carla Freccero (1996b), 'Introduction: Caxton, Foucault, and the Pleasures of History', in Louise Fradenburg and Carla Freccero (eds), *Premodern Sexualities*, xiii–xxiv, New York: Routledge.

Freccero, Carla (1994), 'Practicing Queer Philology with Marguerite de Navarre: Nationalism and the Castigation of Desire', in Jonathan Goldberg (ed.), *Queering the Renaissance*, 107–23, Durham, NC: Duke University Press.

Freccero, Carla (2006), *Queer/Early/Modern*, Durham, NC: Duke University Press.

Freccero, Carla (2011a), 'Forget *Hamlet*', *Shakespeare Quarterly*, 62 (2): 170–3.

Freccero, Carla (2011b), 'Romeo and Juliet Love Death', in Madhavi Menon (ed.), *Shakesqueer: A Queer Companion to the Complete Works of Shakespeare*, 302–8, Durham, NC: Duke University Press.

Freccero, Carla (2016), 'Tangents (of Desire)', *Journal for Early Modern Cultural Studies*, 16 (2): 91–105.

Freeman, Elizabeth (2010), *Time Binds: Queer Temporalities, Queer Histories*, Durham, NC: Duke University Press.

Freud, Sigmund ([1905] 1975), *Three Essays on the Theory of Sexuality*, trans. James Strachey, New York: Basic Books.

Freud, Sigmund ([1920] 1966), *Introductory Lectures on Psychoanalysis*, trans. James Strachey, New York: Norton.

Freud, Sigmund ([1920] 1990), *Beyond the Pleasure Principle*, trans. James Strachey, New York: Norton.

Freud, Sigmund ([1929] 1963), *Civilization and Its Discontents*, trans. James Strachey, New York: Norton.

Freud, Sigmund (1963), *General Psychological Theory*, ed. Philip Rieff, trans. James Strachey, New York: Scribner.

Freud, Sigmund (1997), *Sexuality and the Psychology of Love*, ed. Philip Rieff, trans. James Strachey, New York: Simon and Schuster.

Friedlander, Ari (2016), 'Introduction: Desiring History and Historicizing Desire', *Journal for Early Modern Cultural Studies*, 16 (2): 21–58.

Fuller, Graham (2008), 'Gus Van Sant: Swimming Against the Current', *Focus Features*, 29 July. Available online: http://focusfeatures.com/article/gus_van_sant__swimming_against_the_current (accessed 16 February 2018).

Gajowski, Evelyn (2009), 'The Presence of the Past', in Evelyn Gajowski (ed.), *Presentism, Gender, and Sexuality in Shakespeare*, 1–22, New York: Palgrave.

Gallagher, Catherine and Stephen Greenblatt (2000), *Practicing New Historicism*, Chicago: University of Chicago Press.

Garber, Marjorie (1987), *Shakespeare's Ghost Writers: Literature as Uncanny Causality*, London: Methuen.

Garber, Marjorie (1990), 'Shakespeare as Fetish', *Shakespeare Quarterly*, 41 (2): 242–50.

Garber, Marjorie (1992), *Vested Interests: Crossdressing and Cultural Anxiety*, New York: Routledge.

Garrison, John (2014), *Friendship and Queer Theory in the Renaissance*, New York: Routledge.

Gehl, Robert (2016), 'Ivy League Students Pull Shakespeare Painting, Replace With Black Female Poet', *The Federalist Papers*, 14 December. Available online: http://thefederalistpapers.org/us/ivy-league-students-pull-shakespeare-painting-replace-with-black-female-poet (accessed 28 February 2018).

Gil, Daniel Juan (2006), *Before Intimacy: Asocial Sexuality in Early Modern England*, Minneapolis: University of Minnesota Press.

Gilligan, Carol ([1982] 2003), *In a Different Voice: Psychological Theory and Women's Development*, Cambridge, MA: Harvard University Press.

Goldberg, Jonathan (1990), *Writing Matter: From the Hands of the English Renaissance*, Stanford, CA: Stanford University Press.

Goldberg, Jonathan (1991), 'Sodomy and Society: The Case of Christopher Marlowe', in David Scott Kastan and Peter Stallybrass (eds), *Staging the Renaissance: Reinterpretations of Elizabethan and Jacobean Drama*, 75–82, New York: Routledge.

Goldberg, Jonathan ([1992] 2010), *Sodometries: Renaissance Texts, Modern Sexualities*, New York: Fordham University Press.

Goldberg, Jonathan (1993), 'Sodomy in the New World: Anthropologies Old and New', in Michael Warner (ed.), *Fear of a Queer Planet: Queer Politics and Social Theory*, 3–18, Minneapolis: University of Minnesota Press.

Goldberg, Jonathan (1994a), '*Romeo and Juliet*'s Open Rs', in Jonathan Goldberg (ed.), *Queering the Renaissance*, 218–35, Durham, NC: Duke University Press.

Goldberg, Jonathan, ed. (1994b), *Queering the Renaissance*, Durham, NC: Duke University Press.

Goldberg, Jonathan (1996), 'The History that Will Be', in Carla Freccero and Louise Fradenberg (eds), *Premodern Sexualities*, 1–21, New York: Routledge.

Goldberg, Jonathan (1997), *Desiring Women Writing: English Renaissance Examples*, Stanford, CA: Stanford University Press.

Goldberg, Jonathan (2000), 'The Anus in Coriolanus', in Carla Mazzio and Douglas Trevor (eds), *Historicism, Psychoanalysis, and Early Modern Culture*, 260–71, New York: Routledge.

Goldberg, Jonathan (2003), *Shakespeare's Hand*, Minneapolis: University of Minnesota Press.

Goldberg, Jonathan (2011), 'After Thoughts', in Janet Halley and Andrew Parker (eds), *After Sex? On Writing Since Queer Theory*, 34–54, Durham, NC: Duke University Press.

Goldberg, Jonathan and Madhavi Menon (2005), 'Queering History', *PMLA*, 120 (5): 1608–17.

Grady, Hugh and Terence Hawkes, eds (2007), *Presentist Shakespeares*, New York: Routledge.

Greenblatt, Stephen (1986), 'Psychoanalysis and Renaissance Culture', in Patricia Parker and David Quint (eds), *Literary Theory, Renaissance Texts*, 210–24, Baltimore: Johns Hopkins University Press.

Guy-Bray, Stephen (2002), *Homoerotic Space: The Poetics of Loss in Renaissance Literature*, Toronto: University of Toronto Press.

Guy-Bray, Stephen (2009), *Against Reproduction: Where Renaissance Texts Come From*, Toronto: University of Toronto Press.

Guy-Bray, Stephen (2011), 'The Gayest Play Ever', in Madhavi Menon (ed.), *Shakesqueer: A Queer Companion to the Complete Works of Shakespeare*, 139–45, Durham, NC: Duke University Press.

Guy-Bray, Stephen (2013), 'Animal, Vegetable, Sexual: Metaphor in John Donne's "Sappho to Philaenis" and Andrew Marvell's "The Garden"', in James M. Bromley and Will Stockton (eds), *Sex Before 'Sex': Figuring the Act in Early Modern England*, 195–212, Minneapolis: University of Minnesota Press.

Guy-Bray, Stephen, Vin Nardizzi and Will Stockton (2009), 'Queer Renaissance Historiography: Backward Gaze', in Vin Nardizzi, Stephen Guy-Bray and Will Stockton (eds), *Queer Renaissance Historiography: Backward Gaze*, 1–12, Burlington, VT: Ashgate.

Haber, Judith (2009), *Desire and Dramatic Form in Early Modern England*, Cambridge: Cambridge University Press.

Habib, Imtiaz (2008), *Black Lives in the English Archives, 1500–1677: Imprints of the Invisible*, Burlington, VT: Ashgate.

Halberstam, Jack (2015), 'Straight Eye for the Queer Theorist – A Review of "Queer Theory Without Normativity"', *Bully Bloggers*, 12 September. Available online: https://bullybloggers. wordpress.com/2015/09/12/straight-eye-for-the-queer-theorist-a-review-of-queer-theory-without-antinormativity-by-jack-halberstam/ (accessed 1 October 2017).

Halberstam, Jack (2018), *Trans*: A Quick and Quirky Account of Gender Variability*, Oakland: University of California Press.

Halberstam, Jack [Judith] (1998), *Female Masculinity*, Durham, NC: Duke University Press.

Halberstam, Jack [Judith] (2005), *In a Queer Time and Place*, New York: New York University Press.

Halberstam, Jack [Judith] (2011), *The Queer Art of Failure*, Durham, NC: Duke University Press.

Hall, Kim F. (1993), 'Reading What Isn't There: "Black" Studies in Early Modern England', *Stanford Humanities Review*, 3 (1): 22–33.

Hall, Kim F. (1995), *Things of Darkness: Economies of Race and Gender in Early Modern England*, Ithaca, NY: Cornell University Press.

Halley, Janet (1994), '*Bowers v. Hardwick* in the Renaissance', in Jonathan Goldberg (ed.), *Queering the Renaissance*, 15–39, Durham, NC: Duke University Press.

Halley, Janet (2006), *Split Decisions: How and Why to Take a Break from Feminism*, Princeton, NJ: Princeton University Press.

Halley, Janet and Andrew Parker, eds (2011), *After Sex? On Writing Since Queer Theory*, Durham, NC: Duke University Press.

Halperin, David M. (1993), 'Is There a History of Sexuality?' in Henry Abelove, Michèle Aina Barale and David M. Halperin (eds), *The Gay and Lesbian Studies Reader*, 416–31, New York: Routledge.

Halperin, David M. (1995), *Saint Foucault: Towards a Gay Hagiography*, Oxford: Oxford University Press.

Halperin, David M. (2003), 'The Normalization of Queer Theory', *Journal of Homosexuality*, 45 (2/3/4): 339–43.

Halpern, Richard (2002), *Shakespeare's Perfume: Sodomy and Sublimity in the Sonnets, Wilde, Freud, and Lacan*, Philadelphia: University of Pennsylvania Press.

Hammill, Graham (2000), *Sexuality and Form: Caravaggio, Marlowe, and Bacon*, Chicago: University of Chicago Press.

Hammond, Paul (2002), *Figuring Sex Between Men from Shakespeare to Rochester*, Oxford: Oxford University Press.

Hammonds, Evelynn (1994), 'Black (W)holes and the Geometry of Black Female Sexuality', *differences*, 6 (2–3): 126–45.

Harper, Phillip Brian, Anne McClintock, José Esteban Muñoz and Trish Rosen (1997), 'Queer Transexions of Race, Nation, and Gender: An Introduction', *Social Text*, 52/53 (Fall/Winter): 1–4.

Harris, Jonathan Gil (2009), *Untimely Matter in the Time of Shakespeare*, Philadelphia: University of Pennsylvania Press.

Hayot, Eric (2011), 'Against Periodization; or, on Institutional Time', *New Literary History*, 42 (4): 739–56.

Hemmings, Clare (2011), *Why Stories Matter: The Political Grammar of Feminist Theory*, Durham, NC: Duke University Press.

Hendricks, Margo and Patricia Parker, eds (1994), *Women', Race', and Writing in the Early Modern Period*, London: Routledge.

Heng, Geraldine (2011), 'The Invention of Race in the European Middle Ages I: Race Studies, Modernity, and the Middle Ages', *Literature Compass*, 8 (5): 315–31.

Hinson, Hal (1991), 'My Own Private Idaho', *Washington Post*, 18 October. Available online: www.washingtonpost.com/wp-srv/style/longterm/movies/videos/myownprivateidahorhinson_a0a711.htm (accessed 18 February 2018).

Hocquenghem, Guy ([1972] 1993), *Homosexual Desire*, 2nd edn, trans. Daniella Dangoor, Durham, NC: Duke University Press.

Hodgdon, Barbara (1999), '*William Shakespeare's Romeo + Juliet*: Everything's Nice in America?', *Shakespeare Survey*, 52:88–98.

Holden, Stephen (1999), 'It's a Sort of Family Dinner, Your Majesty', *New York Times*, 24 December. Available online: www.nytimes.com/movie/review?res=9C00E0D71539F937A15751C1A96F95820 (accessed 18 February 2018).

Holderness, Graham (1993), 'Shakespeare Rewound', *Shakespeare Survey*, 45: 63–74.

Holland, Sharon Patricia (2012), *The Erotic Life of Racism*, Durham, NC: Duke University Press.

Howard, Henry, Early of Surrey (2003), *Selected Poems*, ed. Dennis Keene, New York: Routledge.

Howard, Jean E. (1988), 'Crossdressing, the Theatre, and Gender Struggle in Early Modern England', *Shakespeare Quarterly*, 39 (4): 418–40.

Howard, Jean E. and Phyllis Rackin (1997), *Engendering a Nation: A Feminist Account of Shakespeare's English Histories*, New York: Routledge.

Howie, Cary (2011), 'Stay', in Madhavi Menon (ed.), *Shakesqueer: A Queer Companion to the Complete Works of Shakespeare*, 146–51, Durham, NC: Duke University Press.

Irigaray, Luce ([1974] 1985), *Speculum of the Other Woman*, trans. Gillian C. Gill, Ithaca, NY: Cornell University Press.

Irigaray, Luce ([1977] 1985), *This Sex Which Is Not One*, trans. Catherine Porter, Ithaca, NY: Cornell University Press.

Iyengar, Sujata (2005), *Shades of Difference: Mythologies of Skin Color in Early Modern England*, Philadelphia: University of Pennsylvania Press.

Jagose, Annamarie (2009), 'Feminism's Queer Theory', *Feminism and Psychology*, 19 (2): 157–74.

Jameson, Fredric (1981), *The Political Unconscious: Narrative as a Socially Symbolic Act*, Ithaca, NY: Cornell University Press.

Jameson, Fredric (1991), *Postmodernism; or, The Cultural Logic of Late Capitalism*, Durham, NC: Duke University Press.

Jankowski, Theodora (2000), *Pure Resistance: Queer Virginity in Early Modern English Drama*, Philadelphia: University of Pennsylvania Press.

Jardine, Lisa (1991), 'Boy Actors, Female Roles and Elizabethan Eroticism', in David Scott Kastan and Peter Stallybrass (eds), *Staging the Renaissance*, 57–67, London: Routledge.

Jarman, Derek ([1987] 2010), *Kicking the Pricks*, Minneapolis: University of Minnesota Press.

Jarman, Derek (1991), *Queer Edward II*, London: BFI.

Jed, Stephanie (1989), *Chaste Thinking: The Rape of Lucretia and the Birth of Humanism*, Indianapolis: Indiana University Press.

Johnson, David K. (2004), *The Lavender Scare: The Cold War Persecution of Gays and Lesbians in the U.S. Government*, Chicago: University of Chicago Press.

Jones, Ann Rosalind and Peter Stallybrass (2000), *Renaissance Clothing and the Materials of Memory*, Cambridge: Cambridge University Press.

Jones, Melissa (2013), 'Spectacular Impotence: Or, Things That Hardly Ever Happen in the Critical History of Pornography', in James M. Bromley and Will Stockton (eds), *Sex Before 'Sex': Figuring the Act in Early Modern England*, 89–110, Minneapolis: University of Minnesota Press.

Kafer, Alison (2013), *Feminist, Queer, Crip*, Indianapolis: Indiana University Press.

Kahan, Benjamin (2013), *Celibacies: American Modernism and Sexual Life*, Durham, NC: Duke University Press.

Kahn, Coppélia (1981), *Man's Estate: Masculine Identity in Shakespeare*, Berkeley: University of California Press.

Katz, Jonathan Ned (1976), *Gay American History: Lesbians and Gay Men in the U.S.A.*, New York: Meridian.

Katz, Jonathan Ned (1995), *The Invention of Heterosexuality*, New York: Dutton.

Kaufman, David (1987), 'AIDS: The Creative Response', *Horizon*, 30 (9): 13–20.

Kaufmann, Miranda (2017), *The Black Tudors: The Untold Story*, London: Oneworld.

Keach, William (1977), *Elizabethan Erotic Narratives: Irony and Pathos in the Ovidian Poetry of Shakespeare, Marlowe, and Contemporaries*, New Brunswick, NJ: Rutgers University Press.

Kinniburgh, Mary Catherine (2016), 'Equine Erotics, Possible Pleasures: Early Modern Bestiality and Interspecies Queerness in Plate Five of *L'Academie des dames*', *Journal for Early Modern Cultural Studies*, 16 (4): 72–95.

Kleinberg, Seymour (1983), '*The Merchant of Venice*: The Homosexual as Anti-Semite in Nascent Capitalism', in Stuart Kellog (ed.), *Literary Visions of Homosexuality*, 113–26, New York: Hayward Press.

Lacan, Jacques ([1966] 1977), *Écrits: A Selection*, trans. Alan Sheridan, New York: Norton.

Lacan, Jacques ([1973] 1981), *The Four Fundamental Concepts of Psycho-Analysis*, ed. Jacques-Alain Miller, trans. Alan Sheridan, New York: Norton.

Lacan, Jacques ([1986] 1992), *The Seminar of Jacques Lacan, Book VII: The Ethics of Psychoanalysis, 1959–1960*, ed. Jacques-Alain Miller, trans. Dennis Porter, New York: Norton.

Lanser, Susan (2014), *The Sexuality of History: Modernity and the Sapphic, 1565–1830*, Chicago: University of Chicago Press.

Laqueur, Thomas (1990), *Making Sex, Body and Gender from the Greeks to Freud*, Cambridge, MA: Harvard University Press.

Latour, Bruno (2005), *Reassembling the Social: An Introduction to Actor-Network Theory*, Oxford: Oxford University Press.

Levi-Strauss, Claude ([1958] 1963), *Structural Anthropology*, trans. Claire Jacobson, New York: Basic Books.

Lim, Walter S. H. (2010), 'Surety and Spiritual Commercialism in *The Merchant of Venice*', *Studies in English Literature*, 50 (2): 355–82.

Little, Arthur L., Jr. (2000), *Shakespeare Jungle Fever: National-Imperial Revisions of Race, Rape, and Sacrifice*, Stanford, CA: Stanford University Press.

Little, Arthur L., Jr. (2009), '"A Local Habitation and a Name": Presence, Witnessing, and Queer Marriage in Shakespeare's Romantic Comedies', in Evelyn Gajowski (ed.), *Presentism, Gender, and Sexuality in Shakespeare*, 207–36, New York: Palgrave.

Little, Arthur L., Jr. (2011), 'The Rites of Queer Marriage in *The Merchant of Venice*', in Madhavi Menon (ed.), *Shakesqueer: A Queer Companion to the Complete Works of Shakespeare*, 216–24, Durham, NC: Duke University Press.

Little, Arthur L., Jr. (2016), 'Re-Historicizing Race, White Melancholia, and the Shakespearean Property', *Shakespeare Quarterly*, 67 (1): 84–103.

Lochrie, Karma (2005), *Heterosyncrasies: Female Sexuality When Normal Wasn't*, Minneapolis: University of Minnesota Press.

Loomba, Ania (1989), *Gender, Race, and Renaissance Drama*, Manchester: Manchester University Press.

Loomba, Ania (2002), *Shakespeare, Race, and Colonialism*, Oxford: Oxford University Press.

Loomba, Ania (2007), 'Periodization, Race, and Global Contact', *Journal of Medieval and Early Modern Studies*, 37 (3): 595–620.

Loomba, Ania and Jonathan Burton, eds (2007), *Race in Early Modern England: A Documentary Companion*, New York: Palgrave.

Loomba, Ania and Melissa E. Sanchez, eds (2016), *Rethinking Feminism in Early Modern Studies: Gender, Race, and Sexuality*, New York: Routledge.

Lorde, Audre ([1978] 1984), 'The Uses of the Erotic', in *Sister Outsider*, 53–8, Freedom, CA: Crossing Press.

Love, Heather (2000), 'A Gentle Angry People: The Lesbian Culture Wars', *Transition*, 84 (Summer): 98–113.

Love, Heather (2007), *Feeling Backwards*, Cambridge, MA: Harvard University Press.

Lupton, Julia Reinhard (2005), *Citizen-Saints: Shakespeare and Political Theology*, Chicago: University of Chicago Press.

Luxon, Thomas H. (2005), *Single Imperfection: Milton, Marriage, and Friendship*, Pittsburgh, PA: Duquesne University Press.

Lyotard, Jean-François (1979), *The Postmodern Condition: A Report on Knowledge*, Minneapolis: University of Minnesota Press.

MacCabe, Colin (1992), 'A Post-National European Cinema: A Consideration of Derek Jarman's *The Tempest* and *Edward II*', in Duncan Petrie (ed.), *Screening Empire: Image and Identity in Contemporary European Cinema*, 9–18, London: BFI.

MacDonald, Joyce Green (2002), *Women and Race in Early Modern Texts*, Cambridge: Cambridge University Press.

Marcus, Leah S. (1996), *Unediting the Renaissance: Shakespeare, Marlowe, Milton*, London: Routledge.

Marcus, Sharon (2005), 'Queer Theory for Everyone: A Review Essay', *Signs*, 31 (1): 192–218.

Marshall, Cynthia (2002), *The Shattering of the Self: Violence, Subjectivity, and Early Modern Texts*, Baltimore: Johns Hopkins University Press.

Martin, Biddy (1994a), 'Sexualities Without Genders and Other Queer Utopias', *diacritics*, 24 (2–3): 104–21.

Martin, Biddy (1994b), 'Extraordinary Homosexuals and the Fear of Being Ordinary', *differences*, 6 (2–3): 100–25.

Maslin, Janet (1996), 'Soft! What Light? It's Flash, Romeo', *New York Times*, 1 November. Available online: www.nytimes.com/movie/review?res=9C0CE7D91139F932A35752C1A960958260 (accessed 16 February 2018).

Masten, Jeffrey (1997), *Textual Intercourse: Collaboration, Authorship, and Sexualities in Renaissance Drama*, Cambridge: Cambridge University Press.

Masten, Jeffrey (2016), *Queer Philologies: Sex, Language, and Affect in Shakespeare's Time*, Philadelphia: University of Pennsylvania Press.

Matz, Robert (1999), 'Slander, Renaissance Discourses of Sodomy, and *Othello*', *ELH*, 66 (2): 261–76.

McCandless, David (2002), 'A Tale of Two *Titus*es: Julie Taymor's Vision on Stage and Screen', *Shakespeare Quarterly*, 53 (4): 487–511.

McRuer, Robert (2006), *Crip Theory: Cultural Signs of Queerness and Disability*, New York: New York University Press.

Meeker, Martin (2001), 'Behind the Mask of Respectability: Reconsidering the Mattachine Society and Male Homophile Practice, 1950s–1960s', *Journal of the History of Sexuality*, 10 (1): 95–7.

Menon, Madhavi (2004), *Wanton Words: Rhetoric and Sexuality in English Renaissance Drama*, Toronto: University of Toronto Press.

Menon, Madhavi (2008), *Unhistorical Shakespeare: Queer Theory in Shakespearean Literature and Film*, New York: Palgrave.

Menon, Madhavi (2009), 'Afterword: Period Cramps', in Vin Nardizzi, Stephen Guy-Bray and Will Stockton (eds), *Queer Renaissance Historiography: Backward Gaze*, 229–36, Burlington, VT: Ashgate.

Menon, Madhavi (2011a), 'Introduction: Queer Shakes', in Madhavi Menon (ed.), *Shakesqueer: A Queer Companion to the Complete Works of Shakespeare*, 1–27, Durham, NC: Duke University Press.

Menon, Madhavi (2011b), 'The L Words', in Madhavi Menon (ed.), *Shakesqueer: A Queer Companion to the Complete Works of Shakespeare*, 187–93, Durham, NC: Duke University Press.

Menon, Madhavi (2015), *Indifference to Difference: On Queer Universalism*, Minneapolis: University of Minnesota Press.

Mieli, Mario ([1976] 1980), *Homosexuality and Liberations: Elements of a Gay Critique*, trans. D. Fernbach, Boston, MA: Gay Men's Press.

Montaigne, Michel de ([1580] 1987), *The Complete Essays*, trans. M. A. Screech, New York: Penguin.

Montrose, Louis (1983), '"Shaping Fantasies": Figurations of Gender and Power in Elizabethan Culture', *Representations*, 1 (2): 61–94.

Montrose, Louis (1996), *The Purpose of Playing: Shakespeare and the Cultural Politics of the Elizabethan Theatre*, Chicago: University of Chicago Press.

Moraga, Cherríe (1983), *Loving in the War Years/lo que nunca pasó por sus labios*, Boston, MA: South End Press.

Morton, Donald (1996), 'Changing the Terms: (Virtual) Desire and (Actual) Reality', in Donald Morton (ed.), *The Material Queer: A LesBiGay Cultural Studies Reader*, Boulder, CO: Westview.

Muñoz, José Esteban (1998), 'Dead White: Notes on the Whiteness of the New Queer Cinema', *GLQ*, 4 (1): 127–38.

Muñoz, José Esteban (1999), *Disidentifications: Queers of Color and the Performance of Politics*, Minneapolis: University of Minnesota Press.

Muñoz, José Esteban (2000), 'Feeling Brown: Ethnicity and Affect in Ricardo Bracho's *The Sweetest Hangover (and Other STDs)*', *Theatre Journal*, 52 (1): 67–79.

Muñoz, José Esteban (2009), *Cruising Utopia: The Then and There of Queer Futurity*, New York: New York University Press.

My Own Private Idaho (1991), [Film] Dir. Gus Van Sant, USA: Fine Line Features.

Naphy, William (2002), 'Sodomy in Early Modern Geneva: Various Definitions, Diverse Verdicts', in Tom Betteridge (ed.), *Sodomy in Early Modern Europe*, 94–111, Manchester: Manchester University Press.

Neely, Carol Thomas (2004), *Distracted Subjects: Madness and Gender in Shakespeare and Early Modern Culture*, Ithaca, NY: Cornell University Press.

Neill, Michael (1989), 'Unproper Beds: Race, Adultery, and the Hideous in *Othello*', *Shakespeare Quarterly*, 40 (4): 383–412.

Newman, Jane O. (1994), '"And let Mild Women to Him Lose Their Mildness": Philomela, Female Violence, and Shakespeare's *The Rape of Lucrece*', *Shakespeare Quarterly*, 45 (3): 304–26.

Newman, Karen (1987), 'Portia's Ring: Unruly Women and Structures of Exchange in *The Merchant of Venice*', *Shakespeare Quarterly*, 38 (1): 19–33.

Newman, Karen (1991), *Fashioning Femininity and English Renaissance Drama*, Chicago: University of Chicago Press.

Newman, Karen ([1991] 2009), '"And Wash the Ethiope White": Femininity and the Monstrous in *Othello*', in *Essaying Shakespeare*, 38–58, Minneapolis: University of Minnesota Press.

O'Dair, Sharon (2015), 'Cursing the Queer Family: Shakespeare, Psychoanalysis and *My Own Private Idaho*', in Adam Hanson and Kevin J. Wetmore Jr. (eds), *Shakespearean Echos*, 130–41, London: Palgrave.

Orgel, Stephen (1996), *Impersonations: The Performance of Gender in Shakespeare's England*, Cambridge: Cambridge University Press.

Orgel, Stephen ([2004] 2011), 'Ganymede Agonistes', in *Spectacular Performances: Essays on Theatre, Imagery, Books and Selves in Early Modern England*, 251–71, Manchester: Manchester University Press.

Ovid ([1965] 2000), *Ovid's Metamorphoses: The Arthur Golding Translation of 1567*, ed. Frederick Nims, Philadelphia, PA: Paul Dry Books.

Parker, Patricia (1987), *Literary Fat Ladies: Rhetoric, Gender, Property*, Toronto: University of Toronto Press.

Parker, Patricia (1992), 'Preposterous Events', *Shakespeare Quarterly*, 43 (2): 186–213.

Parker, Patricia (1995), 'Fantasies of "Race" and "Gender": Africa, *Othello*, and Bringing to Light', in Margo Hendricks and Patricia Parker (eds), *Women, 'Race,' and Writing in the Early Modern Period*, 84–100, London: Routledge.

Parker, Patricia (1996a), *Shakespeare from the Margins: Language, Culture, Context*, Chicago: University of Chicago Press.

Parker, Patricia (1996b), 'Virile Style', in Louise Fradenburg and Carla Freccero (eds), *Premodern Sexualities*, 199–222, New York: Routledge.

Parsons, Alexandra (2014), 'History, Activism, and the Queer Child in Derek Jarman's *Queer Edward II* (1991)', *Shakespeare Bulletin*, 32 (3): 413–28.

Parvini, Neema (2017), *Shakespeare and New Historicist Theory*, London: Bloomsbury.

Paster, Gail Kern (1993), *The Body Embarrassed: Drama and the Disciplines of Shame in Early Modern England*, Ithaca, NY: Cornell University Press.

Patricia, Anthony Guy (2016), *Queering the Shakespearean Film*, London: Bloomsbury.

Pequigney, Joseph (1985), *Such Is My Love: A Study of Shakespeare's Sonnets*, Chicago: University of Chicago Press.

Pittenger, Elizabeth (1994), '"To Serve the Queere": Nicholas Udall, Master of Revels', in Jonathan Goldberg (ed.), *Queering the Renaissance*, 162–89, Durham, NC: Duke University Press.

Plato (1956), *Protagoras and Meno*, trans. W. K. C.Guthrie, London: Penguin.

Plato (1993), *The Last Days of Socrates: Euthyphro; The Apology; Crito; Phaedo*, trans. Hugh Tredennick Harold Tarrant, London: Penguin.

Preciado, Paul B. ([2008] 2013), *Testo Junkie: Sex, Drugs, and in the Pharmacopornographic Era*, trans. Bruce Benderson, New York: Feminist Press at CUNY.

Prosser, Jay (1998), *Second Skins: The Body Narratives of Transexuality*, New York: Columbia University Press.

Puar, Jasbir (2007), *Terrorist Assemblages: Homonationalism in Queer Times*, Durham, NC: Duke University Press.

Pullman, Joy (2016), 'U-Penn Students Take Down Shakespeare Portrait Because He's Too White and Straight', *The Federalist*, 14 December. Available online: http://thefederalist.com/2016/12/14/u-penn-students-displace-shakespeare-portrait-one-dramatically-inferior-writer/ (accessed 28 February 2018).

Rackin, Phyllis (2005), *Shakespeare and Women*, Oxford: Oxford University Press.

Radel, Nicolas F. (2009), 'The Ethiop's Ear: Race, Sexuality, and Baz Luhrmann's *William Shakespeare's Romeo + Juliet*', *The Upstart Crow*, 28: 17–34.

Rambuss, Richard (1993), *Spenser's Secret Career*, Cambridge: Cambridge University Press.

Rambuss, Richard (1998), *Closet Devotions*, Durham, NC: Duke University Press.

Rambuss, Richard (2003), 'What It Feels Like For a Boy: Shakespeare's *Venus and Adonis*', in Richard Dutton and Jean E. Howard (eds), *A Companion to Shakespeare's Works*, vol. 4, 240–58, Malden, MA: Blackwell.

Rambuss, Richard (2011a), 'Shakespeare's Ass Play', in Madhavi Menon (ed.), *Shakesqueer: A Queer Companion to the Complete Works of Shakespeare*, 234–44, Durham, NC: Duke University Press.

Rambuss, Richard (2011b), 'The Straightest Story Ever Told', *GLQ*, 17 (4): 543–73.

Reid-Pharr, Robert (2001), *Black Gay Man: Essays*, New York: New York University Press.

Rich, Adrienne ([1980] 1986), 'Compulsory Heterosexuality and the Lesbian Existence', in *Blood, Bread, and Poetry: Selected Prose 1979–1985*, 23–75, New York: Norton.

Rich, B. Ruby ([1992] 2013a), 'The King of Queer: Derek Jarman', in *New Queer Cinema: The Director's Cut*, 49–52, Durham, NC: Duke University Press.

Rich, B. Ruby ([1992] 2013b), 'The New Queer Cinema', in *New Queer Cinema: The Director's Cut*, 16–32, Durham, NC: Duke University Press.

Richardson, Bradford (2016), 'Shakespeare Portrait at Univ. of Pennsylvania Removed for Image of Black Lesbian Poet: Report', *The Washington Times*, 12 December. Available online: www.washingtontimes.com/news/2016/dec/12/shakespeare-portrait-at-university-of-pennsylvania/ (accessed 28 February 2018).

Richardson, James ([2007] 2010), 'In Shakespeare', in *By the Numbers*, Port Townsend, WA: Copper Canyon Press.

Roman, David (1994), 'Shakespeare in Portland: Gus Van Sant's *My Own Private Idaho*, Homoneurotics, and Boy Actors', *Genders*, 20 (Fall): 311–33.

Royster, Francesca T. (2000), 'White-limed Walls: Whiteness and Gothic Extremism in Shakespeare's *Titus Andronicus*', *Shakespeare Quarterly*, 51 (4): 432–55.

Rubin, Gayle ([1984] 1992), 'Thinking Sex Notes for a Radical Theory of the Politics of Sexuality', in Carole S. Vance (ed.), *Pleasure and Danger: Exploring Female Sexuality* 2nd edn, 267–319, London: Pandor.

Rubin, Gayle (2010), 'Blood Under the Bridge: Reflections on "Thinking Sex"', *GLQ*, 17 (1): 15–47.

Salamon, Gayle (2010), *Assuming a Body: Transgender and Rhetorics of Materiality*, New York: Columbia University Press.

Sanchez, Melissa E. (2011), *Erotic Subjects: The Sexuality of Politics in Early Modern English Literature*, Oxford: Oxford University Press.

Sanchez, Melissa E. (2012), '"Use Me But as Your Spaniel": Feminism, Queer Theory, and Early Modern Sexualities', *PMLA*, 127 (3): 493–511.

Sanchez, Melissa E. (2016), 'This Field that Is Not One', *Journal for Early Modern Cultural Studies*, 16 (2): 131–46.

Sandoval, Chela (1991), 'U.S. Third World Feminism: The Theory and Method of Oppositional Consciousness in the Postmodern World', *Genders*, 10 (Spring): 1–23.

Sandoval, Chela (2000), *Methodology of the Oppressed*, Minneapolis: University of Minnesota Press.

Saunders, Ben (2004), 'Iago's Clyster: Purgation, Anality, and the Civilizing Process', *Shakespeare Quarterly*, 55 (2): 148–76.

Saussure, Ferdinand de ([1916] 1994), *Course in General Linguistics*, ed. Charles Bally and Albert Sechehaye, trans. Wade Baskin, New York: McGraw-Hill.

Schwarz, Kathryn (2000), *Tough Love: Amazon Encounters in the English Renaissance*, Durham, NC: Duke University Press.

Schwarz, Kathryn (2011), '*Hamlet* without Us', *Shakespeare Quarterly*, 62 (2): 174–9.

Schwarz, Kathryn (2017), 'Held in Common: *Romeo and Juliet* and the Promiscuous Seductions of Plague', in Goran Stanivukovic (ed.), *Queer Shakespeare*, 245–61, London: Bloomsbury.

Sedgwick, Eve Kosofsky (1985), *Between Men: English Literature and Male Homosocial Desire*, New York: Columbia University Press.

Sedgwick, Eve Kosofsky (1990), *Epistemology of the Closet*, Berkeley: University of California Press.

Sedgwick, Eve Kosofsky (1993), *Tendencies*, Durham, NC: Duke University Press.

Sedgwick, Eve Kosofsky (2003), *Touching Feeling: Affect, Pedagogy, Performativity*, Durham, NC: Duke University Press.

Seneca (2004), *Tragedies II*, ed. and trans. John G. Fitch, Cambridge, MA: Loeb Classical Library.

Shakespeare, William (2014), *The Arden Shakespeare: Shakespeare's Complete Works*, rev. edn, ed. Richard Proudfoot, Ann Thompson and David Scott Kastan, London: Bloomsbury.

Shannon, Laurie (2002), *Sovereign Amity: Figures of Friendship in Shakespearean Contexts*, Chicago: University of Chicago Press.

Shapiro, James (1996), *Shakespeare and the Jews*, New York: Columbia University Press.

Sinfield, Alan ([1985] 1994), 'Give an Account of Shakespeare and Education, Showing Why You Think They Are Effective and What You Have Appreciated about them. Support Your Comments with Precise References', in Jonathan Dollimore and

Alan Sinfield (eds), *Political Shakespeare: New Essays in Cultural Materialism*, 158–82, Ithaca, NY: Cornell University Press.

Sinfield, Alan (1992), *Faultlines: Cultural Materialism and the Politics of Dissident Reading*, Berkeley: University of California Press.

Sinfield, Alan (2006), *Shakespeare, Authority, Sexuality: Unfinished Business in Cultural Materialism*, London: Routledge.

Sinfield, Alan and Jonathan Dollimore (1992), 'History and Ideology: Masculinity and Miscegenation: The Instance of *Henry V*', *Faultlines: Cultural Materialism and the Politics of Dissident Reading*, 109–42, Berkeley: University of California Press.

Singh, Jyotsna, ed. (2009), *A Companion to the Global Renaissance: English Literature and Culture in the Era of Expansion*, Malden, MA: Blackwell.

Smith, Bruce R. (1991), *Homosexual Desire in Shakespeare's England: A Cultural Poetics*, Chicago: University of Chicago Press.

Smith, Ian (2009), *Race and Rhetoric in the Renaissance: Barbarian Errors*, New York: Palgrave.

Smith-Rosenberg, Carol (1975), 'The Female World of Love and Ritual: Relations Between Women in Nineteenth-Century America', *Signs* 1 (1): 1–29.

Snorton, C. Riley (2017), *Black on Both Sides: A Racial History of Trans Identity*, Minneapolis: University of Minnesota Press.

Spade, Dean (2015), *Normal Life: Administrative Violence, Critical Trans Politics, and the Limits of Law*, Durham, NC: Duke University Press.

Spillers, Hortense J. (1987), 'Mama's Baby, Papa's Maybe: An American Grammar Book', *diacritics*, 17 (2): 64–81.

Stanivukovic, Goran (2009), 'Beyond Sodomy: What Is Still Queer about Early Modern Queer Studies?', in Vin Nardizzi, Stephen Guy-Bray and Will Stockton (eds), *Queer Renaissance Historiography: Backward Gaze*, 41–65, Burlington VT: Ashgate.

Stanivukovic, Goran V. (2000), '"Kissing the Boar": Queer Adonis and Critical Practice', in Calvin Thomas (ed.), *Straight with a Twist: Queer Theory and the Subject of Heterosexuality*, 87–108, Urbana: University of Illinois Press.

Stewart, Alan (1997), *Close Readers: Humanism and Sodomy in Early Modern England*, Princeton, NJ: Princeton University Press.

Stewart, Alan (2008), *Shakespeare's Letters*, Oxford: Oxford University Press.

Stockton, Kathryn Bond (2009), *The Queer Child: Growing Sideways in the Twentieth Century*, Durham, NC: Duke University Press.

Stockton, Will (2011), *Playing Dirty: Sexuality and Waste in Early Modern Comedy*, Minneapolis: University of Minnesota Press.

Stockton, Will (2012), 'Shakespeare and Queer Theory', *Shakespeare Quarterly*, 63 (2): 224–35.

Stockton, Will (2013), 'The Seduction of Milton's Lady: Rape, Psychoanalysis, and the Erotics of Consumption in "Comus"', in James M. Bromley and Will Stockton (eds), *Sex Before Sex: Figuring the Act in Early Modern England*, 233–61, Minneapolis: University of Minnesota Press.

Stockton, Will (2017), *Members of His Body: Shakespeare, Paul, and a Theology of Nonmonogamy*, New York: Fordham University Press.

Stryker, Susan (1994), 'My Words to Victor Frankenstein above the Village of Chamounix: Performing Transgender Rage', *GLQ*, 1 (3): 237–54.

The Tempest (1979), [Film] Dir. Derek Jarman, UK: London Films.

Thomas, Philip (2015), '*My Own Private Idaho* Review', *Empire Online*, 14 October. Available online: www.empireonline.com/movies/private-idaho/review/ (accessed 20 February 2018).

Thompson, Ayanna, ed. (2006), *Colorblind Shakespeare: New Perspectives on Race and Performance*, New York: Routledge.

Thompson, Ayanna (2008), *Performing Race and Torture on the Early Modern Stage*, New York: Routledge.

Thompson, Ayanna (2011), *Passing Strange: Shakespeare, Race, and Contemporary America*, Oxford: Oxford University Press.

Tillyard, E. M. W. (1959), *The Elizabethan World Picture*, New York: Vintage.

Timpf, Katherine (2016), 'U Penn Removes Shakespeare Portrait Because He Does Not Represent "Diversity"', *National Review*, 14 December. Available online: www.nationalreview.com/article/443049/u-penn-removes-shakespeare-portrait-because-he-does-not-represent-diversity (accessed 28 February 2018).

Titus (1999), [Film] Dir. Julie Taymor, Italy, UK, USA: Clear Blue Sky Productions.

Traub, Valerie (1992), *Desire and Anxiety: Circulations of Sexuality in Shakespearean Drama*, New York: Routledge.

Traub, Valerie (1995), 'The Psychomorphology of the Clitoris', *GLQ*, 2 (1/2): 81–113.

Traub, Valerie (2002), *The Renaissance of Lesbianism in Early Modern England*, Cambridge: Cambridge University Press.

Traub, Valerie (2015), *Thinking Sex with the Early Moderns*, Philadelphia: University of Pennsylvania Press.

Traub, Valerie, ed. (2016), *The Oxford Handbook of Shakespeare and Embodiment*, Oxford: Oxford University Press.

Travers, Peter (1996), 'William Shakespeare's Romeo + Juliet', *Rolling Stone*, 1 November. Available online: www.rollingstone.com/movies/reviews/william-shakespeares-romeo-juliet-19961101 (accessed 18 February 2018).

Turley, Jonathan (2016), 'Penn Students Remove Portrait of Shakespeare With Black Feminist Author', *Jonathan Turley*, 13 December. Available online: https://jonathanturley.org/2016/12/13/penn-students-remove-portrait-of-shakespeare-with-black-feminist-author/comment-page-1/ (accessed 28 February 2018).

Underwood, Ted (2013), *Why Literary Periods Mattered: Historical Contrast and the Prestige of English Studies*, Stanford, CA: Stanford University Press.

Vance, Carol S. (1992), 'Pleasure and Danger: Toward a Politics of Sexuality', in Carole S. Vance (ed.), *Pleasure and Danger: Exploring Female Sexuality*, 2nd edn, 1–27, London: Pandor.

Variety Staff (1996), 'William Shakespeare's Romeo & Juliet', *Variety*, 27 October. Available online: http://variety.com/1996/film/reviews/william-shakespeare-s-romeo-juliet-1200447070/ (accessed 2 March 2018).

Varnado, Christine (2013), '"Invisible Sex!": What Looks Like the Act in Early Modern Drama?', in James M. Bromley and Will Stockton (eds), *Sex Before Sex: Figuring the Act in Early Modern England*, 25–52, Minneapolis: University of Minnesota Press.

Vaughan, Virginia Mason (2003), 'Looking at the "Other" in Julie Taymor's *Titus*', *Shakespeare Bulletin*, 21 (1): 71–80.

Vaughan, Virginia Mason (2005), *Performing Blackness on English Stages*, Cambridge: Cambridge University Press.

Veeser, Harold Aram, ed. (1989), *The New Historicism*, New York: Routledge.

Vicinus, Martha (1993), '"They Wonder to Which Sex I Belong": The Historical Roots of the Modern Lesbian Identity', in Henry Abelove, Michèle Aina Barale and David M. Halperin (eds), *The Gay and Lesbian Studies Reader*, 432–52, New York: Routledge.

Villarosa, Linda (2017), 'America's Hidden H.I.V. Epidemic',
    New York Times, 6 June. Available online: www.nytimes.
    com/2017/06/06/magazine/americas-hidden-hiv-epidemic.html
    (accessed 10 October 2017).
Vitkus, Daniel (2003), *Turning Turk: English Theatre and the
    Multicultural Mediterranean, 1570–1630*, New York: Palgrave.
Walen, Denise A. (2005), *Constructions of Female Homoeroticism in
    Early Modern Drama*, New York: Palgrave.
Warner, Michael (1993), 'Introduction', in Michael Warner (ed.),
    Fear of a Queer Planet: Queer Politics and Social Theory, vii–
    xxxi, Minneapolis: Minnesota University Press.
Warner, Michael (1994), 'New English Sodom', in Jonathan
    Goldberg (ed.), *Queering the Renaissance*, 330–58, Durham, NC:
    Duke University Press.
Warner, Michael (1999), *The Trouble with Normal: Sex, Politics,
    and the Ethics of Queer Life*, New York: Free Press.
Watney, Simon (1987), *Policing Desire: Pornography, AIDS, and the
    Media*, Minneapolis: University of Minnesota Press.
Weeks, Jeffrey (1977), *Coming Out: Homosexual Politics in Britain
    from the Nineteenth Century to the Present*, London: Quartet
    Books.
Wells, Stanley (2004), *Looking for Sex in Shakespeare*, Cambridge:
    Cambridge University Press.
White, Hayden V. (1973), *Metahistory: The Historical Imagination
    in Nineteenth-Century Europe*, Baltimore: Johns Hopkins
    University Press.
Wiegman, Robyn and Elizabeth A. Wilson (2015), 'Introduction:
    Antinormativity's Queer Conventions', *differences*, 26 (1): 1–25.
William Shakespeare's Romeo + Juliet (1996), [Film] Dir. Baz
    Luhrmann, USA: Bazmark Productions.
Winkler, John J. (1993), 'Double Consciousness in Sappho's Lyrics',
    in Henry Abelove, Michèle Aina Barale and David M. Halperin
    (eds.), *The Gay and Lesbian Studies Reader*, 577–94, New York:
    Routledge.
Wittig, Monique (1992), *The Straight Mind and Other Essays*,
    Boston, MA: Beacon Press.
WND (2016), 'Shakespeare Replaced with Black Lesbian Feminist',
    12 December. Available online: www.wnd.com/2016/12/
    shakespeare-replaced-with-black-lesbian-feminist/ (accessed 28
    February 2018).

Worthen, William B. (1998), 'Drama, Performativity, and Performance', *PMLA*, 113 (5): 1093–107.

Woubshet, Dagmawi (2015), *The Calendar of Loss: Race, Sexuality and Mourning in the Early Era of AIDS*, Baltimore: Johns Hopkins University Press.

Zabus, Chantal and Kevin A. Dwyer (1997), '"I'll Be Wise Hereafter": Caliban in Postmodern British Cinema', in Marc Delrez and Benedicte Ledent (eds), *The Contact and the Culmination*, 271–89, Liège: Liège Language and Literature.

INDEX